AMERICAN CARS

PAST TO PRESENT

EDIZIONI WHITE STAR

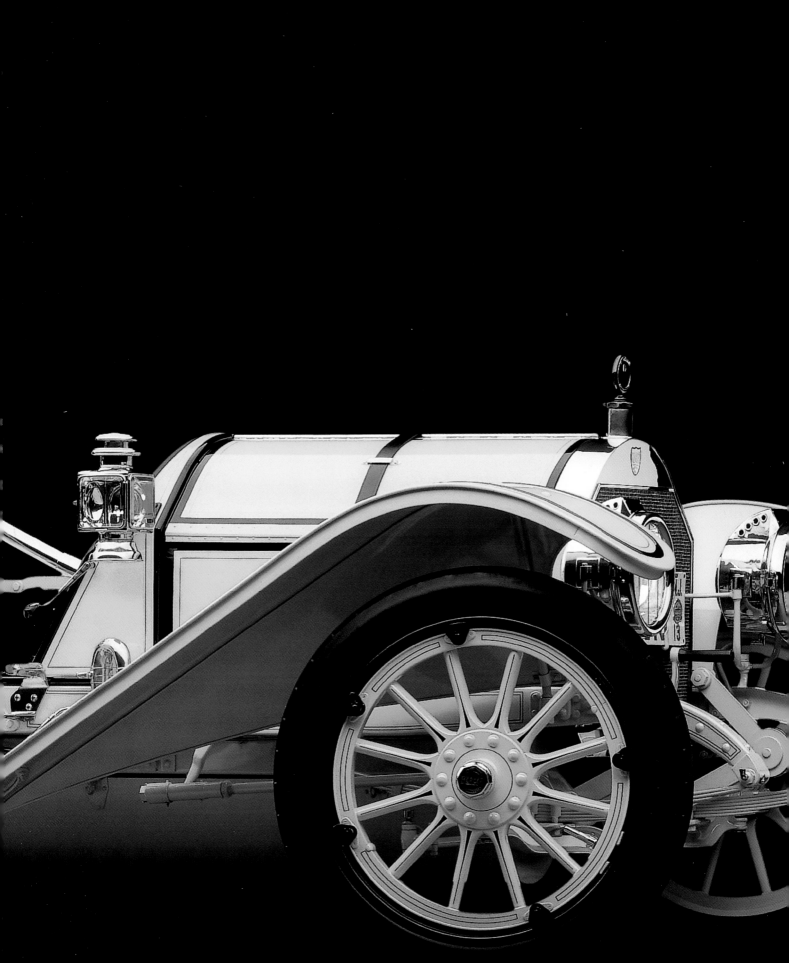

CONTENTS

© 2004, 2007 White Star s.p.a. - Via Candido Sassone, 22/24
13100 Vercelli, Italy - www.whitestar.it

New extended edition

ISBN: 978-88-544-0246-1

REPRINTS:
1 2 3 4 5 6   11 10 09 08 07

Printed in China - Color separation Chiaroscuro, Turin

1 The 1960 Cadillac still
sported a chromed fin.

2-3 The 1913 Mercer
Raceabout was the ultimate
racing machine of its era.

4-5 The 1932 Auburn
Boattail Speedster displayed
a unique blend of style.

6-7 Cadillac celebrated its
50th birthday with a Cadillac
Series 62 convertible called
the Eldorado.

8 The 1932 Imperial
sported a hood mascot that
featured a gazelle.

9 Heny Ford (left) drives
a 999 in a 1903
demostration run.

TEXT
Matt DeLorenzo

EDITORIAL PRODUCTION
Valeria Manferto De Fabianis
Laura Accomazzo - Claudia Zanera

GRAPHIC DESIGN
Maria Cucchi

INTRODUCTION

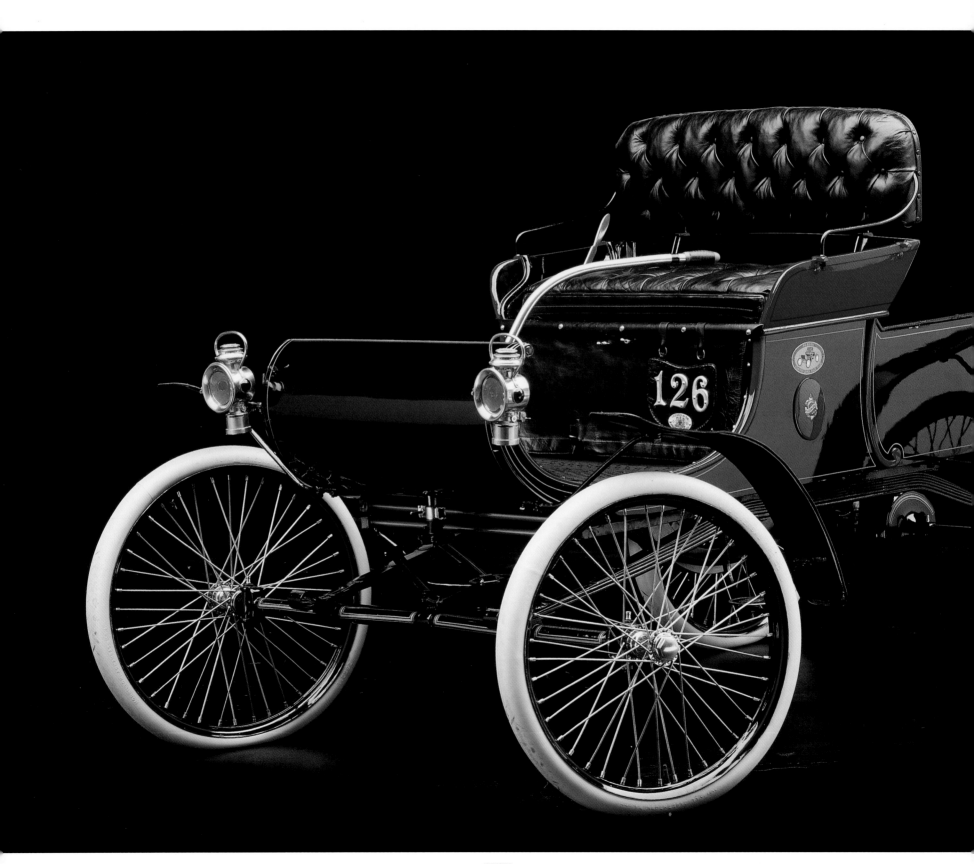

Many books have extensively cataloged the numerous auto companies that have produced cars in America since the turn of the previous century. Yet another encyclopedic treatment of the subject would be redundant. Instead, this work is a broad overview of the history of American cars and establishes a context for how the automobile has evolved and thrived here. Cars may be a universal product, but that's not to say that they are the same everywhere. Viewed from afar, American cars (and trucks) look too big, have engines that are too large and are considered impractical for solo commuting. Considering America's vast continent with its wide, open roads, readily available parking and low energy prices, one begins to understand why automobiles here differ from those found elsewhere in the world.

The car may have been invented in Europe, but it was America that set the stage for its mass production. Good old-fashioned American ingenuity as demonstrated by Cadillac's mastery of interchangeable parts and Henry Ford's invention of the moving assembly line helped make the personal transportation as ubiquitous as it is today. The first automobiles look remarkably the same worldwide—essentially motorized carriages. But as technical sophistication grew, with the invention of such features as the self-starter, electric lighting and closed bodies, each company's offerings began to take on individual characteristics that reflected not only a particular firm's identity, but also the country of origin. One of the first steps in this process was the fact that America settled on left-hand drive, while Britain chose right-hand drive. As automobiles became a foundation of American society in the 1920s and 1930s, these vehicles began to take on a personality all their own, especially as styling became as important a selling point as a vehicle's function. American cars on average tended, even then, to be a larger and more expressive, than their European coun-

terparts. In the wake of World War II, American cars became unlike those seen anywhere else. The United States' large land mass and low energy prices resulted in a culture that was built upon the automobile as its primary mode of transportation. Cars were the catalyst in the move from an urban to a suburban lifestyle.

Post-war prosperity and a highly competitive industry combined to make the annual model change a standard business practice in the American market. Meanwhile, a devastated Europe, with crowded urban areas and a road system that predates all of American history, needed smaller, more efficient cars.

And while some of these European designs were more "sensible," American cars from that era were and

10-11 The 1901 Curved Dash Oldsmobile by virtue of its light weight and low cost, was the first automobile with mass appeal that would eventually lead to the motorization of America.

11 The striking hood ornament of the 1954 Packard Panama Clipper.

still are revered for their almost whimsical, space-age designs. America's contribution to worldwide automotive design in this era can be summed up in a few short words: the tail fin.

This automotive exuberance couldn't last as a severe economic downturn and the increasing popularity of imported European cars at the end of the 1950s led the U.S. makers to consider the compact car and less ostentatious designs in the 1960s. But while styling was somewhat subdued, the quest for more power had just begun. This was the era of muscle cars, vehicles powered by huge, tire-smoking V-8s. Gasoline prices were at an all-time low, the push further into the suburbs continued, and new highways seemed to pop up overnight.

During the 1970s, it took two energy crises, and government edicts to clean up the air and to build safer vehicles to rein in the manufacturers' ability to make the large, powerful cars that the average Americans demanded. And while the new smaller, front-drive vehicles began to look like their European counterparts, lower fuel economy standards and less stringent emissions regulations for trucks provided the loophole manufacturers needed to build the large, powerful vehicles still craved by the American market. Trucks, ranging from cargo-carrying pickups to large four-door sport-utility vehicles, are every bit as likely to provide daily family transportation as cars.

Close examination of the history of the car in America is also an exercise in déjà vu. Even among the earliest car companies, one could find the same names over and over again—Henry Ford was involved with his own company, as well as Cadillac. Henry Leland left Cadillac to start Lincoln, a company later bought by Henry Ford. Ransom E. Olds, after being ousted from his own company, started REO. Walter P. Chrysler worked for Buick, as did Louis Chevrolet.

Even seemingly new ideas have all been tried before. In the industry's infancy, the internal-combustion gasoline engine competed with both electric and steam power before prevailing as the powerplant of choice. Today manufacturers are spending untold sums to develop electric or fuel cell technology vehicles in a bid to move beyond internal combustion power. In the early 1900s, Rolls-Royce, Fiat and Mercedes assembled cars in the United States, faint echoes of the larger Japanese and

German plants that would be built in the U.S. during the last two decades of the 20th century. Chrysler sought to use the aerodynamically styled Airflow in 1934 to gain a leg up on its competitors; Ford revolutionized automotive design in the 1980s with its aero-styled Taurus family sedan. Even the establishment of General Motors in 1908, combining the forces of Chevrolet, Buick and Oldsmobile set the stage for other mergers that are a daily fact of life.

Every so often, a manufacturer would look around the landscape and decide that what America needs is another new car division to satisfy some unmet need. Oldsmobile had its Viking, Cadillac, the LaSalle, Ford the Edsel and GM the Saturn. Conversely, in bad economic times, the same manufacturers would decide that there were too many divisions to satisfy the market and would give the ax to some legendary names—like Chrysler to DeSoto and Plymouth, and most recently, GM to

Oldsmobile. And every generation has a visionary who declares that he or she will re-invent the automobile, from Buckminster Fuller and his Dymaxion, to Preston Tucker and his Torpedo to John DeLorean and his DMC12. The history of the American industry is a rich tapestry of cars, characters and corporations. And like most tapestries, it's best enjoyed by not examining each individual thread, but by stepping back and taking in the broad strokes of the entire work.

14-15 Although exaggerated in proportion, many of the styling details on the Mako Shark, such as the hood treatment, chrome bumperettes and fender contours, were used on the production Sting Ray.

16-17 More than just a show car turned production model, the Dodge Viper gave Chrysler Corporation a much-needed lift in employee morale and public image during the early 1990s.

12-13 GM Design favored the predominance of jet age styling cues, as is most evident in the rear end of this 1960 Cadillac Series 62 convertible.

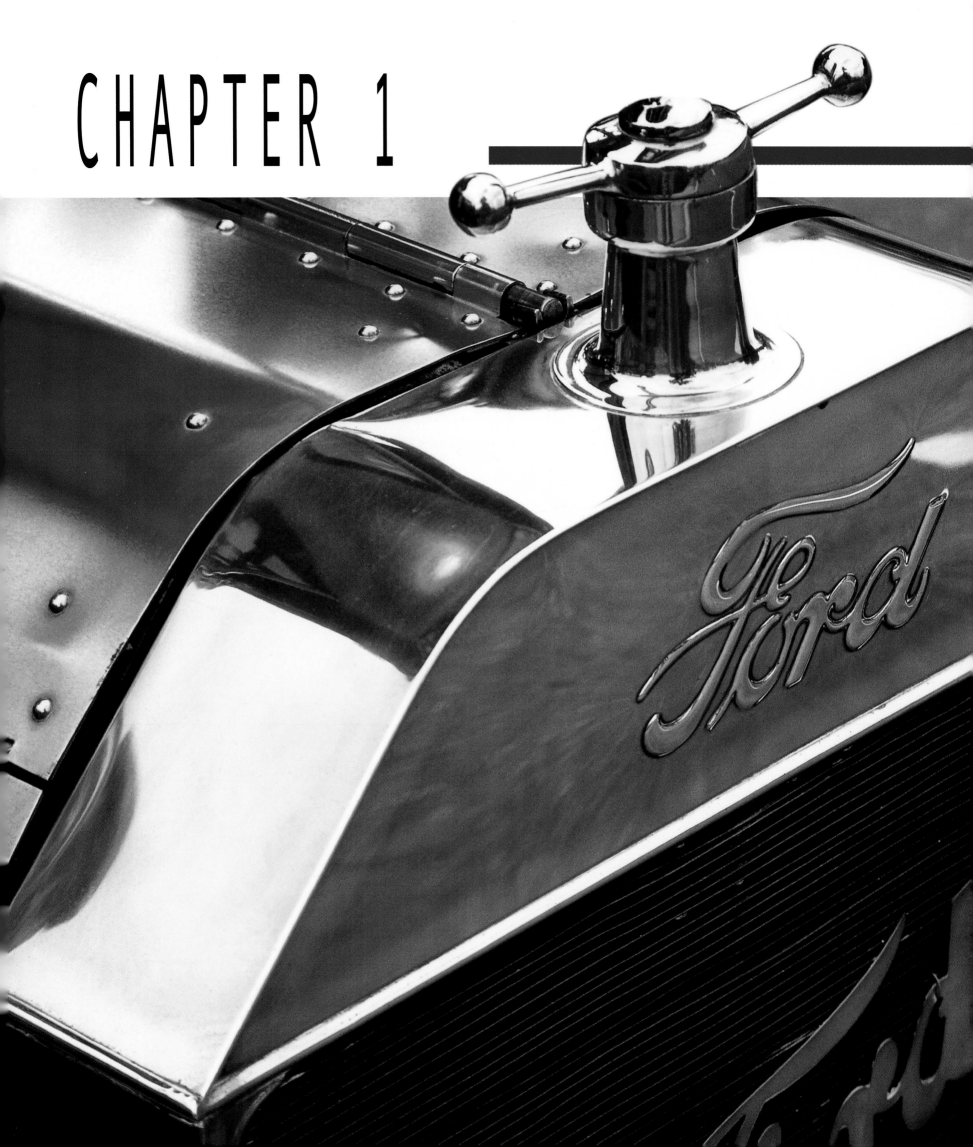

CHAPTER 1

1896 - 1911
An Industry
Stirs
to Life...

18-19 America's fascination with the automobile predates the turn of the 20th century, but it wasn't until Henry Ford developed the low cost Model T that the love affair blossomed. More than 15 million were built.

ike so many things in America, the automobile can trace its roots back to Europe. In the mid-1880s, two men working quite independently of each other, Carl Benz and Gottlieb Daimler, fitted four-stroke internal combustion engines onto wheeled conveyances. The horseless carriage was born and along with it, a new industry.

While Benz and Daimler were among the first, they weren't alone in their tinkering. All across America, men with names like Ransom E. Olds, Henry Ford and David Buick as well as Charles and Frank Duryea, Alexander Winton and Elwood Haynes, all dreamed of putting their names on cars. Some would become immortal—Henry Ford is generally credited with putting America on wheels. Collectors and historians would remember others like Winton, who produced fabulous automobiles in his time. And the rest, like Haynes, would become postscripts in local archives—a snapshot in the Indiana Historical Society of a man and his early automobile ready to make a trial run in Kokomo, Indiana, on July 4, 1894.

The early attempts at auto making in America can be described as chaotic at best. Unlike today's industry that employs hundreds of thousands and calls Detroit its home base, American auto making started out as a cottage trade scattered across the land. Every town that had a blacksmith, a carriage maker or any sort of industry that used a gas or steam engine most likely could boast one or two enterprising fellows seeking to perfect the automobile. Automotive News in its "100 Events that Made the Industry," quotes Hiram Percy Maxim, an engineer who worked on his own car in Lynn, Massachusetts, writing in his memoirs: "As I look back, I am amazed that so many of us began to work so nearly at the same time, and without the slightest notion that others were working on the problem. It has always been my belief that we all began work on a gasoline-propelled road vehicle at about the same time because it had become apparent that civilization was ready for [it]."

Civilization may have been ready, but convincing investors to commit the necessary capital to develop the automobile business was altogether another matter. More than once, racing would prove pivotal in moving the industry along.

In 1895 the Chicago Times-Herald, inspired by a race sponsored by Le Petit Journal from Paris to Rouen a year earlier, proposed a November race from Chicago to Waukegan, Illinois, a distance of about 90 miles. First prize would be $5,000. While the initial entry list was long, only two cars showed up at the starting line on November 2, a Benz and a Duryea wagon, entered by brothers Charles and Frank Duryea. Because of the lack of entrants, the race was rescheduled for Thanksgiving Day, November 28. Still, on November 2, the paper offered $500 for the first vehicle to drive to Waukegan and back. The Benz won after Frank Duryea swerved to avoid hitting a carriage and landed in a ditch.

On November 28, only six of the 100 or so contestants who registered for the race showed up at the snowy start/finish line—three Benz automobiles, two electric cars and the Duryea. Because of the weather, the course was shortened to a 54-mile roundtrip between Chicago and Evanston, Illinois.

Two of the Benzes and both electric vehicles fell by the wayside with Frank Duryea winning the race an hour and a half ahead of the remaining Benz with an average speed of just over 6 mph.

20 Two Germans, working independently of each other, Carl Benz and Gottleib Daimler (seated in the rear of his machine piloted by his son Wilhelm) are credited with inventing the automobile.

20-21 On Thanksgiving Day, 1895, J. Frank Duryea overcame the elements to win America's first race. That victory helped put the car that he built with his brother Charles into production.

22 Charles E. Duryea pilots the third car built by the fledgling Duryea works in 1895. Still more carriage than automobile, this model was the first to be equipped with pneumatic tires.

23 top left The first creation from the Duryea brothers was this motorized buggy built in 1892 powered by a two-stroke, one-cylinder engine. However, it took Frank Duryea nearly a year of tinkering to get the car to run consistently.

23 top right What could be called a 1930s "barn find" is this dilapidated motorized carriage, built in the 1892-1893 period.

23 bottom The Duryea brothers are credited with creating the U.S. auto industry by building 13 vehicles in 1896, the nation's first series production car. Here one of these first autos sees service with the Barnum & Bailey Circus.

Parlaying the fame from this and other races, the Duryeas began building vehicles in Springfield, Massachusetts. They are credited with the first mass-produced automobile in America, building 13 vehicles in 1896. That year, according to Automotive News, 19 vehicles were built: the 13 Duryeas and one each of Ford, Winton, Crouch, Daily, King and Overman. Duryea's success was not long lived. The cars were expensive, costing between $1,000 and $2,000 and the quality indifferent. In fact, only three of the cars were built at the Duryeas' shop. The other 10 were built by students at the nearby Springfield Industrial School and literally had to be rebuilt before they could be sold.

Still, the Times-Herald race and other demonstrations of the automobile's potential had a huge effect on investment. By 1898, it's estimated that more than 200 automobile companies had been organized with total capitalization of a half billion dollars. And in 1900, the New York Auto Show—the nation's first—hosted 40 manufacturers representing over 300 models and drew a crowd of 48,000.

The Curved Dash Breakthrough

The grandfather of popular American automobiles, though, was the Curved Dash Olds, named for its toboggan-like front end. Ransom E. Olds, the son of Pliny Olds, a Lansing, Michigan, machine-shop operator who built gas and steam engines, founded the company in 1897. He did so at the urging of his father who wanted him to "build one motor carriage in as nearly a perfect manner as possible."

By 1899, he was prepared to build cars at a factory set up in Detroit. Fire would later claim that plant, a blaze credited with creating the supplier industry in the U.S. Since Olds needed space to assemble automobiles, he converted the foundry into a factory and then assembled engines and bodies supplied by outside companies, headed by such people as Henry Leland (who would start both Cadillac and Lincoln), Benjamin Briscoe and the Dodge brothers. Later all production would be consolidated back in Lansing.

In a further twist, that Detroit factory site is mere yards from Detroit's Renaissance Center, corporate headquarters of General Motors and the place where the decision was made in 2000 to drop America's oldest surviving nameplate by the end of 2004. In 1900 the Curved Dash Olds made its debut. Powered by a 1-cylinder engine with a displacement of 95.4 cu.-in., it delivered 4 bhp. The water-cooled motor was located beneath the seat and ignition came from four dry-cell telephone batteries. With a wooden body, seats for two and a tiller for steering, the Curved Dash rode on a 60-inch wheelbase and a 56-inch track. The car employed chain drive, had a 2-speed planetary gear transmission, plus reverse and 28-inch tall wire wheels. Weighing just 700 lbs., the Curved Dash was lightweight, powerful and easy to drive with an amazing capacity to go just about anywhere. In fact,

early demonstrations often had the car bouncing up and down steps of the Michigan State Capitol building in Lansing to show the car's capability on steep inclines. The Curved Dash Olds was an unqualified hit, selling in volumes as high as 5,000 a year for just $650, although that price would drop to just $260 by the time the car went out of production in 1907. The first American car was true to its type—a car for the masses. In a turn of events that would repeat again and again throughout the industry, Ransom Olds was forced out of the company he owned in 1904. He would go on to found REO Motor Company, which would produce cars and trucks until 1936.

24-25 With 4 bhp and weighing 700 lbs, the Curved Dash Oldsmobile proved to be a rugged and versatile automobile. To showcase the vehicle's climbing ability, Ransom Olds devised this giant teeter-totter as a publicity stunt.

25 top Not only did cars need improvement, so did roads. In May 1905, Oldsmobile sent two cars, Old Scout and Old Steady, on a 45-day transcontinental drive from New York to Portland, Ore. to promote road construction.

25 bottom The 1901 Olds Curved Dash, so called for its toboggan-shaped nose, sports the first use of the famous Oldsmobile crest on its flanks. This particular model is fitted with the optional top and fenders.

Race for Survival

Some 90 miles away in Cleveland, Ohio, Alexander Winton also had a dream to produce his own car. Although his company would last only until 1924, it made its mark in competition as well as the manner in which the cars were built. Not only was he one of the first men to organize his business around an orderly production process, he also recognized the publicity value of demonstration runs and racing. His first car, built in 1897, hit a top speed of 33 mph in the measured mile. He capitalized on that attention by later driving the car from Cleveland to New York. Two years later he repeated the trip, this time accompanied by a reporter who sent dispatches back repeatedly referring to Winton's machine as an automobile. The name stuck. In 1899 Winton sold 100 cars. But unlike the Curved Dash Olds, a vehicle with mass appeal, Winton's cars were larger, heavier and more expensive. In 1901, as part of his ongoing program of promotion through racing, he participated in an event held in Grosse Pointe, Michigan that would change the future of the auto industry.

26-27 Henry Ford (left) passes Alexander Winton to win a 10-mile race held in October 1901 on a track in the Detroit suburb of Grosse Pointe. The victory earned Ford financial backing for his first automotive venture, which later became Cadillac.

27 Horatio Nelson Jackson (at wheel) and Sewall Crocker were the first to drive coast-to-coast in 1903, aboard Jackson's two-cylinder Winton. The 63-day journey was the result of a $50 bet Jackson made at San Francisco's University Club that it could be done.

At that time, 38-year-old Henry Ford was struggling. His first venture in auto making, the Detroit Automobile Company, was bankrupt after producing 20 vehicles. He had built another car, a 2-cylinder motorized carriage, slightly larger than the Curved Dash Olds but much in the same vein, as a means of providing transportation that the average worker could afford.

The Detroit Driving Club offered a $1,000 prize to the winner of a 25-lap race on its one-mile dirt oval in suburban Grosse Pointe. Ford saw the race as an opportunity to showcase his talents and perhaps pick up some cash to get back on his feet. Thirteen vehicles, including the heavily favored Winton, were entered. The preliminaries took much longer than expected, so the feature race was shortened to 10 laps, and through attrition only three cars were ready to start the main event. At the start, the third entry suffered mechanical problems and withdrew, leaving the race between the 70-bhp Bullet of Winton and Ford's 26-bhp car.

At the beginning of the race Winton pulled away handily, but Ford persevered, closing the gap after five laps. Suddenly the Winton began to sputter and falter. The car was suffering from electrode fouling. Ford, who used the services of local dentist Dr. W.E. Sandborn to fashion a ceramic insulator for his spark ignition coil to provide a hotter, more consistent spark, had no such problems. This spark coil system paved the way for the modern spark plug.

Ford's victory in the car, later dubbed "Sweepstakes" to commemorate the win, provided much needed publicity and attracted enough inventors to allow him to incorporate the Ford Motor Company in June 1903.

30 top left With its boiler positioned at the front, the 1908 Stanley Steamer did not have a conventional grille, but instead sported a coffin nose with the script Stanley name proudly displayed.

30 top right Produced three years after the company's establishment in 1898, the 1901 Baker electric proved to be a reliable city car whose ultimate utility, like today's electric vehicles, was hampered by its short range.

Steam or Electric?

While many of the cars produced during this period used Nicholas August Otto's petroleum-fueled 4-stroke internal combustion engine, it wasn't the only power source available in America's fledgling industry. Steam and electric were two viable, though not necessarily ubiquitous, alternatives.

Perhaps the most famous was the Stanley, a steam car built by twin brothers Freeland O. and Francis E. Stanley. A Newton, Massachusetts shop was established after the pair purchased the rights to a steam engine from a Rhode Island inventor. The brothers' two partners had a falling out, and the twins went in separate directions, one into a failing concern, while the other helped established Locomobile, which began building steamers. However, blood proved thicker than boiling water, and the twins reunited a year later, building their own steam car. Locomobile sued, but the brothers had changed their design enough to avoid a ruling against them. Locomobile abandoned steam power in 1904 in favor of gasoline engines and produced cars until 1929.

The Stanley Steamers were quite sophisticated in design from their gasoline counterparts. Since there was no need for a radiator for cooling, the cars sported a coffin nose boiler emblazoned with the script

Stanley. During its brief run, Stanley had the distinction of holding the land speed record in 1906 when Fred Marriott pushed a modified steamer to 127.66 mph in the measured mile.

Another familiar automobile name, Studebaker, got its start producing Conestoga wagons in the 1850s and its first vehicle was actually an electric.

However, Studebaker soon turned to internal combustion as a power source.

Two of the more serious and sustained efforts to produce an electric car were by the Baker Motor Vehicle Company of Cleveland and Anderson Carriage Company, which produced the Detroit Electric. Walter Baker built his first electric vehicle in 1898 and continued to build town cars until 1921, when the firm abandoned the car market to focus on building electric trucks.

Anderson began business as a high-end carriage maker in 1884 and later moved operations from Port Huron, Michigan, to Detroit in 1907 when it began building electric cars. Starting with an initial run of 125 cars, Detroit Electric's output grew to 650 per year, but the vehicles were pricey. At $1,400 they were more than double the cost of a Model T.

Ironically, Detroit Electric's owner body included one Clara Ford, Henry's wife. Rechristened the Detroit Electric Car Company when founder William Anderson retired in 1918, the company built cars until 1939, with the later models based on Dodge bodywork. Despite years of technological innovation, the electric vehicle today still faces the same challenge that Baker and Anderson did a century ago: limited range. Back then, the wet-cell lead acid batteries made them impractical for anything but in-town use.

Besides experimenting with batteries or steam, other manufacturers had unorthodox ideas on how Otto's 4-stroke engine should work. Adams-Farwell, a Dubuque, Iowa automotive pioneer, turned the idea of a reciprocating engine on its head, literally.

Rather than having a stationary block in which pistons moved to turn a crankshaft, the 1904 Adams-Farwell had a stationary shaft around which the cylinders rotated, acting as a flywheel. This 20 bhp 3-cylinder rotary engine was mounted horizontally, and circular motion of the cylinders helped cooling. Power was transmitted via bevel gears to a 4-speed transmission. In 1906, a 45 bhp 5-cylinder model, fitted with a 3-speed transmission, was introduced. The car was sold with few changes until 1913.

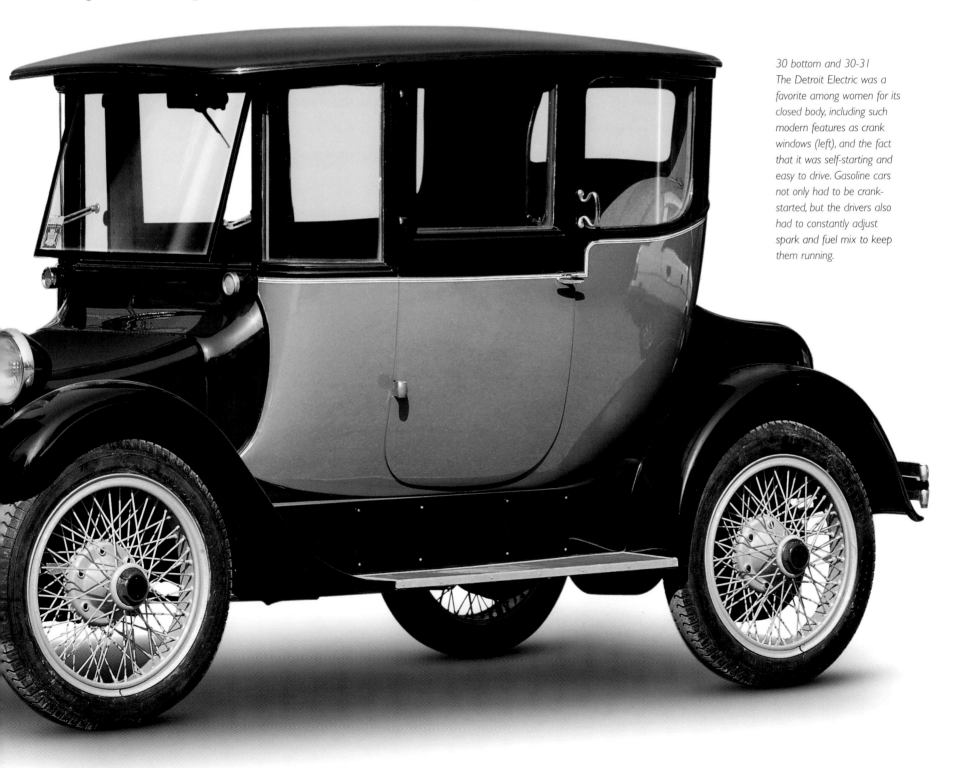

30 bottom and 30-31
The Detroit Electric was a favorite among women for its closed body, including such modern features as crank windows (left), and the fact that it was self-starting and easy to drive. Gasoline cars not only had to be crank-started, but the drivers also had to constantly adjust spark and fuel mix to keep them running.

convince Motor magazine about the interchangeability of Cadillac parts and urged the publication as well as the Royal Automobile Club to test this capability. It took several years for the RAC to develop a standardized test. On February 29, 1908, three 1907 Cadillacs with non-sequential serial numbers were driven to the Brooklands racetrack, lapped the circuit 10 times and then locked in a brick garage. The following Monday, mechanics began disassembling the cars. Two days later, the cars were in 721 separate pieces each. RAC members mixed the parts, removed 89 different components from the pile and

Standard of the World

As the American industry evolved, technical innovation in the vehicle itself was no longer the deciding factor in whether or not a company would survive or fail. Knowing how to build a vehicle in an efficient manner with high quality became equally relevant. As the Duryeas proved before the turn of the century, being first didn't automatically guarantee success.

Henry Leland was an experienced machine tool engineer who studied his craft in the textile industry, at Colt firearms and finally at the Rhode Island machinery firm of Brown and Sharpe, before moving to Detroit in the 1890s. There he founded Leland and Faulconer, a producer of steam engines, gears and marine engines. As noted earlier, when Oldsmobile needed engine parts following the disastrous fire at their Detroit works, Leland and Faulconer was one of the suppliers.

In 1902 Leland formed Cadillac, named for Antoine de la Mothe Cadillac, the French explorer who founded Detroit in 1701. The company was built from the remains of Henry Ford's Detroit Automobile Company, the bankrupt venture Ford departed before building his Sweepstakes winner.

Though common in the production of firearms and industrial machinery, the art of precision machining was not highly practiced in the realm of the automobile. Each vehicle was hand crafted with individual pistons and cylinder honed for fit. The idea of interchangeable parts was understood but thought unachievable since it would require strict tolerances in mass-produced parts. According to *Cadillac, Standard of the World: The Complete History*, Maurice D. Hendry wrote that when Leland produced engines for Oldsmobile, he would require that engine bores be meticulously measured. If the piston was too big, it would be honed to fit, but if too small, the part would be scrapped, as would blocks with oversize bores, while narrow bores would be honed out.

This differed from the usual industry practice of matching large pistons with oversize bores and small pistons with narrow cylinders. His goal was the complete interchangeability of parts. This philosophy was carried over into the newly formed Cadillac Motor Car Company.

Seizing on this potential, Cadillac's sales agent in Britain, a Frederick Stanley Bennett, tried in 1903 to

substituted them with spares from Bennett's agency. Over the next several days the cars were reassembled (the mismatched colors of the body panels caused the cars to be nicknamed Harlequins) and driven 500 miles around the Brooklands track. By establishing the practicality of interchangeable parts, Cadillac was awarded the prestigious Dewar Trophy, an award that recognized leadership in automotive technology. As a result, Cadillac would rightly claim its cars were "the standard of the world." Cadillac would win its second Dewar five years later for the electric self-starter.

32 top Cadillac's 1902 prototype came from what remained of the Detroit Automobile Co., Henry Ford's first unsuccessful venture in the auto industry, whose assets were taken over by Henry Martyn Leland, an experienced tool engineer.

32-33 A 10 hp single-cylinder engine powered the first Cadillac, a 1903 model called the Model A Runabout. Unlike earlier cars, the Cadillac used a steering wheel instead of a tiller, although on this model, it was mounted on the car's right-hand side.

33 top In winning the prestigious Dewar Trophy for parts interchangeability, three Cadillacs were disassembled at the Brooklands racetrack in 1908, their parts mixed and reassembled. Once together, all three cars were driven 500 miles.

Ford's Better Idea

The idea that parts could be interchangeable paved the way for the mass production of cars and again, Henry Ford would step forward into the spotlight. Ford's first real factory was located on Piquette Avenue in Detroit on property acquired in April 1904 for $23,500. Piquette Avenue was becoming the hub of auto manufacturing—Ford was located on the same block as the Everitt-Metzger-Flanders auto company, while the Wayne Automobile factory and later Packard would be located nearby.

The three-story building plus a separate powerhouse were built for $70,000. Learning a lesson from the Olds factory fire, the facility was equipped with firedoors, a sprinkler system and fire escapes.

The long, narrow building (it was 402 feet long and 56 feet wide) was patterned in the New England textile mill style, which allowed for large windows and good natural lighting. Cars were built in workstations with teams building complete vehicles from the ground up. Production began in 1904.

The company's first car to come out of the Piquette factory was the Ford Model B, which was assembled on the second floor, while the third floor was used for subsequent smaller cars, the Model C and F. At the insistence of Alexander Malcomson, Ford's partner and financial backer, Ford began to build larger and more complex vehicles culminating in the 1905 Model K, a 6-cylinder tourer that retailed for $2,500. Ford had seen other car companies that catered to the wealthy fail for lack of volume. His vision was to create a car for the masses, one that his own workers could afford.

The failure of the Model K in 1906 and continuing disagreements led to Malcomson's departure. Ford increased his stake in the company and set about to develop his people's car. An interim step was the Model N, which marked the return of a simpler, less expensive design (it retailed for $600, even less than the Curved Dash Olds) powered by a 4-cylinder engine. In 1907, more than 8,000 units of the Model N were sold, quintupling the previous year's sales. Variations of the slightly more expensive versions called Model R and S soon followed.

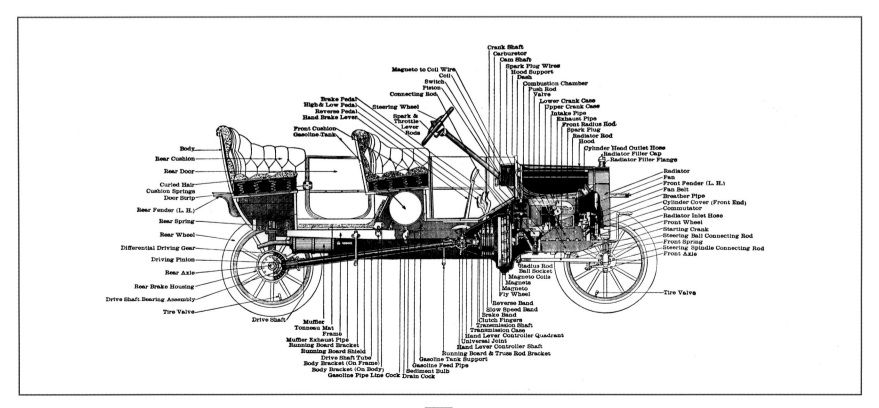

Meanwhile, on the third floor of Piquette plant, Ford built a partition beyond which only certain trusted employees were allowed to pass. It was in this room where the Model T would be developed. The reason for secrecy had as much to do with the factory's location as anything else. Naturally, with so many car companies in such close quarters, there was plenty of interaction between employees and just as much friendly spying. In fact, Ford's office, which had been on the first floor facing the street, was later moved up to the second to discourage people from dropping by to see what was going on.

Ford planned to make the Model T not only affordable, but also lighter and stronger and therefore more durable than anything else on the market. The way he would do it would be with the use of vanadium steel, a special alloy he observed on a French car and a material virtually unknown in America.

Ford convinced a foundry in Ohio to adopt the process and took delivery of his first shipment of the steel in the spring of 1907. The first Model T was introduced on October 1, 1908. Other innovations on the Model T included the use of a single casting for the 4-cylinder engine rather than casting the barrels separately. The engine was also one of the first applications of the detachable head.

The Model T's 4-cylinder engine displaced 3.0 liters and produced 26 bhp, enabling the car to hit speeds as high as 45 mph and yet return nearly 30 miles on a gallon of gasoline. The Model T had a 2-speed transmission controlled by a foot pedal. Priced initially at $850, the car was an instant success, thanks to its low weight, good performance and durability. In the first year, the Model T sold 10,660 units.

36-37 By 1916, the Model T added features like doors, electric lights and even an electric starter to keep pace with the competition.

37 top Prior to the development of the Model T, Ford built a large six-cylinder touring car, the Model K, that met with limited success.

37 bottom Even with its top up, the Model T offered limited protection from the elements. Still, the car proved popular for its low purchase price, which dropped as low as $260, as well as the ease with which it could be repaired and maintained.

Meanwhile, a new larger factory was being constructed in Highland Park, a suburb located a few miles north of the Piquette facility, with operations shifting to the plant in 1910. It was there that Ford experimented with a rope pulling a chassis across the floor and workers, assigned to a specific station doing one task over and over again, would assemble the vehicle. Instead of individual teams building cars from the ground up, the cars themselves would be moved along an assembly line, the same basic process used today in manufacturing plants around the world. By 1911, Ford had established its first branch assembly plant in Kansas City, Missouri. Meanwhile, the moving assembly line at Highland Park began to dramatically speed up the production process. In 1913, the plant assembled more than 100,000 cars. The following year output tripled. Eventually, the line would produce one car every 10 seconds. As volumes increased, prices dropped so that by 1925, two years before the Model would finally go out of production, a roadster could be had for just $260. In its 19-year lifespan, 15,007,033 Model T cars were built and sold in the United States alone.

38-39 The use of a moving assembly line was the key to the Model T's low cost. The system, installed in Ford's Highland Park assembly plant, also featured overhead conveyor belts to power the tools to build the cars as well as move the line itself.

39 top While the cars themselves evolved, note the closed body style on these later Model Ts, the basic concept of the assembly line has remained unchanged to this day.

39 bottom The efficiency of the moving assembly line allowed Ford to increase production to the point where one car was being built every 10 seconds. Here completed cars await shipment.

40-41 Early on the "body drop" where the body of the car is mated to its chassis, was actually performed outside the Highland Park assembly plant. Later that operation was moved indoors.

41 top Though an efficient means of producing cars, Ford's moving line meant that workers performed repetitive tasks assembling specifics components such as the steering system.

41 bottom Components assembled on smaller lines, such as this one building magnetos, would feed into the larger, main assembly line.

The Sporting Life

In this early stage of the auto industry, the adage "racing improves the breed" was more a case of "racing proves the breed." The most famous and grueling race was the 1908 New York to Paris race that traversed 20,000 miles across America, Asia and Europe. An American car, a 1907 Thomas Flyer from Buffalo, New York won the race, thereby elevating the reputation of U.S. engineering and manufacturing.

Erwin Thomas purchased the Globe Cycle Company in 1900 and two years later began pro-

42 top and 42-43 One of the greatest adventures in early motoring was the 1908 New York Times Round-the-World Race from New York to Paris, which featured six cars from America, France, Germany and

Italy. The event won by the Thomas Flyer, built in Buffalo, N.Y. In the image above the Thomas Flyer is bogged down in mud somewhere in the America West during the 169-day New York to Paris Race.

43 top left Traveling west, the cars were shipped across the Pacific for the Japan leg (here the Thomas drives through Kobe) before landing by ship at Vladivostok for the trek across Asia.

43 top right Crowds close in the on the Thomas Flyer in Paris. Although a German Protos actually arrived in Paris on July 26, four days before the Americans, they had been penalized 15 days for skipping the Japan leg, which handed the victory to the Thomas Flyer.

ducing light 1- and 2-cylinder cars. His first Flyer appeared in 1904 followed the next year by cars with 40 and 50 bhp 4-cylinder engines and a 60 bhp six. A new body style, patterned after European cars of the time, appeared in 1906 and provided the basis for the race winning '07 Model Flyer.

Though the publicity garnered by the win enabled sales to peak at 1,908 cars in 1909, the company's first shaft-drive car, the Model L Flyabout, suffered from poor quality. Thomas sold the company to bankers in 1910 and by 1912 the company was in receivership.

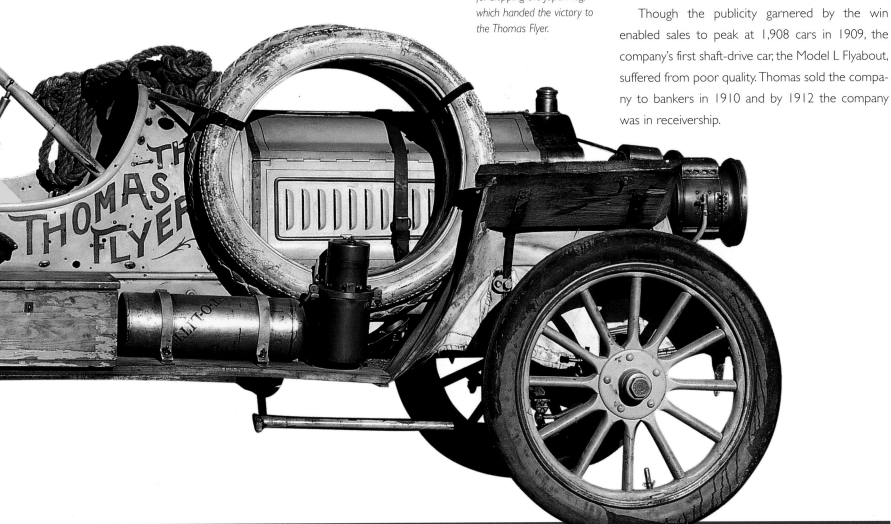

44-45 *East meets West as the Thomas Flyer drives through an Oriental village.*

45 top *The Thomas Flyer, as indicated by this early advertisement, was hardly a car for the average working man with a price tag of $3,500 in 1907.*

19 EXPENSIVE EFFICIENT BEARINGS.

THE THOMAS FLYER
50 H.P. $3500.00
A CAR THAT'S FULL JEWELLED.

The Jewels in a watch and the bearings in a motor car exercise practically the same function. One is just as vital as the other. The cheaper the watch the fewer the jewels—the better the car the better the bearings.

Short sighted economy suggests to the automobile manufacturer that he keep the number of expensive bearings down to the minimum. Regard for the perfection of his product demands that the number be brought to the maximum.

The efficiency of a car—all other essentials being adequate—increases in proportion to the increase of high grade and high priced bearings.

That is one of many points in Thomas Flyer construction in which cost has been utterly ignored. The Thomas contains 19 efficient and expensive bearings.

Get the 1906 Thomas Catalogue and learn more about this invaluable feature

THE E. R. THOMAS MOTOR COMPANY
1200 Niagara Street, BUFFALO, N. Y.
Members Association Licensed Automobile Manufacturers

45 bottom *The Thomas Flyer had been shipped to Valdez, Alaska for a 1,000-mile leg in the Yukon Valley. But, an early thaw made passage impossible and the car was sent on to Japan.*

Another company built on racing success was Marmon and, unlike Thomas, it had a longer run.

The Indianapolis-based company, with roots going back as far as 1851, built air-cooled V-4s from 1902 to 1908. A 1908 60 bhp V-8 was followed by two larger fours in 1909. In 1911 the Marmon Wasp, a single seat racer powered by a six, won the first Indianapolis 500. Piloted by Ray Harroun, the Wasp competed against a field of cars that all carried riding mechanics. In addition to winning the first 500, the Marmon also marked the first use of a rearview mirror on an automobile. Marmon would go on to produce larger 6- and 8-cylinder cars culminating in a large, 8-liter V-16 limousine, its only model in its last year of business, 1933. The benefits of winning races were not con-fined to the promotional aspects alone. People were not buying cars just because of the durability that a race winner exhibited, but for the excitement promised by that level of performance. Cars were no longer just a means to get from Point A to Point B. The idea that getting there is half the fun was taking hold. And automakers were more than willing to make purpose-built cars to satisfy these desires.

The epitome of these early open speedsters were the Mercer Type 35-R Raceabout and the Stutz Bearcat. Mercer, founded by Brooklyn Bridge builder G.C. Roebling, took its name from the county in which its Trenton, New Jersey works were located. The Type 35 debuted in 1910 with a T-head Beaver engine displacing 299 cu.-in. Roebling's son, Washington (who would later die on the Titanic) suggested a lightweight speedster for 1911. Finlay Robertson Porter, an engineer who would go on to found FRP and Porter car companies, designed a car called the Raceabout. It proved to be as fast as it was spartan. The only bodywork was a hood that covered the engine and fenders connected by running boards that shielded the wheels. The open-air cockpit (the windshield consisted of a steering column monocle) was equipped with two simple bucket seats placed ahead of a drum-like gas tank. There was a small tool kit behind the tank along with two spare tires. Mercer boasted that the car was designed to be "safely and consistently driven" above 70 mph. After Washington Roebling's death and Porter's departure, Erik Delling

46-47 *The Inaugural Indianapolis 500 run in 1911 went to Ray Harroun in the Marmon Wasp, who averaged 74.59 mph. He* *was the only racer without a riding mechanic and the Marmon was the first car ever equipped with a rear view mirror.*

the low-slung profile unsettling, the company offered an American Tourist version of the same car with a conventional frame-over-axle design.

In 1911, Stutz built his own racing car in five weeks and entered it into the inaugural Indy 500 placing 11th. Under the sobriquet of "the car that made good in a day," Stutz formed the Ideal Car Company to build his Bearcat. The 1912 Bearcat, though similar in appearance to the Mercer—no bodywork around the cockpit, twin bucket seats, monocle windshield and barrel-shaped gas tank—was much heavier and offered a choice of 4- or 6-cylinder power. The large 6.3-liter Wisconsin six made about 60 bhp, roughly the same as the Mercer.

It was also $500 cheaper than its main competitor, with prices starting at $2,000. The 6-cylinder model listed at $2,125. In addition to winning numerous road races and hillclimbs (Stutz automobiles won 25 of 30 events entered in 1921), a Bearcat broke the transcontinental speed record in 1915 when Cannonball Baker drove it from San Diego, California, to New York in 11 days, 7 hours and 15 minutes. Nick Georgano, writing in "The American Car—A Centenary," noted that the Bearcat was the source of intense rivalry with Mercer owners. Stutz owners would shout, "There's no car worser than a Mercer," to which the Mercer camp would respond, "You have to be nuts to drive a Stutz."

Harry Stutz left his company in 1919, three years after banker Alan A. Ryan bought the firm. Ryan subsequently sold Stutz in 1922 to Charles M. Schwab, president of Bethlehem Steel. The Bearcat continued in production until 1924. One of Stutz's biggest racing wins came in the Le Mans 24 Hours in 1928 when a single entry was leading with one hour left before a transmission failure. The car limped home in second behind a Blower Bentley. In the meantime, management decided to refocus the company with the 1926 Safety Stutz, a car featuring shatterproof glass, 4-

wheel hydraulic brakes and a year's free passenger insurance. In 1931, the company tried to restore its image by reintroducing the Bearcat, which was guaranteed to run at 100 mph. A Super Bearcat riding on a shortened 116-in. wheelbase was also introduced, but it was too little, too late. Stutz ceased manufacturing efforts in 1935.

Another sporting car, though not as racy as the stripped down Mercer Raceabout and Stutz Bearcat, was the Pope-Hartford Roadster. Winner of the 1911 Oakland-Panama Pacific Road Race, the Pope-Hartford was one of three brands by Colonel Albert A. Pope. A Civil War veteran who had used his Army pay to start what would become the nation's largest bicycle company, he looked to diversify his Pope Manufacturing Company by getting into the automobile business.

He started not one, but three companies: Pope-Tribune, a maker of economy cars; Pope-Hartford, a mid-range of vehicles that became the most famous and best sold; and a luxury car firm known as Pope-Toledo, which was actually the gasoline-powered successor to the Toledo Steamer, known for its 60 mph top speed. Both Pope-Tribune, which made small 1- and 2-cylinder runabouts, and Pope-Toledo failed by 1909. Still, by 1913, Pope-Hartford had earned a good reputation, although the company's ambitions had gotten out of hand. More than 14 different models with either 4- or 6-cylinder engine were offered, and the confusing array of vehicles actually hurt sales. By 1914, Pope had quit the car business.

The industry had moved beyond building cars for basic transportation and began looking for other needs to satisfy, be they the desire to go fast or to surround oneself in luxury. In this environment, Pope found itself the victim of trying to offer too many models of cars across a broad spectrum. It wasn't a bad idea as General Motors would later prove. It seems that Pope was just a bit ahead of the times.

designed a new line of raceabouts called the 22-70. Still open top cars, these new models had more traditional bodywork with doors and a conventional windscreen. The cars were equipped with 4-cylinder engines and later were fitted with sixes. By 1925, however, Mercer was out of business due to low demand.

Harry Stutz was an Indianapolis carmaker whose first claim to fame was the American Underslung, which was produced from 1905 to 1914. What made this car unusual was the routing of the car's frame rails underneath rather than over the axles, hence the name "Underslung." This construction technique resulted in a car that was much lower in height without sacrificing ground clearance. For those who found

CHAPTER 2

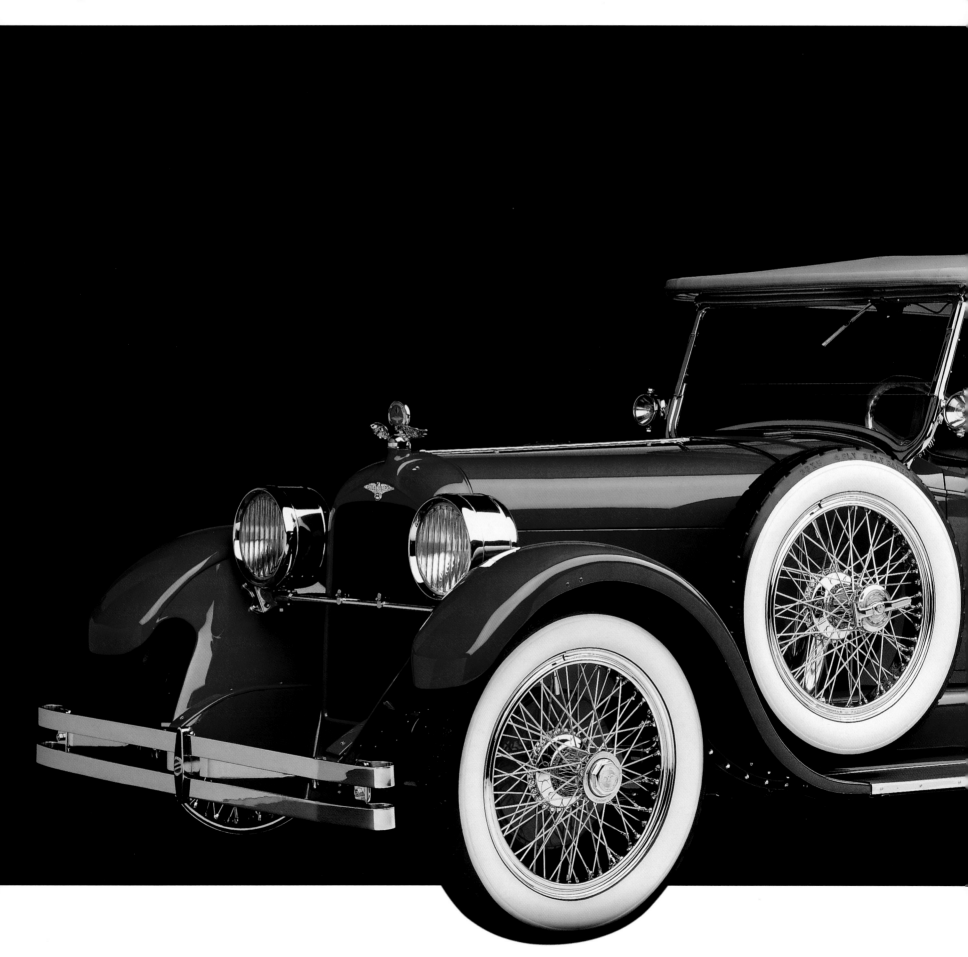

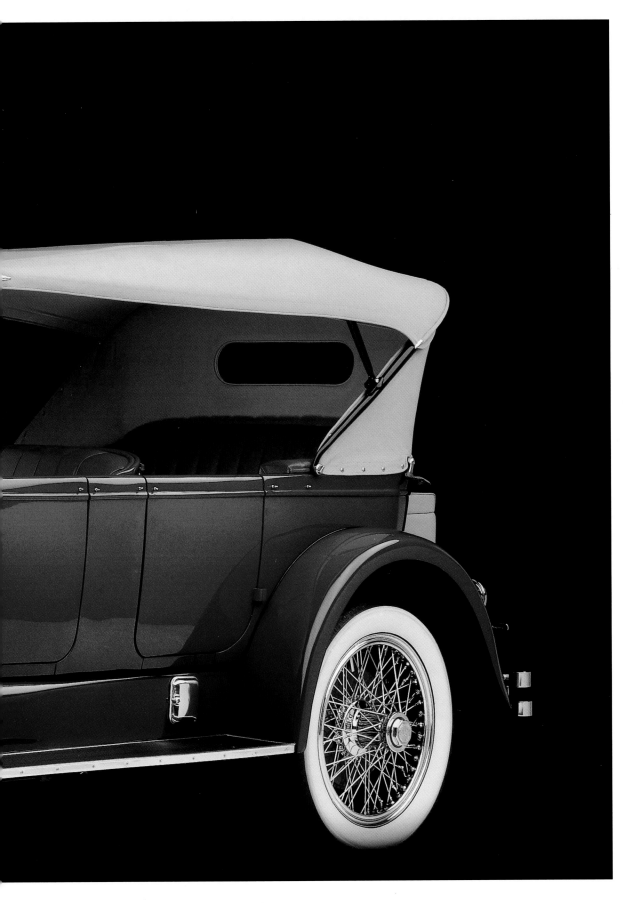

1912 - 1929
Cars for
the Masses

48-49 While Duesenberg
would come to represent the
pinnacle of American luxury
cars, its first offering, the
Model A (introduced in
1921; pictured is a 1923
model), didn't sell well, forcing
Fred and August Duesenberg
to sell their company in
1926.

T he moving assembly line and interchangeable parts enabled mass production of cars, but they did little to spur the demand for automobility by the average American. It would take another innovation to ensure that automobiles would become a household necessity in America. That invention would be the electric self-starter.

Henry Leland's Cadillac prided itself on adapting new technology. The firm was the first to use Johannson Gauges (so-called Jo-Blocks) that provided precise measurements needed to make interchangeable parts. Cadillac also offered the first closed-body automobile, showing the Osceola prototype in 1905 and offering closed bodies as an option in 1906 and standard equipment in 1910. So it was inevitable that Charles Kettering, head of Dayton Engineering Laboratories, would approach Leland in 1911 with plans for a self-starter. Both men

had known people who had been injured by the kick-back from hand cranks, and they also knew that it was a difficult task hand-spinning the engine and quickly running back to the steering wheel to adjust the throttle and spark advance to keep the engine running. There had to be a better way and Kettering believed his system, which used battery power to crank the engine, was the answer.

Leland subsequently ordered 12,000 starting sets for his car and both men set about finding the

money to make the starter a reality. Kettering needed the investment to tool up production of the systems, while Leland had to convince the bankers who controlled Cadillac (now part of a fledgling General Motors) yet didn't want to spend money on this newfangled contraption.

At a particularly stormy meeting, the bankers produced various "experts" who said the electric starter was a non-starter. Leland had anticipated their arguments and had an electric-starter equipped Cadillac in the room. After the presentation, he reached in the car, turned a switch, adjusted the throttle and punched a button. The Cadillac chugged to life and idled smoothly, quelling the bankers' objections.

The self-starter also ushered in the concept of the modern electrical system. In addition to a starter, cars were equipped with generators that provided voltage to the ignition system, recharged the battery used to crank the engine in the starting process, and powered lights, replacing acetylene gas lamps. These developments would earn Cadillac its

second Dewar Trophy, the only manufacturer ever to win the honor twice.

By the 1912 New York Auto Show, every vehicle on display was equipped with an electric starter except those of Henry Ford, who thought the system was too heavy for his lightweight Model T. Later, even Ford relented, offering the self-starter as an option and then as standard equipment.

Although Ford resisted advances like the self-starter, on the labor relations front he was progressive. He revolutionized pay scales in the industry by offering his workers $5 a day in 1914.

This nearly doubled the industry's going rate and virtually ensured that everyone working for Ford Motor Company could afford the cars they were building. Henry's dream of cars for the masses had become a reality.

The success of the Model T almost proved to be its undoing. After a period in which Ford introduced more than one new model a year until the Model T's debut in 1908, the company would stick with the Tin Lizzy for almost two decades.

50-51 Born in the back shops and barns all across America, auto making soon evolved into a highly specialized business as evidenced by the 1915 photo of a dynometer testing station where the cars received their final check before being shipped.

51 The key to making the modern assembly line work was standardized parts. Cadillac was the first manufacturer to use Johansson Gauges, known as Jo-Blocks, to check tolerances. Here a workman measures the gauge on tooling.

Body by Fisher

THE familiar phrase *"as good as Buick"* suggests that you see and drive the car that others use as the Standard of Comparison before you spend your money.

"WHEN BETTER AUTOMOBILES ARE BUILT · · · BUICK WILL BUILD THEM"

The Better Buick

VALVE-IN-HEAD
Buick
MOTOR CARS

Bigger Is Better

The teens were volatile years in the auto industry. Fortunes were made and lost as new companies sprung up and pioneering firms faltered. Consolidation was in the air.

The master of the deal was William Crapo Durant, an enterprising Flint businessman who gained control of Buick in 1904. Founded by David Dunbar Buick, a Scot who also lived in Flint and invented the process that bonded porcelain to cast iron bathtubs, Buick was noted for its advanced engineering, thanks to Walter Marr, who conceived the powerful valve-in-head design.

Durant, who had made a fortune in the carriage trade and later on Wall Street, was a savvy businessman when it came to sales and marketing. He took a gamble in 1908, continuing to build cars as industry sales plummeted. When the market turned around in the spring, Buick was one of the few with inventory to sell and he profited handsomely. It was during this downturn that Durant first proposed a merger of the four largest automakers: Ford, Maxwell-Briscoe, REO and Buick. The deal died when Ransom Olds and Henry Ford demanded cash for their companies instead of a stock swap.

Flush with cash from his sales successes, Durant then set about to buy up a number of automakers, including Cadillac and the troubled Oldsmobile and Oakland works, and in September 1908 he incorporated General Motors.

In addition to the carmakers, Durant overextended himself by buying a large number of suppliers, many of which were in financial trouble. By 1910, he was forced out of General Motors by bankers, who took control of the firm. But that wasn't the last GM would hear from Durant.

52 and 53 bottom left In the industry's infancy, getting customers to buy their first car was the challenge, as the business matured, getting their repeat business was the goal as shown by these "Better Buick" ads.

53 top Flint businessman William Crapo Durant established General Motors in 1908 using his success with Buick as a foundation and adding the troubled Cadillac,

Oldsmobile and Oakland to his empire. He was forced out of GM twice, but later built his own car, the Durant, which he inspects outside his Long Island City, N.Y. factory with William Poerter (right).

53 bottom right Flint was a one-company town thanks to Buick. Here in 1910, workers leave the factory on foot or by streetcar. The automobiles they built were still out of reach.

54 top and 54-55 Louis Chevrolet made a name for himself driving for the Buick factory racing team. Below he pilots a Buick Model 10 in 1910. He clashed with William C. Durant and was eventually ousted from the company that bore his name.

55 top The Chevrolet Classic Six was the brainchild of carried, Louis Chevrolet (second from left), but company owner Durant felt that it was too big and overpriced for the mass market.

Louis Joseph Chevrolet and his brother, Arthur, had been drivers for the Buick factory racing effort. Born in Switzerland, Louis Chevrolet arrived in the U.S. in 1900 as a mechanic and later earned a reputation as a fearless racer. But Chevrolet also dreamed of being a car builder and it was Durant who backed him. Ousted from GM but still wealthy, Durant set up a number of automakers besides Chevrolet in the period between 1911 and 1914. These included Mason Motor, Little Motor, Republic Motor, Sterling Motor and Monroe Motor, and Durant had hopes that one or all would hit the big time. Durant's first car came from Little Motor—the Little Four, a small, 4-cylinder car based on a design from the failed Whiting Company. It debuted in early 1912 and sold for $650. Its successor, the Little Six, was slated for a 1913 introduction using an engine developed by Durant's Sterling unit. Meanwhile, Louis Chevrolet was busy building prototypes for his first effort, a large 6-cylinder touring car called the Type C or better known as the Classic Six. Riding on a 120-in. wheelbase, the 3350-lb. vehicle was powered by a 299 cu.-in. inline six making on the order of 35 to 40 horsepower with a hefty $2,500 sticker price. Durant was not a big fan of the Classic Six, thinking that Chevrolet stood a better chance of building smaller and less expensive cars that appealed to the same wide market as Ford's Model T. Durant valued the inherent recognition in the Chevrolet name due to Louis' racing successes and felt that it had much more cachet than the Little brand.

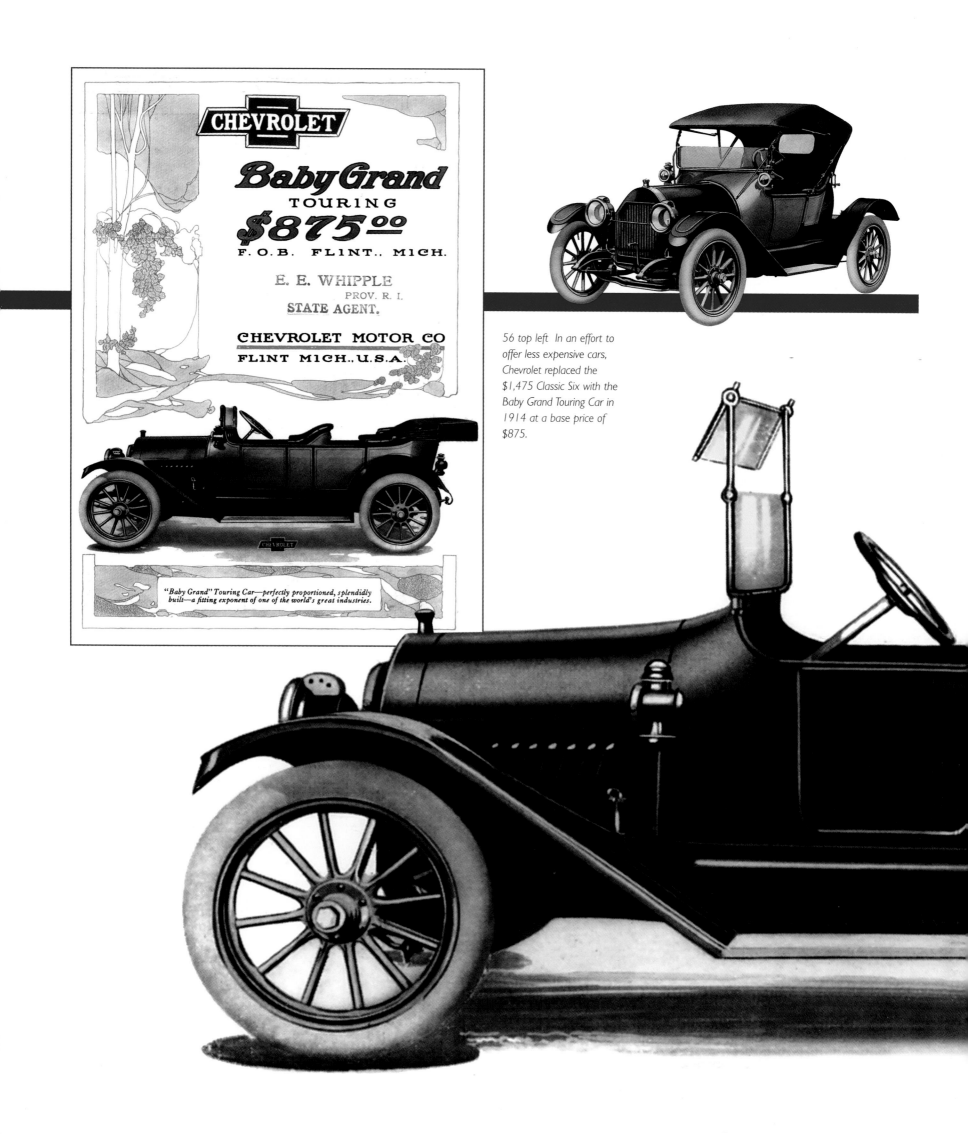

CHEVROLET

Baby Grand
TOURING
$875⁰⁰
F.O.B. FLINT., MICH.

E. E. WHIPPLE
PROV. R. I.
STATE AGENT.

CHEVROLET MOTOR CO
FLINT MICH..U.S.A.

"Baby Grand" Touring Car—perfectly proportioned, splendidly built—a fitting exponent of one of the world's great industries.

56 top left In an effort to offer less expensive cars, Chevrolet replaced the $1,475 Classic Six with the Baby Grand Touring Car in 1914 at a base price of $875.

The Classic Six made it to production and was moderately successful during its brief production run through 1913 and into the early months of 1914. But Durant and Chevrolet were at loggerheads, the two having completely different ideas on everything ranging from the types of cars the company should build to personal comportment. According to Lawrence Gustin in the biography *Billy Durant, Creator of General Motors*, it was a tiff over cigarettes that may have proved to be the breaking point in the relationship. "Late in 1913, Louis Chevrolet and Durant parted company."

The real reason perhaps, was that Durant had decided not to continue the large luxurious car of Louis Chevrolet's dreams. Instead, he wanted to compete more directly with the low-priced Ford. But a more immediate reason was an ongoing, and petty, dispute over Chevrolet's cigarette smoking habits. Louis Chevrolet's version is that Durant told him he wouldn't make any money until he became a gentleman, that he should smoke

cigars, not cigarettes. Every time they talked, Durant would mention this. Finally Chevrolet could contain his irritation no longer: 'I sold you my car and I sold you my name, but I'm not going to sell myself to you. I'm going to smoke my cigarettes as much as I want. And I'm getting out.' And very shortly he did."

Chevrolet would return to racing, joining his brothers Arthur and Gaston to build a series of winning Indy cars called the Frontenac. The car won the Indy 500 back-to-back in 1920 and 1921, but Gaston's death in November 1920 during a race led to the surviving brothers' eventual retirement from competition. With Louis Chevrolet out of the picture, Durant concentrated on making the Series H a mass-market car. The 1914 model, also known as the Baby Grand, had a 24 horsepower 171 cu.-in. 4-cylinder engine and retailed for $875. A roadster known as Royal Mail sold for even less at $750. At the top of the range, the Type C was replaced by the Series L Light Six

which was considerably less expensive at $1,475, but that car was dropped a year later.

Chevrolet's first in-house Model T fighter, the model 490, would debut in mid-1915. Similar in appearance to the Model T, the car was named for its price, $490, which was the going rate for the competing Ford. An optional electrical kit, which included a self-starter (which Ford didn't offer) was listed for $60 and later became part of the car's standard list price of $550 by 1917. Though Ford remained the sales leader, the 490 pushed Chevrolet output past 60,000 units in 1916 and to 125,000 in 1917, landing it fourth in industry sales. Durant was back.

In 1917 Chevrolet began to revamp and expand its model lineup, redesigning the Series H and resurrecting the Baby Grand name for this new car called the Series F. At the top of the line, it introduced the Series D powered by a V-8 engine, which displaced 288 cu.-in. and produced 55 bhp. The high cost—it sold for $1,385—limited its appeal. By 1918, the Series D V8, which now cost $1,550, was dropped and Chevrolet wouldn't offer another V-8 in its line until the birth of the legendary small-block in 1955.

During this period, Durant used the success of Chevrolet to buy his way back into General Motors, the conglomerate he formed in 1908. By April 1916, he had acquired a majority stake in the firm and by 1918 merged Chevrolet with General Motors. His triumph was relatively short-lived. The economic downturn at the end of World War I, combined with his personal fortune evaporating in the stock slide of 1920, led to his ouster.

56 top right A two-door roadster called the Royal Mail was Chevy's least expensive car at $750, which included such features as electric lights, speedometer, windshield, top and side curtains.

56-57 The smaller car for the masses dreamed up by Durant for Chevy was the 490 introduced in 1916, a name inspired by the car's base price and exactly the price of a Ford Model T.

Steinway. That alliance dated back to the personal relationship between William Steinway and Gottleib Daimler. The two were introduced by Daimler's chief engineer Wilhelm Maybach, whose brother had emigrated to America and worked for Steinway. It was Steinway who helped incorporate Daimler Motor Company in the U.S. in 1888 and built marine engines and boats for the German company for many years, since he was convinced that America would not be ready for cars for a long time. Cars were finally built in the years leading up to World War I, although production ceased once hostilities began.

In 1920, another famous European make decided to set up shop in Springfield, Massachusetts, hometown to that original run of 13 Duryeas.

Over Here

The burgeoning U.S. market was a tempting target for European manufacturers, especially for those who had come across the Atlantic to compete at Indianapolis as well as for other famous prizes, such as the Gordon Bennett Cup and the Glidden Trophy. It was through the publicity of the speed events that names like Peugeot, Renault, Mercedes and Fiat were becoming just as much household names here as they were in Europe. And while U.S. production of foreign makes may seem to be a recent development (Honda, for instance, opened its U.S. plant in 1982), in the early 1900s several European makes not only exported cars to America, but set up manufacturing facilities as well.

The first was Italian automaker Fiat, which established a factory in Poughkeepsie, New York. Established with American backers in 1910, the facility initially produced the 5.9-liter Type 54, the famous Type 55 with its huge 9.0-liter 4-cylinder engine, and in 1912, an 8.6-liter U.S.-designed Type 56. In 1918, production was halted and the plant was sold to Rochester-Duesenberg to build airplane engines.

The other American-built car during this period was the Mercedes, which was manufactured under license by Long Island, New York piano maker

Rolls-Royce moved 50 craftsmen and their families from England to build the Silver Ghost, going as far as moving the steering wheel from right-hand to left-hand-drive in 1925.

In 1926, the company introduced the New Phantom model and also acquired the Brewster & Company coachworks to build custom bodies. Regular series production ceased when the factory in England introduced the Phantom II in 1929, although several hundred cars were built from existing stocks of parts.

An additional hundred or so imported Phantom II chassis were bodied by Brewster. In 1934, the venture was dissolved and the facilities taken over by Springfield Manufacturing Company which built Brewster cars for two more years.

58 top and 59 top Fiat, which built a U.S. factory in 1910, enjoyed some popularity in the U.S. until World War I, when the works were sold to Rochester-Duesenberg to build aero engines. In addition to the assembly operation, Fiat set up this large factory garage in New York City to service its automobiles.

58-59 In 1920, Rolls-Royce moved 50 craftsmen over to Springfield, Mass., to built the Silver Ghost. This 1921 model retained its right-hand drive, but by 1925, the factory was turning out left-hand drive models.

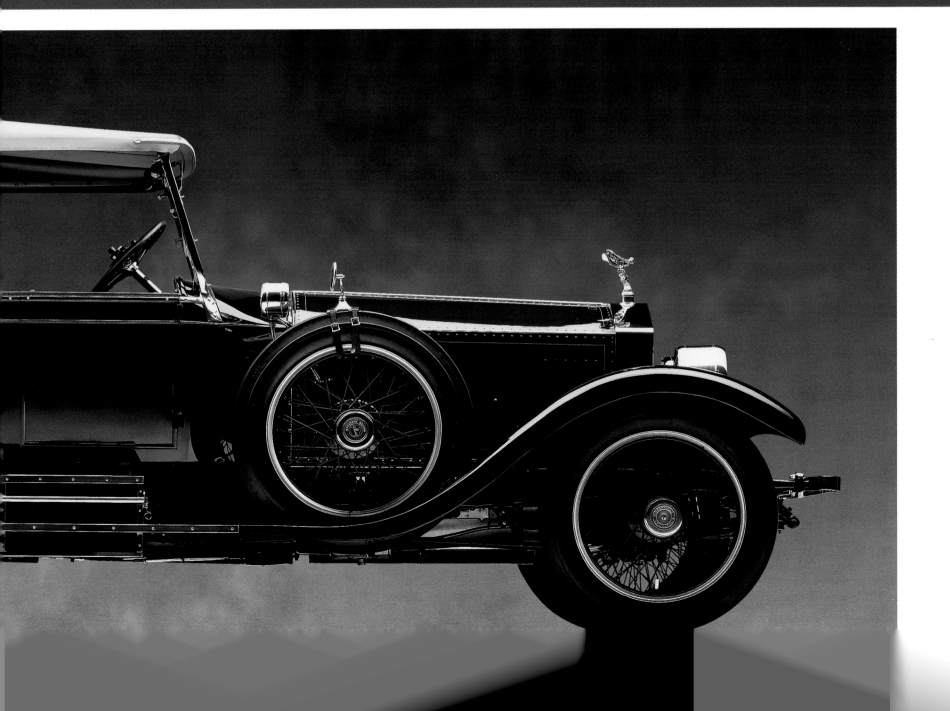

Over There

The "War to End All Wars" would be a temporary boon to companies like Dodge that supplied vehicles to the military. The firm was founded by brothers John and Horace Dodge from rural Niles, Michigan. The pair had learned to be machinists from their father, who operated a small shop. Their first big break came as a result of the Olds factory fire, which gave them a chance to supply transmissions. In 1903

the Dodges had branched out, winning a contract to deliver 650 chassis to Henry Ford. When the automaker couldn't pay a $10,000 invoice, Ford gave the brothers stock worth 10 percent of the company. By 1919, Ford repurchased the stock for $25 million, while the Dodge brothers had received nearly $10 million in dividends over that period.

In 1913, they quit their supplier contract with

Ford and a year later the first Dodge car was produced. Although never the top seller (it did manage to rank second in sales behind Ford with 141,000 units in 1920), Dodge cars were successful against Buick, Chevrolet and Willys-Overland. One of the innovations was the use of an all-steel body developed by Edward Budd of Philadelphia, Pennsylvania. Still suspicious of the welds, the Dodge brothers

added rivets to the car bodies just in case. The use of steel bodies meant that Dodge cars were rugged, and they found a home in the armed services. Dodge cars were popular staff cars for Gen. John J. "Blackjack" Pershing during his incursions into Mexico to chase Pancho Villa in 1916 and during World War I as well. Sadly, John Dodge died of pneumonia in January 1920, followed within 11 months by Horace, also from illness. The Dodge brothers would never know that the company they founded would be one of the few pioneering American nameplates that would endure.

Trying to help with the war effort would prove the undoing of Henry Leland. While at Cadillac, Leland tried unsuccessfully to convince the newly returned Durant that the company should build aircraft engines to help with the war effort. Henry and his son Wilfred quit Cadillac and set up their own factory to produce aircraft engines and called their new venture Lincoln and the engine it would produce the Liberty. The war ended before Leland made any significant number of the engines he had contracted to build for the government. Consequently, he went back to building cars, the first of which, the Series L, appeared in 1920. The cars were expensive, ranging from $4,600 roadsters to $6,600 town cars. The Lelands were again victims of poor timing. Not only did they start too late on Liberty

engines to meet the nation's war requirements, they had launched an expensive car in the midst of a postwar recession. On top of this development, the government began hounding the Lelands for payment on the unfulfilled airplane contract. Within two years, Lincoln was on the brink of bankruptcy. Leland's unlikely savior was Henry Ford, who at the urging of his 28-year-old son, Edsel, promised to bail Lincoln out and keep the Lelands in control. Remember that Leland had worked with Ford at the Detroit Automobile Company in 1902, which became Cadillac after Ford left. In 1922 Ford took control of Lincoln, never allowing the Lelands to exercise the control he promised. Within four months, they were gone, never to work in the industry again.

61 top Henry Leland, who made Cadillac the "standard of the world," was ruined during World War I when he tried to build Liberty aircraft engines for the U.S. government. Here he poses with the first closed body car, the Cadillac Osceola, a 1903 prototype.

61 bottom left After the Dodge Brothers died in 1920, the company was adrift with only minor changes to its lineup until the operation was taken over by Walter P. Chrysler in 1928.

60-61 John and Horace Dodge built rugged cars favored by the military, building on that success in the retail market. The Dodge Main works in Detroit boasted its own test track.

61 bottom right Not quite as inexpensive as the Ford Model T, the four-cylinder Dodge Type-A Sedan was designed to appeal to the middle class.

The death of the Dodge brothers and the departure of industry pioneers like the Lelands and Durant were signs of change in a maturing industry. Marques like Winton, Locomobile, Mercer, Wills St. Clair and Simplex would disappear. The basics of manufacturing and engineering had been established, from the moving assembly line to the H-pattern of the manual shift, as first patented by James Packard and William Hatcher in 1902. Packard, which was started as the Ohio Automobile Company in Warren, Ohio, was a pioneer of another sort by moving its operations to Detroit in 1903. By the 1920s, Michigan's largest city was consolidating its role as the hub of auto manufacturing in the United States. There were still some significant manufacturers located elsewhere—most notably Buffalo's Pierce-Arrow as well as Indiana-based Auburn, Cord, Duesenberg and Studebaker. Wagon-maker Studebaker took the reverse tack, buying Detroit-based EMF as a way to get into the auto business, but it eventually chose its hometown of South Bend as a manufacturing base and sold off its Michigan-based holdings.

A New Generation Takes Over

The industry was changing quickly. Industry pioneers—the inventors and entrepreneurs—were being replaced by a new breed of professional management trained within the industry itself. Durant's departure marked the rise of Alfred Sloan, who had come to General Motors from the Hyatt Roller Bearing division. Promoted to chief executive officer in 1923, Sloan devised a system of decentralized operating divisions, which designed, manufactured and sold cars, backed by a centralized finance structure. It was Sloan who devised a hierarchy among the divisions, providing cars that would allow buyers to make their way up through General Motors' offerings based on their life stage and income. "A car for every purse and every purpose," Sloan would say. By 1927, General Motors had passed Ford in sales. While Sloan worked in relative anonymity at General Motors, Walter P. Chrysler proved that someone who worked in an industry of established nameplates could still build a car company based on one's name.

Walter Chrysler worked for American Locomotive in Pittsburgh before moving to Flint, Michigan to manage Buick. Over his eight-year career at Buick, Walter would see his wages skyrocket. Tight-fisted GM President Charles Nash brought him into the company at $6,000, half his railroad wages.

After Chrysler threatened to quit, Nash quadrupled his pay and by the time Durant resumed control in 1916, Walter was making $50,000 a year. Even though Chrysler still wanted to start his own firm, Durant enticed him to stay for $500,000 a year. But later disputes with Durant forced Chrysler to leave. At the urging of bankers, and with a hefty $1 million salary, he took over ailing Willys-Overland. He soon left to take control of financially troubled Maxwell-Chalmers, a merger of two sick car companies.

While at the reins of Maxwell-Chalmers, Chrysler relied on the talents of Owen Skelton, Carl Breer and Fred Zeder (known as the Three Musketeers) to develop a high compression, 6-cylinder tourer that he wanted to bear his name. In the meantime, he put Maxwell-Chalmers into receivership and formed the Maxwell Motor Company to develop his car.

Denied space at the New York Auto Show in 1924 because neither Maxwell-Chalmers nor Maxwell Motor produced cars at the time, Chrysler showed his prototype at the Commodore Hotel. The car was a hit and Chrysler renamed Maxwell after himself, forming what would become the third member of America's Big Three.

64-65 *By the 1920s, the automobile had become firmly embedded in American society as reflected by its starring role in films of the day such as Laurel and Hardy features.*

The Upper Crust

While many sought to emulate Henry Ford's success of selling cars to the masses at a low price (in 1924, Ford produced its 10 millionth car and sold more than half of the 4 million cars produced in the U.S. that year), there were a few that catered to a more wealthy clientele. Among these more exclusive makes were Cunningham, Duesenberg and the three P's: Packard, Peerless and Pierce-Arrow.

Cunningham, based in Rochester, New York, evolved from a carriage business that started in 1834 by a Canadian, James Cunningham. The firm grew to be a preeminent builder of fine carriages and began building cars as a sideline in 1907. Using Buffalo or Continental engines, Cunningham would build custom bodywork for its cars and in 1916 introduced its own V-8, a 442 cu.-in. brute.

Cunninghams were prized by the wealthy for their bespoke bodywork built on huge 132- or 142-in. wheelbases. In 1919, a Cunningham Touring Victoria sold for $9,000. By the Great Depression, the market for vehicles catering to the upper crust began to dry up and Cunningham concentrated on building cars and hearses for the funeral trade, although it did supply custom bodywork on other chassis, such as the Ford V-8. Cunningham ceased production in 1936.

65 top left The versatility of the Model T is displayed by this "snow cat" version of a pickup truck where the front wheels are replaced by skis and dual rear wheels fitted with a track.

65 top right As late a 1921, dealers still employed stunts like driving a Model T up stairs to underscore the ruggedness of Henry Ford's machine.

65 bottom Edsel Ford inspects the 10 millionth Model T while Henry Ford reflects on the car that started his career, the 1896 Quadricycle.

Duesenberg, which was started by a group of bankers in 1916, employed Frederick and August Duesenberg, self-taught engineers from Germany. They built aircraft engines during World War I from a New Jersey plant. Their first car, the Model A, debuted in 1920 sporting a straight eight engine, the industry's first until Packard offered one in 1923. The marque found success on racing circuits from Indy (where it won the 500 in '23, '25 and '27) to Europe, where Jimmy Murphy became the first American to win a grand prix in an American car when he captured the 1921 French Grand Prix. The brothers moved the venture to Indianapolis where it was renamed the Duesenberg Automobile and Motors Company and reorganized yet again in 1925 as Duesenberg Motors. E.L. Cord purchased the company in 1926 and asked the brothers to produce the finest car money could buy.

This begat the Model J, which debuted at the 1928 New York Auto Show, ushering in the era of

what would become known as the Grand Classic. The Model J chassis retailed for between $8,500 and $9,500 and on it any number of coachbuilders would fit custom-built bodies to specification. Duesenberg models bodied at the factory featured coachwork by noted designer Gordon Buehrig and retailed for $17,500.

66-67 The Duesenberg 1930 Model J Le Baron Phaeton is considered the epitome of 1930s classic American luxury car design.

67 top Heavyweight boxing champ Jack Dempsey takes his turn at the wheel of a 1921 Duesenberg straight-eight racer.

68-69 Details like the side-mount spares and flex hose exhaust on this 1929 Murphy-bodied Duesenberg Model J Dual Cowl Phaeton turn a simple automobile into a work of art.

70 Cars like the Peerless may have been expensive, but the high prices commanded allowed the manufacturer to pioneer technologies such as using shaft drive instead of chain drive.

70-71 Storied '30s classics like Packard established their roots in early in the industry's history with models like the 1916 Twin Six, which was powered by a V-12 aircraft engine.

71 top Part of the allure of Pierce-Arrow was its high quality engineering and durability. Not only did Pierce-Arrow cars serve in the military, the American Red Cross used this particular model as a staff car in 1919.

THE BOOKLOVERS MAGAZINE ADVERTISER

The Joys of Touring

Come in fullest measure to those who know the sense of absolute safety, the thrill of measureless speed, and the feeling of luxurious comfort that abound in

Peerless
Direct Drive
Touring Cars
$3,700 to $6,000

Peerless Cars are easy to handle. They are sent out

Ready to Run and Stay So

Photogravure of the "Peerless Girl V" here illustrated, size 18x29 inches, without advertising and suitable to frame, mailed you for ten cents stamps or coin. Write for new illustrated catalogue.

The Peerless Motor Car Co., Cleveland, Ohio.
Member Association Licensed Automobile Manufacturers.

Duesenberg's erstwhile rival was Packard, which, after it flirted with racing, concentrated on building luxury cars. Packard would be known for its trademark hexagon hubcaps and unique shape of its radiator shell. In 1916, Packard earned its reputation with the Twin Six, a V-12 model based on the Liberty aircraft engine design that became Henry Leland's undoing. Strapped for resources, Leland had enlisted Packard to help with the engineering of that powerplant.

However, the Twin Six proved to be a difficult sale—prices were actually cut from $6,000 in 1921 to $3,850 in 1922. A year later, the twelve was dropped in favor of a new straight eight. In addition to the eight, Packard offered a 6-cylinder model, the Single Six, which the company advertised as a 10-year-car for its high quality materials and craftsman-

ship. Peerless was a Cleveland-based maker of bicycles and wash wringers when it entered the car business in 1900. Its biggest contribution came two years later when the company mounted the engine up front and used a shaft to drive the rear wheels, a layout that would become an industry standard. It began to offer progressively larger engines, moving from fours and sixes to an 80-bhp eight in 1916.

All Peerless models featured V-8 power from that year through 1924. A year later a six was reintroduced to the line, followed in 1926 by another called the Continental. In 1929, a straight eight replaced the V-8. However, Peerless was caught up in the economic upheaval caused by the Great Depression and ceased operation in 1931, although its factory was converted to a brewery for Carling's at the end of Prohibition.

Like Peerless, Pierce-Arrow had its start in bicycles and other non-transportation goods, such as birdcages. The Buffalo-based company was run by George Pierce and offered its first car, the 1-cylinder Motorette, in 1901. In 1904 the Pierce Great Arrow was introduced, and beginning in 1905, the car virtually owned the Glidden Tour, winning that event five times in a row.

Calling itself Pierce-Arrow, the company was known for its trademark radiator mascot, an archer bent over a drawn bow. In 1914, the company patented its design for a fender-mounted headlamp, a design other manufacturers refused to copy to avoid paying royalties. Aiming for the upper reaches of the car market, Pierce-Arrows retailed for over $8,000 and by 1920 sported such amenities as dash-mounted Waltham clocks, dual ignition, dual valves and by 1926, power brakes.

In the mid-1920s, a smaller, less expensive series called the 80 appeared. While it broadened the appeal of the Pierce-Arrow brand, it was felt by some that it diminished the cachet of the larger, more expensive models. Pierce-Arrow ran into financial difficulties and the board decided to sell the company to Studebaker in 1928. For five years, Pierce-Arrow operated as an autonomous division and in 1933 split from Studebaker when that company ran into financial difficulties.

Selling the Sizzle

The 1920s set the stage for two other developments that would define the course of the industry for years to come: the use of advertising and the establishment by manufacturers of in-house styling departments. While advertising was as old as the automobile itself, its effectiveness in pitching the emotional aspect of car ownership was something that was developed much later.

One of the first makers to quote something other than vehicle specifications and price in its sales literature was Roamer, a Kalamazoo, Michigan-built luxury car that sought to position itself as an American Rolls-Royce.

The company went as far as to pattern its radiator shell after the legendary British automobile. In its sales brochures, it quoted the likes of Oscar Wilde and used the language of the snobby elite to create an aura around the brand. But it wasn't until automaker Ned Jordan penned a series of ads in the 1920s that the idea of using imagery to sell cars was unleashed. Jordan developed a mid-priced 2-seat roadster, complete with rumble seat and powered by a 6-cylinder Continental engine in 1919 called the Playboy.

Named after Millington Synge's play *Playboy of the Western World*, the Jordan was undistinguished as cars go, but the series of 4-color ads with copy written by company chief Ned Jordan broke new ground. His ad, "Somewhere West of Laramie," captured the spirit of a Wyoming cowgirl

72-73 *This 1928 ad for the Ford Phaeton portrays the car in a static situation, but still part of everyday life.*

73 top left *Although the car is moving gracefully through countryside in this Cadillac ad from the Saturday Evening Post in 1928, there is little to convey driving excitement.*

JUST as Cadillac beauty created a vogue in motor car style, so has Cadillac's incomparable performance re-created a vogue for driving. There is an irresistible desire to take the wheel of the Cadillac and enjoy what none but a Cadillac-built car, with its 90-degree, V-type, 8-cylinder engine, can give—performance seemingly unlimited in range and variety, so unlabored, so easily controlled, so zestful yet restful, that once again Cadillac has given the idea of luxury in motoring a new meaning.

More than 50 exclusive body styles by Fisher and Fisher-Fleetwood

CADILLAC
A NOTABLE PRODUCT OF GENERAL MOTORS

A SINGLE glance at the aristocratic lines and regal appointments of the new Cadillac must of necessity determine at once all question of social supremacy in motoring hereafter. The car bespeaks everything that is fine and substantial. In addition there is the assurance of the lithe and lightning-like performance and prodigious power of the highly developed 90-degree, V-type, eight-cylinder engine. Such a reservoir of instantaneously tapped energy no Cadillac and no other fine car has ever had.

More than 50 exclusive body styles by Fisher and Fisher-Fleetwood

CADILLAC
A NOTABLE PRODUCT OF GENERAL MOTORS

73 top right *Yet another 1928 ad, where the star is the car. By contrast, Jordan automobiles were being sold with ads evoking the spirit of freedom that autos could bring.*

Jordan saw riding by his private railcar as he traveled to San Francisco. The gist of the ad was that the Jordan Playboy was built with that free-spirited girl in mind. Other ads like "A Million Miles from Dull Care" read in part: "I am sick of four walls and a ceiling…I have business with the sunshine and the summer wind. I am weary of dishes and doctors.

I am tired of going to the store and helping with meals. I am going somewhere if it is the last thing I ever do in my life. I want to start somewhere in the early morning and be somewhere else when it is time to go to bed." Ned Jordan was not selling a tangible good like an automobile, he was selling the concept of what his automobile, or rather automobility, could do for one's state of mind. Advertisers called it selling the sizzle and not the steak. But even strong imagery could do little to ensure the success of a mediocre car. Even though he lowered prices to $1,750 in 1924 and later offered an 8-cylinder model, the unremarkable Jordan met with limited success and the company ceased operation in 1932.

Besides imagery, celebrity was also used to sell cars during this period. While racers had long been associated with various marques, it was an aviator's turn with the Rickenbacker. Advertised as "the car worthy of its name," it carried the famed hat-in-ring logo of Capt. Eddie Rickenbacker, America's ace of aces in World War I. Introduced in 1922, the 58-bhp 6-cylinder mid-market car sported dual flywheels and internal expanding brakes on all four wheels, an innovation in its class.

According to David Burgess Wise's *New Encyclopedia of Automobiles*," Rickenbacker suffered from a vicious whispering campaign from other manufacturers that said the brakes were dangerous because they were too powerful. When Walter Flanders, one of the key figures behind the development of the car, accidentally died, Rickenbacker decided to halt production.

The last Rickenbacker, built in 1927, was powered by a 107-bhp 4.4-liter straight eight, giving the car a top speed of 90 mph. The design for the car was sold to J.S. Rasmussen in Germany and formed the basis for two Audi models.

74 This 1912 ad for the Ford Model T not only demonstrates the many uses for the vehicle, but also shows how quickly it had woven itself into the very fabric of American life.

75 top left Although the wheels are turning on this 1925 Buick ad, there's little else to suggest that the car is moving.

75 top right Few luxury car makers actually built their own bodies, as this Lincoln ad shows in its boasting of its use of Le Baron coachworks.

75 bottom left Most auto advertising of the era was understated and static as in this 1914 Stevens-Duryea pitch.

75 bottom right Many early luxury cars, with bodies that resembled elegant coaches of a bygone era, were designed to be chauffeur-driven, as displayed in this 1910 Pierce-Arrow ad.

76 The "bandwagon effect" in which prospects are told

that everyone else is buying one was a popular marketing tool of the era.

77 Willoughby was another coachworks that developed bodies for Lincoln, as shown in this 1928 advertisement, which also stresses the division's ties to Ford Motor Co.

FOUR-PASSENGER TOWN SEDAN—By Willoughby

The fact that more Lincolns have been sold than any other car costing as much or more is convincing evidence that Lincoln value, quality and appearance are appreciated by those who buy fine cars.

78 top As indicated in the ad, Fisher still built the bodies for GM's cars, but the overall design of the car was done in-house.

78 bottom Harley Earl (seated behind the wheel) was lured from California in 1927 to head GM design, a job he held for 30 years.

78-79 The LaSalle was a breakthrough for the auto industry because it was the first automobile styled specifically by a factory design staff, GM's Art & Colour Section, headed by Harley Earl.

The 1920s was a period in which established luxury makes discovered that they could not survive on a diet of champagne and caviar and sought to carve out niches in mid-priced segments, such as Pierce-Arrow's 80 series cars.

Other lower and mid-priced entries included Hudson's Essex and Oakland's Pontiac, which was slotted between Chevrolet and Oldsmobile. Cadillac was no different in launching the LaSalle, a lower priced line of cars. The significance is that the car, when it debuted in 1927, was the first regular production model to be designed by an in-house styling studio. That studio was headed by Harley Earl.

In the 1920s, Earl had made a name for himself in Hollywood, designing custom-bodied cars for stars like Tom Mix and Fatty Arbuckle. He was a Stanford graduate in law and the son of a Michigan native who moved west to start a carriage works. Earl helped his father in the family business and stayed on when Don Lee, the California distributor for Cadillac, acquired the shop.

Earl's work, which included a limited run of 100 custom-bodied Cadillacs, caught the eye of Lawrence Fisher, who was running the division at the time. He convinced Earl to move to Detroit to start the Art & Colour Section at GM.

The LaSalle design was patterned directly on the Hispano-Suiza, especially in the prominent grille.

Two wheelbases were offered, 134 and 125 inches, and all models sported two-tone paint schemes. From this modest start, Earl would go on to assemble a styling operation that by the late 1930s and especially during the 1950s would give American cars a look unlike anything else in the world.

In these coming years, General Motors would displace Ford as America's largest automaker, thus giving Earl this power. Still, Henry Ford would prove to be a tenacious competitor.

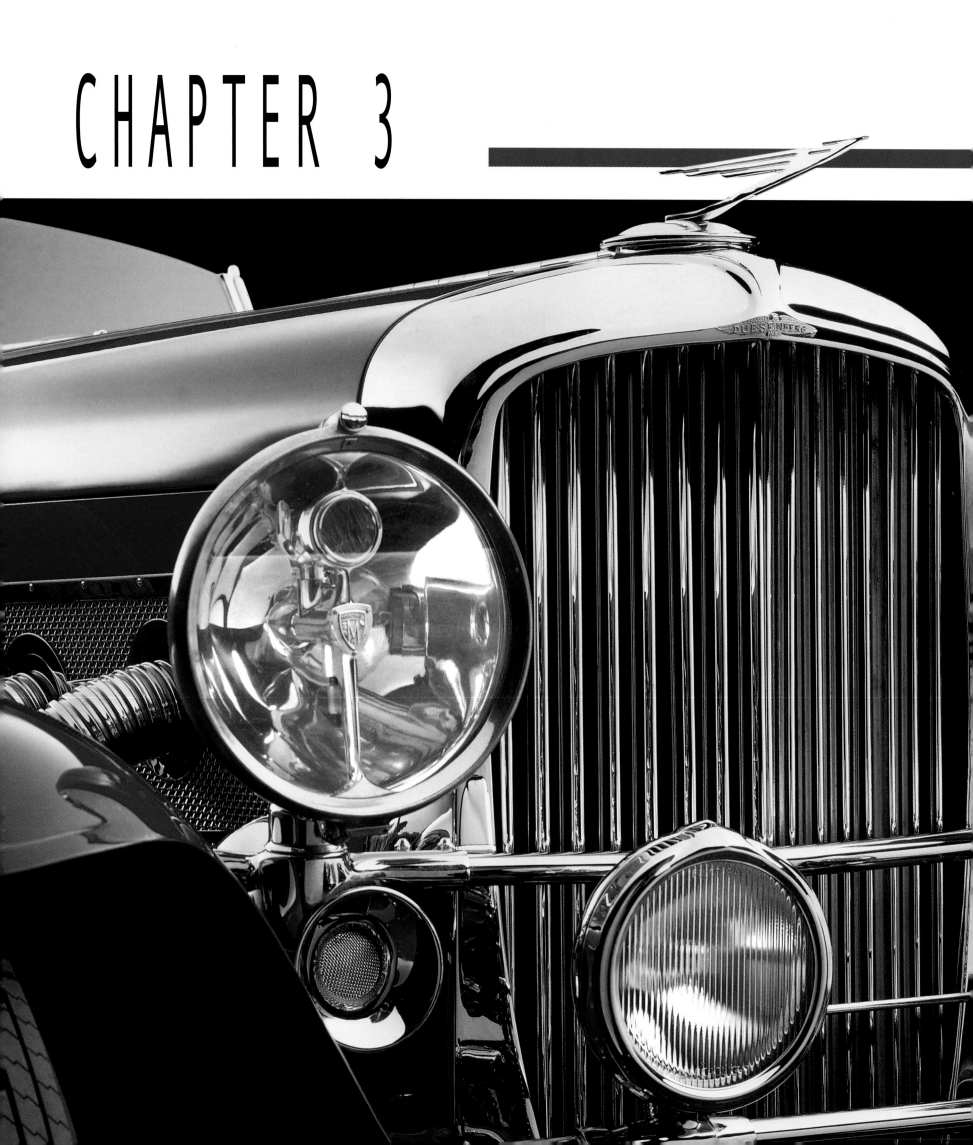

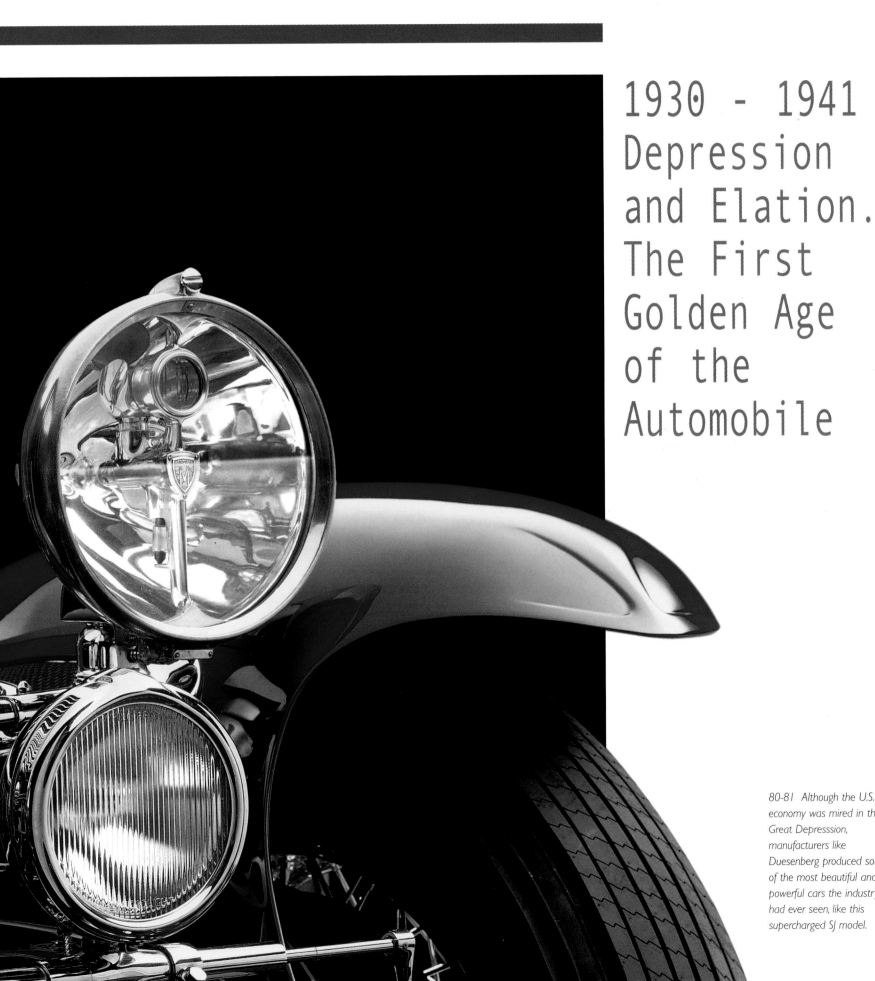

CHAPTER 3

1930 - 1941 Depression and Elation. The First Golden Age of the Automobile

80-81 *Although the U.S. economy was mired in the Great Depresssion, manufacturers like Duesenberg produced some of the most beautiful and powerful cars the industry had ever seen, like this supercharged SJ model.*

T he introduction of the 1927 LaSalle ushered in a new age for the auto industry. It was the first product from an in-house design studio at a major manufacturer. The 1930s would be a golden age in which designers would take center stage. It was also an era in which some of the greatest bodywork from coachbuilders would be produced. But as the automakers depended more on the expertise of their own designers, the market for custom bodies shrank until most coachworks were absorbed by automakers or simply ceased operation. Against this backdrop, there was fierce competition in the mainstream market as Ford sought to reassert itself as the industry leader. Further roiling the waters was the 1929 stock market crash and the Great Depression, which caused more consolidation in the industry and spelled the demise for many other companies. Ford could have been one of those victims had it not decided to reinvent its mass market offering before the nation's economic woes began. The Model T had soldiered along for nearly two decades. Its simple design, low cost and production at far-flung plants throughout the world had turned it into the ubiquitous everyman's car. Over 15 million had been built at 34 assembly plants in North America alone.

But the overwhelming success of the Model T stifled innovation. Adhering to the adage, "If it isn't broken, don't fix it," Ford resisted change even as its closest competitor, Chevrolet, began to offer 6-cylinder power, larger sleeker bodies, battery ignition, softer riding balloon tires and roll-up windows. Not only that, Chevys were available in a wide range of colors versus the Model T's basic black. That's not to say that Ford didn't experiment with alternatives. The company tried to develop an 8-cylinder engine with an X configuration; however, after six years of development it was abandoned as too heavy, too complex and too expensive.

While Ford executives knew the company was falling behind, none dared to challenge Henry Ford about a replacement car. And even though Ford still led Chevrolet in sales, Henry figured out that the Model T's days were numbered. Abruptly, he announced in early 1927 that Model T production would cease in May and a new car would be developed to replace it by year's

end. The industry practice was to develop new models while keeping current cars in production, something Ford himself did back in the days of his Piquette Avenue operation. This time around, he took the unprecedented step of shutting down his works for nearly half a year, idling with no pay tens of thousands of workers and leaving his 10,000 dealers with nothing to sell. It's a testament to how powerful Ford had become in the marketplace. There was no other manufacturer who could do that and hope to survive.

The Model A debuted on Dec. 2, 1927 and caused a national sensation, although historians say there was little about the car that made it remarkable. The fact that the Model T had become such an icon and the largest manufacturer had shut its doors for most of 1927, thereby allowing Chevrolet to pass it in the sales race, created tremendous curiosity. Thousands of people turned out to see the car.

The Model A was longer and lower than the T and featured a more powerful 200 cu.-in. 4-cylinder engine that nearly doubled horsepower to 40 and provided a top speed of 65 mph. Other improvements included 4-wheel brakes (the T used brakes only on the rear wheels) and a conventional 3-speed manual instead of the planetary gear set with its 3-pedal setup. Much of the car's styling, from its curved radiator shell with widow's peak, the hood line and even the shape of the headlamps, were similar to Lincoln. And Ford introduced shatter-resistant safety glass for the first time on a mass-market car, all for $495. The car was a hit and more than 400,000 orders were taken. But it took awhile for production to hit full stride and Chevrolet again repeated as sales leader in 1928, though Ford came back in 1929 and 1930 to eclipse its rival. But, by that time the stock market had crashed, the economy soured and the industry would go through another round of consolidation. Even the Model A wasn't immune, with sales plunging from 2 million in 1929 to half that number a year later.

82-83 Workers on this Ford Motor Co. assembly line in Minnesota do body preparation work prior to the painting process in 1935.

Even in the 1930s, ergonomics was an issue, note that the workers stand on wooden benches rather than the hard concrete floor.

A V-8 Is Born

Unlike the Model T, Ford would refresh the Model A's styling and offer technical innovation at a much more rapid pace. The next trump card he played came in 1932. To counter the popularity of the Chevrolet Confederate Series BA with its 60 hp "stovebolt" six, Ford decided that the Model A would be equipped with a V-8. The 221 cu.-in. engine had a 90-degree V and produced 65 horsepower. The car was sold alongside the Model B, a 4-cylinder version, and the only distinguishing characteristic was the V-8 badge on the Model A's headlamp tie-bar. With only a $50 price differential, the V-8 proved so popular that by 1935 the four was no longer available in passenger car models.

The so-called flathead V-8 had a long run with the only significant change being an increase in displacement to 236 cu.-in. in 1946. The company would keep the motor in production until 1954. Still, even with V-8 power to Chevy's six, Ford was able to surpass its rival in sales for just one year, 1935.

Ford also embarked on a program of updating its bodies. While the car's mechanical base remained unchanged, the 1930s would see the standard car evolve from an open tourer style to a closed body. Roof construction on these closed body cars would change from wood and canvas to all steel roofs. The grilles sported a V shape and the formerly freestanding fenders would blend into the body.

During this period of the late 1920s and early 1930s, new nameplates began to appear as older marques disappeared. During this time, GM's Oakland

Division spawned Pontiac, which would later become the name of that unit, while Walter P. Chrysler, who acquired Dodge in 1928, also introduced DeSoto and later Plymouth.

The Great Depression was a case of good news/bad news for car lovers. The bad news was that the poor economy pitted company against company in a pitched battle for survival, with many venerable makes succumbing to bankruptcy. The good news was some extraordinary cars were produced due to the intensity of this competition.

Much of this artistry came from the coachbuilders, many with histories that pre-date the automobile. Names like Brewster, Derham, Judkins and Biddle & Smart were products of the carriage trade. Others, like Brunn, Willoughby, Fleetwood, Murphy, LeBaron and Rollston, developed along with the automakers.

In addition to doing customer-specified work, many of these coachbuilders had standard designs they would produce. It was the Don Lee Studio's run of 100 Cadillacs that brought designer Harley Earl to the attention of General Motors' management. Other coachbuilders would build vehicles penned by designers working with manufacturers.

86-87 The 1932 Auburn Boattail Speedster displayed a unique blend of style, craftsmanship and innovation that helped propel the U.S. industry to what is considered its Golden Age. The two-passenger Speedster had an elegant sweep to its design and included such artful touches as contrasting paint scheme accents and polished chrome wire wheels. The cut-down windshield and high cowl and rear-hinged doors gave the Speedster a sporty flair that few cars of the time possessed. Beneath the massive hood of the 1932 Auburn Boattail Speedster, buyers could choose between a 100-horsepower straight-eight or a 160 horsepower V-12. From the rear, the Auburn has the look of a road-going speedboat thanks to its radically tapered rear end.

Dawning of a Golden Age

Perhaps the greatest contributor to this Golden Age was Errett Lobban Cord, a young entrepreneur who, like a small scale Billy Durant, had made and lost several fortunes before he reached his mid-20s.

In 1924, he assumed control of Auburn and sought to upgrade the car's image with a trademark two-tone paint scheme and a beltline that swept up into the hood. These 8-88 models used powerful Lycoming in-line 8-cylinder engines. In 1928, the company introduced a car that would become synonymous with the brand, the Auburn Boattail Speedster. Designated the 851/852 model, the 115 bhp Speedster was capable of speeds in excess of 108 mph.

Auburn was on a roll, selling more than 22,000 cars in 1929. And although the volume was cut in half in 1930 following the stock market crash, Auburn bounced back to set a new record of 28,000 in 1931, thanks to the restyled 8-98 models and the introduction of low-priced V-12 models, including the 1932 12/160A which retailed for $975. But then, the 6.4-liter Lycoming V-12 Speedsters of 1932-33 flopped, and the company never recovered. The last 851/852 Speedsters, which were designed by Gordon Buehrig and featured exposed flex hose exhausts, sold at a loss in 1935-36. E.L. Cord's attention was focused elsewhere, and Auburn ceased production by 1937.

Cord's flamboyant flair also left an imprint on Duesenberg, which he acquired in 1926. By 1932, the supercharged 320 bhp model SJ, which was built on the shorter, 142.5-in. standard wheelbase, joined the impressive Model J. SJ models, another Buehrig design, were distinguished by four hood-mounted external flex hose exhaust pipes similar to those found on the Auburn Speedster. Two two-passenger SSJs were also made, one going to Gary Cooper and the other to Clark Gable.

88-89 In addition to its massive size, the 1935 Duesenberg SJ produced immense power from its supercharged 420 cu. in. straight eights, as much as 400 bhp in some cases.

89 top This Dual Cowl Phaeton gets its designation from the second cowl fitted with it own windscreen behind the driver's compartment.

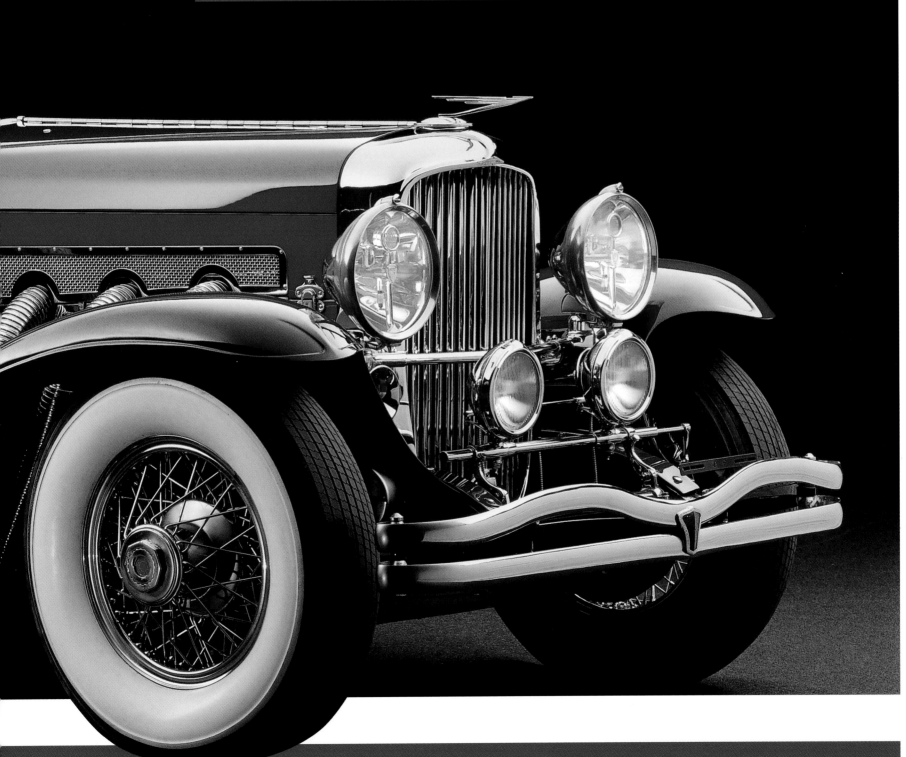

Cord is also responsible for the first serious attempt at building a front-wheel drive car in America. The 1929 Cord L-29 was intended to slot in between the Auburn and Duesenberg. The front-wheel drive configuration allowed for a car that was only 61 inches tall, nearly a foot shorter than most cars of the era. It was powered by a 125 bhp 300 cu. in. Lycoming straight eight and was one of the first cars to use X-shaped cross bracing to stiffen the chassis.

The L-29 was priced between $3,095 and $3,295 and was offered in four body styles: sedan, cabriolet, brougham and phaeton. While it was a hit at introduction with 4,400 cars sold the first year, sales worsened as the economy soured and the L-29 went out of production in 1932.

90-91 E.B. Cord introduced the first mass-produced front-wheel drive car in America with the 1929 Cord L-29. Because the front-drive layout didn't require a driveshaft beneath the body, the Cord L-29 stood appreciably lower than conventional cars when it was introduced in 1929.

92-93 Power was delivered to the front wheels on the 1930 Cord L-29 via a three-speed sliding pinion gearbox mounted behind the front differential, a design similar to Miller racing cars of the era.

93 top Like all L-29 models, a 125-horsepower inline eight-cylinder engine powered this 1930 Phaeton.

93 bottom A two-door cabriolet, four-door sedan and five-passenger brougham models also joined the 1930 Cord L-29 Phaeton in the maker's lineup.

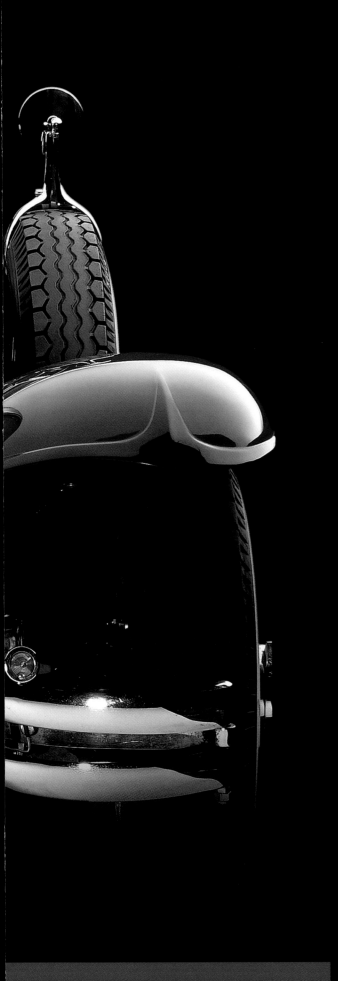

At the same time, Wall Street wizard Archie Andrews was trying to launch the Ruxton, which was also front drive. Always a wheeler-dealer, he named his car after V.C. Ruxton, a large Wall Street investor, in hopes of attracting his backing. Ruxton never put a nickel into the firm, but that didn't stop Andrews from trying to put the Ruxton into production at an existing manufacturer.

After being rebuffed by Hupp Motors, he formed New Era Motors and approached Moon, a St. Louis manufacturer that had been struggling for survival. In an ironic twist, E.L. Cord had gotten his start in the auto business as a leading salesman for Moon in the Chicago area. Unbeknownst to Moon management, Andrews had swapped the rights to the Ruxton design for a controlling interest in the company, which led to a showdown in which Moon executives barricaded

themselves in the factory's headquarters. Andrews won a court order that evicted the managers. He put the Ruxton into production at Moon and later struck a deal with Wisconsin-based Kissel to build both Moon and Ruxton automobiles in June 1930. However, Kissel soon went into receivership and production of both cars ceased since Kissel was the sole supplier of transmissions and drive units.

The Ruxton, which rode on a 130-in. wheelbase, was low slung like the Cord L-29 and it, too, was powered by a straight eight, which was supplied by Continental. A distinguishing feature was the lack of running boards. A factory-offered paint scheme (which only saw the light of day on two show cars) was comprised of eight bands of color going from light on top to dark at the bottom. It's estimated that only 500 Ruxtons were built.

94 top The other front-wheel-drive car of note was the 1930 Ruxton, which lasted only one year on the market. Its look was much lower than other cars of the day.

94 bottom The Ruxton logo first appeared in 1929 to herald the following year's launch of the car.

94-95 Underscoring the complicated relationships that existed in the early auto industry, Ruxtons were actually assembled at the Moon auto works in St. Louis, Missouri.

Meanwhile, Cord wasn't giving up on the idea of front drive, and in 1936 the landmark 810 debuted, another design by Gordon Buehrig. Originally planned as a junior Duesenberg, the car was rechristened the Cord just prior to production.

The striking design featured a coffin-like louvered nose, hide-away fender-mounted lights and no running boards. Despite its beauty, the Cord 810 was a mechanical beast. The front-drive 214-cu.in. Lycoming V-8 was powerful, producing 125 bhp, but it took a ter-rible toll on U-joints and transmissions. In 1937, the updated 812 came along and offered, in addition to a standard wheelbase model, a long-wheelbase berline. Optional supercharging of the Lycoming eight bumped horsepower to 195.

After 2,300 Cord 810/812 models were built, E.L. Cord abruptly closed shop and retired to England. The tooling for the cars were sold to Hupp and later Graham, which incorporated some of the Cord's body panels on their late 1930s offerings.

96-97 Envisioned originally as a Duesenberg, the Cord 810 was introduced in 1936 with V-8 power and in four body styles, two sedans, a cabriolet and a phaeton. The 1936 Cord Beverly Sedan is equipped with a large integrated trunk, a feature lacking on the less expensive Westchester sedan.

98-99 The finely crafted and finned, "coffin nose" hood contributed to the Cord's unusually clean exterior design. The front-drive allowed the Cord 810 be low, a stance that Gordon Buehrig capitalized on by removing the traditional running boards and fitting the car with hide-away headlamps.

The Graham-Paige was offered in a choice of 4, 6 or 8 cylinders with such advanced features as a 4-speed transmission and hydraulic brakes. In 1931, when the car was simply known as the Graham, sales had plummeted to less than a third of the pre-Crash volume. Still, Graham distinguished itself with industry-0leading styling, offering in 1932 the first fully skirted fenders on a series called the Blue Streak. That year, sales dropped to 12,967 and Ray Graham took his life. The other two brothers continued in the business and Graham's second-generation cars appeared in 1934. They offered a supercharger for the first time, which boosted the eight's output and provided a top speed of 95 mph. It was an inexpensive option at $130. The eights were dropped the following year, although supercharging was offered on the six, again for only $130 more. The Graham was rated at 89 bhp for a normally aspirated and 112 bhp with forced induction. Three models were offered: Crusader, Cavalier and Supercharged. Graham's 6-cylinder engine proved of interest to foreign manufacturers—Nissan made a copy, while Lammas-Graham of England used the supercharged version for a small run of sports cars, and the French maker Voision used the normally aspirated six in its last model run of 1937. In 1936 Graham introduced its "sharknose" body style that had a snout that reminded people of the predatory fish, although the company's official name for the design was "the spirit of motion." Although the last Grahams were built in 1940 (2,895), the name lived on when it was acquired in 1944 by Joseph Frazer of Willys-Overland and later transferred to Kaiser-Frazer. In 1950 Graham-Paige became an investment company and later transformed itself into Madison Square Garden Corporation.

THE *Graham* FOUR DOOR SEDAN

Other survivors of the 1930s included Studebaker and Hudson. Studebaker persevered despite the hardships of the Great Depression and some rather tragic circumstances that could have easily ended the venture. In 1931 it retained hometown legend and Notre Dame football coach Knute Rockne as a spokesman and named the 1932 model after him. Unfortunately, Rockne died in a plane crash in the spring of 1931. The Rockne was offered in two wheelbases of 110 and 114 in. with inline sixes producing 66 or 72 bhp and was attractively priced at $585-$795. However, the Ford Model A, which had the advantage of V-8 power, still undercut the Rockne on price.

In 1933 Studebaker went into receivership and the Rockne, after two years of disappointing sales, was discontinued. The Rockne's sixes were used in a new series of cars, which reintroduced two earlier names, the Commander and the Dictator, which survived until 1938.

Retaining the services of Raymond Loewy, Studebaker introduced the first modern economy car, called the Champion in 1939. Powered by a 2.7-liter six, the car was priced at $765 and promoted for its fuel economy, which was between 20 and 22 mpg. It was a huge hit, propelling the firm's volume beyond 100,000 units in 1940-41. The popularity of the Champion enabled Studebaker to survive beyond World War II and into the 1960s.

Hudson, which traces its name back to Detroit department store magnate J.L. Hudson in 1909, had a long history of success with 6-cylinder cars since introducing its Model 6-54 in 1912. Its lower priced Essex models in the 1920s proved popular, and by 1929 the Hudson-Essex combine was third in industry sales. By the early 1930s, sales began to falter, the six was dropped in favor of straight-eight power and the 1932 Essex was called the Terraplane. Subsequent models dropped the Essex nomenclature altogether. The Terraplane, which offered 8-cylinder power on a lightweight, 106-in. wheelbase, earned a reputation as a good performer for less money than the Model A. In 1933, a 113-in. wheelbase Terraplane with a more powerful 94 bhp straight eight was offered.

The next year, the eight was dropped and the Terraplane became a twin of the Hudson Six. In 1938 Terraplane became a Hudson model and disappeared a year later. In the meantime, Hudson's new entry-level car was the 112, named for the car's 112-in. wheelbase. Hudson replaced that model with the Series 40 Six in 1940.

116 Even though its cabriolets were offered with six- and eight-cylinder power, the Studebaker line suffered greatly in 1932 with total sales dropping to under 26,000.

117 top Amelia Earhart promotes the 1933 Essex Terraplane, a low-cost car whose sales success helped support its parent, Hudson Motors. So successful was the car, that Hudson later dropped Essex from the name and the cars were simply sold as Terraplanes.

117 bottom In this sketch of the 1932 coupe with aircraft imagery is ironic because Studebaker's sister car, the Rockne, would last for the '32-'33 model years because its namesake, Notre Dame coach Knute Rockne had died in a plane crash a year earlier.

The General Earns Its Stripes

While the Great Depression is often cited as the force that drove companies out of business during the 1930s, the fact remains that General Motors thrived at the expense of many weaker companies and that, more than anything else, changed the face of the industry. The GM juggernaut was made possible by the organizational skills of Alfred P. Sloan, Jr., who fashioned a stair step arrangement of divisions to provide cars for "every purse and purpose."

Sloan recognized in the 1920s that the market was changing. For the first 20 years of the industry, conventional wisdom held that there was a small market for luxury cars and a vast market for rudimentary vehicles like the Model T. For a while the model worked. Luxury makers thrived by catering to their segment, and mass-market manufacturers prospered while putting cars in the hands of average Americans. And even Ford was able to cater to both with the acquisition of Lincoln. But, as Ford painfully discovered in the late 1920s when his Model T became outdated, people wanted more than

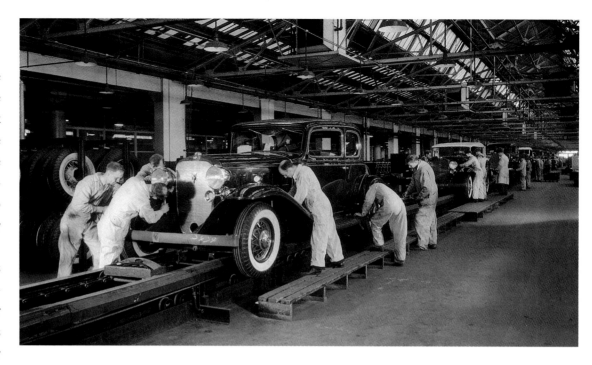

118 top Luxury manufacturers like Cadillac move beyond bespoke bodywork, using the assembly line to turn out its 1932 lineup.

118 bottom left Auto assembly moved beyond its cottage industry roots with the use of advanced and expensive technology like this front end alignment system on a 1936 Buick assembly line.

118 bottom right Chevrolet pistons destined for use in 1937 six-cylinder models are closely inspected after machining.

119 A giant press turns out body stamping that would feature General Motors' unique "turret top" design, the first use of an all-steel roof.

basic transportation. The 1930s would prove that there were many "purses and purposes" between the Model A and the Lincoln. Trying to appeal to this new middle-class buyer with a less costly version of a premium brand could be just as disastrous as ignoring these buyers altogether, as demonstrated by Pierce-Arrow's introduction of the Series 80 and Packard's 120.

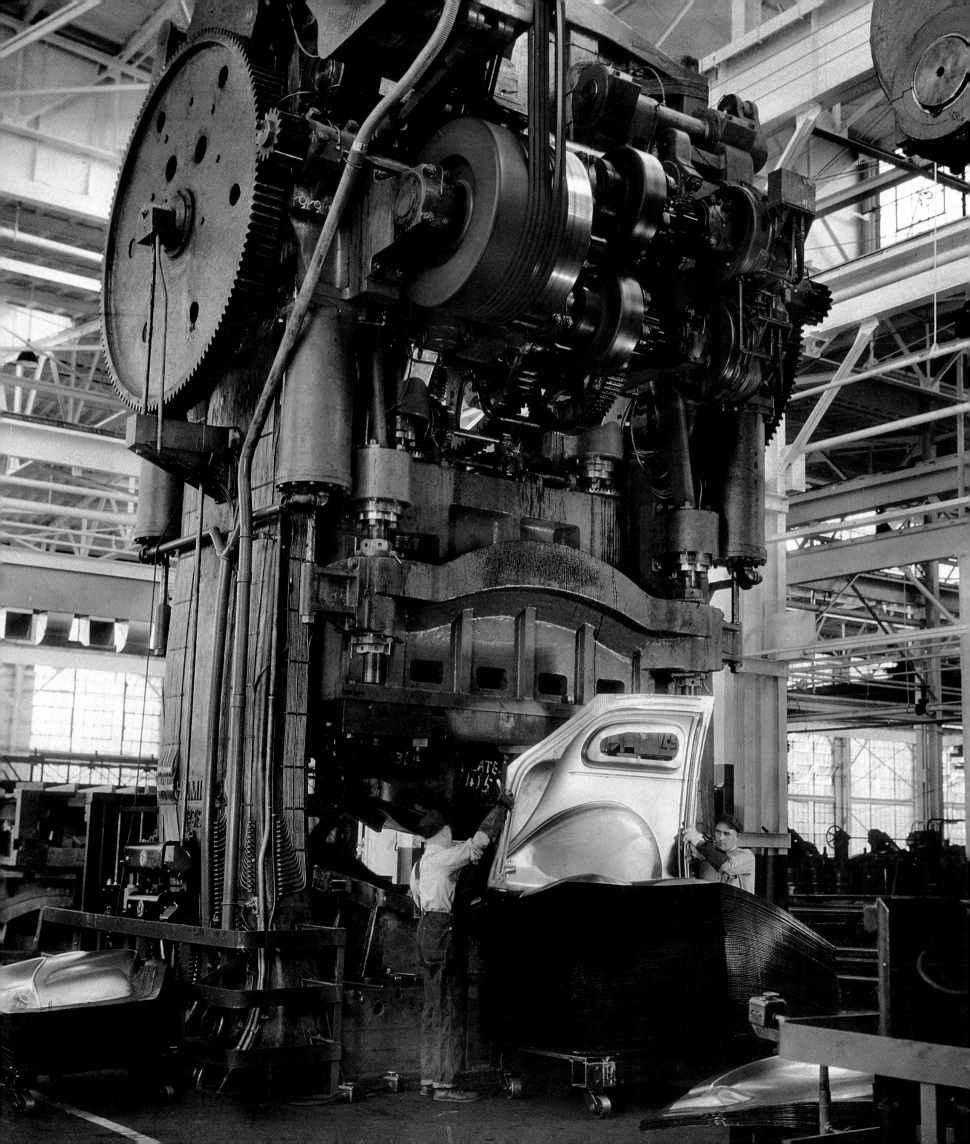

Therein lies the genius of Sloan's approach to GM. Each division was given a piece of the market and could become specialists in appealing to that particular segment. Therefore Chevrolet could concentrate on the mass market and not be distracted by trying to build a luxury to compete with Lincoln and Cadillac. At the other end of the spectrum, Cadillac could concentrate solely on luxury car buyers and not worry about having a mass-market vehicle to compete with Ford. And for every "purse and purpose" in between, Pontiac, Oldsmobile and Buick would be there with specific offerings. On the other side, General Motors enjoyed huge economies of scale, sharing components and even body stampings, while Harley Earl's designers worked diligently to give each division its own unique look. General Motors cars shared everything including "no draft" ventilation, independent "knee action" front suspensions and "turret top" steel roofs. The formula worked. Throughout the Great Depression, General Motors was profitable.

Going places . . a

120 top Although LaSalle would not survive after World War II, in the 1930s, it touted itself as a junior Cadillac with its affordable luxury.

120-121 In this 1935 ad, Buick, as a more upscale division, highlights the fact that its owners are going places in the world. In other words, Buick buyers have "made it."

121 top General Motors emerges as a marketing juggernaut with cars for every segment of the market. In this ad, Chevrolet emphasizes its low price.

121 bottom Oldsmobile was considered a step up from Chevrolet and Pontiac, but a step below Buick. In this 1930 ad, Olds stresses its dependability.

nd *how!*

industry's first styling department, its designs and cars in the early 1930s weren't particularly daring, especially when compared to Chrysler's aerodynamic Airflow or Cord's pioneering work in front-wheel drive. Given the lack of success of those two efforts, it was probably a good thing. Instead, GM's lower range cars, particularly at Chevrolet, Pontiac and Oldsmobile, hewed to the Sloan philosophy of being good enough rather than class leading. In his autobiography, *My Years with General Motors*, Sloan wrote: "It was not necessary to lead in technical design or run the risk of hurried experiments [provided] our cars were at least equal in design to the best of our competitors in grade." In other words, build a car equal to the competition, price it low and GM's economies of scale and huge distribution network would take care of the rest.

In Sloan's organization, Chevrolet was the low-priced, entry-level vehicle pitted directly against Ford. The 6-cylinder Confederate Series BA held its own against the Model A and helped regain the sales crown for Chevy in 1931. Despite having two fewer cylinders than the '32 and later Model As, Chevy trailed Ford in sales only once more during the decade in 1935, when Ford sold over 942,437 cars to Chevy's 793,437.

In 1934, the Master and Standard ranges, as they were informally called a year earlier, become official series, with the Master being offered on a larger 112-in. wheelbase. Chevrolet's line was redesigned in 1937 around a new 112.3-in. wheelbase and a larger bore 216 cu.-in. Blue Flame six producing 85 bhp.

Next up Sloan's ladder was Pontiac, which grew out of General Motors' Oakland division in 1926. The lower priced 6-cylinder Pontiac was such a hit that it replaced the Oakland name entirely. Pontiac was viewed as a step up from Chevy in terms of equip-

ment, offering both 6- and 8-cylinder power for value conscious buyers (although 6-cylinder powerplants disappeared briefly during 1933-34). The last Oakland used an Olds Viking V-8 and was renamed a Pontiac in 1932. The engine was dropped in favor of straight eight power in 1933, and Pontiac became the first eight priced less than $600. The 1935 models featured "Silver Streak" styling that included skirted fenders and the first application of a die-cast side grille. Also of note is the 1935 Pontiac Improved Eight Business Coupe, a lightweight, straight-eight 2-seater.

Oldsmobile's mission was to be a technology leader. Priced higher than Pontiac but below Buick, Oldsmobiles generally were fitted with advancements likes hydraulic brakes and semi-automatic transmissions at least a full model year before the other divisions. In 1929-31, Oldsmobile offered a lower priced V-8 line called the Viking, but it was dropped in 1932 when a new straight eight was introduced. Other than under-the-skin technical advances and minor differences in body trim such as grilles, there was little in outward appearance to distinguish '30s Oldsmobiles from the standard Pontiacs and Buicks.

While GM kept pace with the technological innovations of the time and is credited with having the

122 top Just as LaSalle was a lower priced Cadillac, Oldsmobile briefly experimented with a higher priced model based on the LaSalle called Viking. It was sold for only two model years, 1929 and 1930.

122 bottom Even in 1930, safety was a concern. One of the features of Olds Viking was the use of non-shattering plate glass, as this demonstration points out.

122-123 Even though styling progressed, as shown by this 1937 Chevrolet Master Deluxe Business Coupe, Chevy still relied on six-cylinder power and would do so until 1955, a distinct disadvantage to the Ford V-8s.

123 top The Pontaic proved so popular as a model in 1926 that its name soon supplanted Oakland as a GM division. The 1937 model was positioned as a step up from Chevrolet, thanks to its eight-cylinder engine.

While Buick shared bodies with its sister divisions, as a more upscale division (this is the era it earned its reputation as a doctor's car), it was provided a bit more latitude from Sloan's dictum.

Starting in 1931, Buicks were powered by 8-cylinder engines exclusively and the cars became quite popular in Europe. King Edward VIII ordered two Canadian-built Buick limousines, one of which famously carried his paramour, Mrs. Wallis Simpson off to France in 1936 prior to his abdicating the throne.

New division general manager Harlow Curtice (who would later become GM chairman) teamed up with Harley Earl in 1936 to create a four-vehicle line— the Special, Century, Roadmaster and Limited—which further burnished Buick's image as an upscale marque. In 1938 Earl built the industry's first concept car, the Buick Y-Job, which was a pure styling exercise. Although manufacturers had produced show cars in the past such as the Pierce-Arrow Silver Arrow and Cadillac's V-16 Aerodynamic Fastback, usually these cars were sold to the public, followed by limited series production.

The Y-Job was a one-off dream car that became Earl's personal transportation for many years. This sleek, two-place convertible was long, low and wide, with hideaway headlamps, flush door handles, no running boards and front fenders that flowed into the doors.

The grille, instead of being vertical, laid horizontal, complementing the full-length bumper. Rather than spawning a specific line of cars, the Y-Job was different in that it pointed to a direction in which all of GM styling was headed. Leon Mandel, writing in his book American Cars, quotes Harley Earl's styling premise thusly: "My primary purpose…has been to lengthen and lower the American automobile, at times in reality and always at least in appearance."

Sixty-five years after the Y-Job appeared, Buick again

124-125 Harley Earl, who had created the first in-house design staff in the auto industry, also introduced the first concept car with his 1938 Buick Y-Job, a study that influenced overall design direction rather than a promise of a new model.

is invoking the image of Harley Earl and holding the car up as an example of what modern Buicks should look like. The odd car out in all these developments, ironically, was the LaSalle, which had brought Earl to General Motors in the first place. By the late 1930s, it had essentially become a junior Cadillac V-8 with an Oldsmobile body and fell afoul of Sloan's ironclad rule of "no duplication by the corporation in the price fields or steps." It was dropped in 1940.

Cadillac would close out the 1930s with a landmark design, the Series 60 Special, a compact-sized car designed by Earl protégé William Mitchell, who would himself head GM Design after Earl's retirement.

The 60 Special embodied the philosophy of the Y-Job, eschewing running boards and excessive chrome trim. The greenhouse was now a separate element and the trunk was integrated into the body for a distinct three-box look that would influence car design for decades to come.

By this time, Fisher Body was the sole supplier to GM (although there was still some bodywork being done on Buicks and Cadillacs by the few remaining coachworks). Bodies were now categorized by letters: the A-Body 4-door sedan and coupe was shared by Chevy and Pontiac, while the larger B-Body could be found in the Olds 60, Buick Century and Pontiac Deluxe lines.

The Cadillac Series 60 became the C-Body and was used for Buick's Series 50 and Series 70 Roadmaster, Olds' 90 and the Pontiac Torpedo 8, as well as the last LaSalle, the 1940 Special. As the clouds of war gathered in Europe, General Motors created a car company that was the model of efficiency. That model would later prove to be invaluable as the auto industry switched gears from building transportation for the masses to becoming an arsenal for democracy.

CHAPTER 4

1942 - 1948
The War
Years and
Recovery

126-127 Le Baron, a
renowner coachbuilder owned
by Briggs Body, created the
Chrysler Newport Dual Cowl
Phaeton in 1940. Six of these
parade cars were built, one of
which was used to pace the
Indy 500.

On Sept. 1, 1939, war broke out in Europe with the simultaneous invasion of Poland by Nazi Germany and Soviet Russia. An ocean away in America, it was business as usual in an auto industry that was still struggling with the effects of the Great Depression.

In this period before the United States would enter the war, there were two significant developments in American cars that would distinguish them for decades to come from cars produced anywhere else in the world, namely, air conditioning and automatic transmissions. America, a land of large spaces and untold natural resources, wanted comfort and convenience from cars, while other countries, with crowded urban areas and limited resources, demanded vehicles that prized space efficiency and economical operation.

Packard introduced air conditioning to the industry in the fall of 1939 in its 1940 models. The bulky Packard system coupled a compressor to refrigeration coils mounted behind the back seat. Referring to its cars as "Air Cool-ditioned," Packard boasted that its system only took up as much space as a large suitcase in the trunk. Packard installed the option on 1,500 cars from 1939 to 1942 and probably would have produced more had it not been preoccupied with a shifting in production to war material, landing a contract to build Rolls-Royce aero engines in 1940.

Air conditioning took some time to catch on as a universal feature in American cars. By 1965, less than a quarter of new cars were fitted with the option, although by 1973 that number had grown to 60 percent. In 1994, nearly 99 percent of all new cars sold in the United States had air conditioning.

At the same time Packard took the wraps off its "Air Cool-ditioned" cars, Oldsmobile offered a fully automatic transmission as a $57 option.

Although the idea of an automatic transmission had been toyed with since the beginning of the industry (in 1901 the Sturtevant brothers of Massachusetts patented a 3-speed automatic with centrifugal clutch and built cars from 1905-1907), the invention of syn-

cromesh gears made using manual transmissions much easier. Against the dependability and low cost of manual gearboxes, automatic transmissions had a hard time catching on.

Ironically, it was Earl Thompson, the inventor of syncromesh gears hired by Cadillac in 1928, who began work on the first automatic transmissions using a fluid coupled clutch. Another program at Buick, to develop a continuously variable transmission, was scrapped by Alfred Sloan as too costly.

By the mid-1930s, Thompson's team had developed a semi-automatic transmission that still needed a manual clutch to start, but would shift on its own between first and second and also third and fourth. The driver still had to manually shift between second and third. Called the "Safety Transmission," it debuted as a $59.75 option on 1937 Oldsmobiles.

A year later, Buick offered the option but dropped it midway through the model year because of durability concerns.

The big breakthrough came in 1938 with the development of the first fully automatic transmission called the 180, or Hydra-Matic. It was offered on the Oldsmobile Sixty, Seventy and Custom Eight models in 1940. That year Olds installed 25,000 Hydra-Matics in its cars. A year later Cadillac offered the gearbox as an option. Unlike air conditioning, which took some time to catch on, by the 1950s automatic transmissions were offered on the majority of American cars.

128 The 1942 Oldsmobile B-44, which featured fenders swept back into the doors and a two-tier grille, reappeared with few changes in 1946 as post-war car production resumed.

129 top In 1940, Oldsmobile began to offer four-speed automatic transmission as a $57 option. Called Hydra-Matic, this new gearbox would forever change the American car.

129 bottom Plymouth essentially resumed production in 1946 with the 1942 model, a car that featured wider grilles and front fenders as well as the elimination of running boards.

Doing the Continental

While the Series 60 Cadillac had set the tone for future design with its well-defined three-box shape, both Ford and Chrysler produced cars in 1940 that demonstrated that General Motors wasn't alone in setting style. Edsel Ford had long toiled in the shadow of his father and was never successful in taking over the reins of the family business. In the late 1930s, Edsel proposed a reorganization of Ford patterned after Alfred Sloan's GM hierarchy that had proved so successful. Henry Ford rejected it out of hand.

130-131 The concept of the "personal luxury car" was conceived by Edsel Ford as the Zephyr-based Lincoln Continental and executed in a landmark design by Robert Gregorie in 1940 (above). Along with the new Lincoln Continental, the Zephyr was also restyled in 1940 with an envelope body that covered the running boards.

Edsel was a patron of the arts and a student of design. At Lincoln, he could combine this passion with luxury cars, a business in which his father had shown little interest. Edsel had championed the acquisition of Lincoln and was the prime mover behind the creation of the Lincoln Zephyr. That car would provide the basis for a new kind of personal luxury car, the Continental.

The project was begun as a one-off design for Edsel's personal use. While there are similarities to the Zephyr, the Continental was influenced by European luxury cars as well as a late '30s hot rod based on a Ford Model A designed by Edsel.

Eugene "Bob" Gregorie, the designer who had taken John Tjaarda's original design for the Zephyr and converted it into the production model, is credited with the Continental's look. The modified '39 Zephyr convertible built for Ford was nearly a foot longer, had a larger and boxier truck and sported a bumper-mounted spare in the rear, which was known as a Continental kit. The car was a sensation among Edsel's wealthy friends, and in 1940 the Continental Cabriolet went into production. According to the *American Automobile, A Centenary*, author Nick Georgano notes that the production Continental "was three inches lower and

seven inches longer than the standard Lincoln Zephyr... The Continental sold on its styling and image, for its performance was no better than that of the regular Lincoln Zephyr.

There were hardly any modifications to the V12 engine and the cabriolet weighed about the same as the Zephyr convertible... Continental buyers paid a hefty premium for their stylish cars, $2,280 for the 1940 cabriolet, while the Zephyr convertible cost a mere $1,770." Only 404 were sold in 1940, but it created a class for a standard personal 2-door luxury car, as opposed to the many custom-bodied 2-doors typical of the 1920s and '30s.

Chrysler's contribution to design was also a swan song of sorts for custom coachbuilder LeBaron, which was now a department in Briggs, a Detroit supplier of bodies to Chrysler and Ford. The firm was commissioned to build six each of two show cars created by designers for Chrysler: the Newport Dual-Cowl Phaeton and the Thunderbolt. Also known as a parade car, the Newport was aluminum bodied with hideaway headlamps and an envelope body that was completely flush with no running boards. The Newport's other claim to fame was its use a pace car at the 1941 Indianapolis 500. The Thunderbolt was even more futuristic with completely enclosed wheel wells, a retractable hardtop and concealed headlamps. An interesting feature on the Thunderbolt was the stepped hood, a look that designer Alex Tremulis would use after the war on Preston Tucker's Torpedo.

132 top The Thunderbolt was another 1940 show car, this one designed by Alex Tremulis, who would go on to pen the Tucker Torpedo. It featured hideaway headlamps and

an complete envelope body with fully skirted wheels.

132 bottom Another groundbreaking feature of the Thunderbolt was its

fully retractable, power hardtop, something that had never been tried on an American car before.

132-133 The Chrysler Newport Dual-Cowl

Phaeton was designed by Ralph Roberts of LeBaron and based on an Imperial chassis fitted with a 143 bhp straight eight.

Small Wonders

In the years leading up to World War II, many European companies and countries answered the call to put the masses on wheels with tiny cars like the Citroën 2CV, the Fiat Topolino and the Volkswagen Beetle. In America, most entry-level transportation consisted of much larger cars that cost $500 to $600. One car modeled after these small European economy cars was the Crosley, a Cincinnati-produced minicar powered by a 2-cycle, 2-cylinder engine. Powel Crosley had tried building automobiles early in the century, having a hand in the 1909 Marathon Six and the DeCross cycle car in 1913. He was much more successful making radios and refrigerators, and by the 1930s, he thought he'd give the auto industry another shot. Measuring just 120 in. long, the Crosley was rated at 15 bhp and boasted a top speed of 50 mph. Its $350 sticker price was $250 cheaper than a 6-cylinder, 2-door Chevrolet business coupe, yet the car didn't make much of an impact.

In the car-starved postwar years, Crosley resumed production, this time using a Navy-developed 4-cylinder 772 cc engine. The motor was made of brazed copper and sheet steel with a fixed head, and it suffered badly from quality problems, including holes in the cooling system. A cast iron block solved the problem and Crosley went on to develop an entire line of cars ranging from a station wagon to a sports car.

The latter, called the Hotshot, won its class at the Sebring 12-hour race in 1950. However, as production of more mainstream cars caught up with public demand, the market for Crosley's tiny cars dried up and the firm ceased production in 1952.

Emulating Crosley's postwar efforts on a much smaller scale was the Athens, Ohio maker of the King Midget, a small, 2-passenger kit car. With Jeep-like styling, King Midgets were powered by 8.5 bhp 1-cylinder Wisconsin engines (which were replaced in 1966 by 9.5 bhp Kohler motors). About 5,000 were sold from 1946 to 1969.

134 top Powel Crosley, Jr., who had made a fortune selling radio equipment, stands with one of his two-cylinder minicars in 1940, which he hoped would repeat the success of Henry Ford's Model T.

134 bottom The original Model I King Midget was designed as a single-place one-cylinder kit car to be built by the owner. It later gave way to the larger, and more popular two-seat Model II that remained in production for over 25 years.

135 Originally designed by American Bantam, the all-purpose Jeep would be built by Willys-Overland and Ford for the U.S. war effort. A study in simplicity, the four-cylinder four-wheel drive Jeep was the equivalent of an all-purpose automotive tool for the military. It could be outfitted for any number of jobs from ambulance to assault vehicle.

A Jeep Is Born

There were two other small 4-cylinder cars on the market in the 1930s and ironically, both companies would have a hand in developing and building the iconic vehicle of World War II, the Jeep.

The Willys Four, produced by Willys-Overland, was the last remaining American-designed 4-cylinder car on the market after the Model A shifted over to exclusive use of V-8s. Priced $200 less than the entry-level Chevrolet, the Willys was powered by a 134.2 cu.-in. inline four that produced 48 bhp and later was upgraded to make 67 bhp. That engine would become the heart of the Jeep's drivetrain.

The Austin America was the U.S.-built version of the Austin Seven with a twist. It sported U.S. designed and built bodywork mimicking more expensive roadsters of the era on a diminutive 75-in. wheelbase. When it was introduced in 1930, it sold for $445, $10 more than the Model A.

Never selling more than 10,000 cars in a single year, the company was taken over in 1933 by Roy Evans, who four years later reorganized the company as American Bantam. Alexis de Saknoffsky, who designed the original Austin America, penned the shape of the American Bantam, while Indy car designer Harry Miller tweaked the engines to boost displacement to 50 cu.-in. and output to 22 bhp. However, the American Bantam never caught on and the company halted production after the 1940 model year.

At that time, American Bantam was deeply involved in developing its concept for the Jeep, a lightweight, 4-wheel drive truck sought by the Army. The Jeep name is said to come from one of two sources, a character in a Popeye cartoon or, more likely, a phonetic pronunciation of the Army's GP or General Purpose designation for the vehicle.

Bantam built a quarter-ton 4x4 Jeep to meet the Army's requirements for a fast, rugged, all-terrain reconnaissance vehicle and received an order to develop 70 of the vehicles in 1940 for further testing by the military. Standing 36 in. tall and with an overall length of just 132 in., Bantam's Jeep impressed the Army enough to earn an order for 1,500 vehicles.

However, there was a faction within the government that felt American Bantam was too small to build the large quantity of vehicles that would be needed for the war effort. As a result, the Army showed the vehicle to two other companies, Willys-Overland and Ford, which were also building prototypes to compete for the contract.

Eventually, the Willys design was standardized and the company submitted the low bid for a contract of 16,000 vehicles. Even Willys was hard pressed to meet production quotas, so at the Army's direction, it turned over the design to Ford and both companies turned out more than 640,000 Jeeps by the end of the war. American Bantam, squeezed out of the project entirely, was given a contract to produce small trailers.

The Jeep was a model of simplicity, in many ways

like the Model T. Built from just 1,500 parts, the Jeep's power came from Willys' durable 60 hp inline four mated to a 3-speed manual transmission. The 4-wheel-drive system had a 2-range transfer case and the entire vehicle weighed just over 2,100 lbs.

As popular as the Jeep was among servicemen, it didn't find a large market after the war, no doubt because of its rugged, crude nature. Jeeps were popular war surplus buys, however, and one urban legend still making the rounds as late as the 1970s held that you could buy an original Jeep knockdown kit for $50—all you had to do was assemble it yourself.

Willys-Overland made the transition back to the civilian market as a maker of the industry's first civilian sport/utility vehicles, a category that would become

immensely popular almost 50 years later. In addition to building the standard Jeep, which was called the Universal, Willys also offered a wagon on a longer wheelbase and an even more car-like roadster in 1948 called the Jeepster. Designed by Brooks Stevens, the Jeepster was a convertible 5-passenger vehicle powered by a choice of 4- or 6-cylinder engine. It was built until 1951.

While the Jeep was important to the overall war effort, it represents just a fraction of the material Detroit's manufacturers produced from 1942-45. According to Automotive News, GM produced 13,000 bombers and fighters, 206,000 aircraft engines, 38,000 armored vehicles, 854,000 trucks, 190,000 artillery pieces, 198,000 diesel engines and 1.9 million machine guns. Oldsmobile made 48 million artillery shells, while Pontiac built torpedoes.

Ford built 8,685 B-24 bombers in a huge, purpose-built facility at Willow Run. It also built 57,851 aircraft engines, 277,900 Jeeps, 93,217 trucks, 2,718 tanks, 26,954 tank engines and 12,500 armored cars as well as a number of gliders and amphibious vehicles. Chrysler produced 25,000 tanks, 18,000 Wright engines for B-29 bombers, 43,500 6-by-6 trucks, 29,000 marine engines and 12,000 tank engines, while Packard built powerplants for PT boats and aircraft.

Postwar Priorities

When World War II ended, the manufacturers wasted little time in pulling out their tooling from storage and cranking up their assembly lines. But during those war years, very little could be done to develop new cars. The 1946, '47, and '48 models would look like 1942 all over again.

Still, there were several significant changes in 1941 that would serve the automakers well in this transition period. At General Motors, fastback styling was introduced across the range (although Chevrolet wouldn't get the design until 1942), which gave the cars a sleeker, more modern look. Buick in particular introduced a new fender treatment called the "airfoil" on the Super model. The fender swept back and down through the door, ending low in front of the rear wheel arch. In later styling, this look, when coupled to the line running over the rear wheel arch, would become know as a "sweep spear." Oldsmobile was the first division to show 1946 models when in early 1945 workers hand-assembled several cars, which were displayed around the country to whet the appetite of buyers who hadn't seen a new

car in three years. It wouldn't be until October that most GM divisions had their assembly lines back in production. Both Chrysler and Buick introduced wood-sided station wagons in 1941, and the Buick returned in 1946 joined by Chevrolet. Chrysler dropped its wagon and continued with wood-bodied Town & Country sedans and convertibles. Ford also embraced the woodies with the Sportsman series of 2-door convertibles sold through Ford and Mercury divisions. The irony is that a little more than a decade after the industry finally advanced to all-steel body construction, wood would return as a styling element. Unfortunately, woodies didn't sell in any great volumes since the upkeep was difficult and expensive.

136-137 After World War II, the industry made cars for the mass market, abandoning the bespoke bodywork that had made the cars from the 1930s so memorable. An exception is the 1948 Chrysler Town & Country Convertible, the first in a series of "woodies."

Packard, having sold the tooling for the 180 to the Soviets during the war, resumed production with its Clipper, a mid-market sedan offered with a base model six and three straight eights.

Though basically a prewar design, the Clipper had a bold grille and smoothly contoured body that didn't seem as dated as some of the other reconstituted offerings by Detroit. Offered on either 120- or 127-in. wheelbases, the Clipper was restyled in 1948 with an envelope-styled body that many likened to an upside-down bathtub. The lack of a senior car further diminished Packard's luster—it was now perceived as just another car in the market and sales began a long

decline. Studebaker was the first manufacturer to offer an all-new postwar car in the Raymond Loewy-designed Champion. It was powered by updated versions of the pre-war sixes, with a choice of 80 bhp 170 cu.-in. or 94 bhp 226 cu.-in. units.

The Champion's rounded, streamlined front and rear with equal length hood and trunk combined with a wraparound back window raised the question, "Is it coming or going?" It stuck as a nickname. Still, with its 6-passenger seating, relatively compact dimensions of 193 in. overall length, and three body styles (2-door, 4-door and convertible), the Champion proved quite popular. The only other established maker to offer a

The No. 1 Glamour Car of America

138 top Studebaker, which at the time had one of the oldest locals in the United Auto Workers representing its employees, promoted a family atmosphere by hiring father-son teams.

138-139 Like all its competitors, Packard reintroduced its 1942 model as a 1946, picking up where it had left off before the war with the Clipper. The company's inability to match all new designs from other makers by the end of the 1940s eventually led to the firm's demise.

NEW 1947 STUDEBAKERS

new body design in this period was Hudson, which converted quickly to the smooth-sided "envelope" body style in its 1948 models. These Hudsons used unit body construction, combining both body and chassis frame in a single piece. A further innovation was the "step down" design of the floor. Rather than having the floor level with the top of the frame rails that formed the door sills, Hudson lowered the floorpan to the bottom of the integrated frame rail providing "step down" access into the vehicle.

139 top Studebaker reportedly invested $11 million in the redesign of its Commander and Champion series in 1947, among the first all-new postwar designs.

139 bottom Studebaker Commanders come off the final assembly line in South Bend, Indiana, as the company quickly ramps up to meet the skyrocketing demand in a car-hungry country.

One White Chip

The pent-up demand for automobiles was not only good business for the existing automakers, it also encouraged others, industrialists and everyday dreamers alike, to become the next Henry Ford. One of the most successful of these was another Henry—Henry J. Kaiser, who had built a fortune before the war in construction and cement, building many dams throughout the American West. During the war, alarmed at the slow pace of shipbuilding, Kaiser plunged ito building Liberty ships at an astounding rate of one every 39.2 days, compared to the national average of 52.6 days.

Kaiser acquired the assets of Graham-Paige Motors and took in its chairman, Joseph Frazer, as a partner to form Kaiser-Frazer. The new company purchased the huge B-24 plant Ford had built at Willow Run in suburban Detroit. Supposedly, Kaiser rented the ballroom at the Detroit Athletic Club to announce his entry into the auto business. At this cocktail reception to which he invited members of the automaking establishment, Kaiser boasted that his company was investing $100 million in the venture. To which a voice reportedly called out from the back of the room, "Give that man one white chip." Nevertheless, Kaiser-Frazer was a worthy, if overly ambitious, effort. The original Kaiser, conceived before the partnership with Frazer, was styled in California by noted designer Howard "Dutch" Darrin and engineered by William Stout (of Stout Scarab fame). It featured front-wheel drive, torsion bar suspension and a composite body. The Frazer would be more of a standard luxury car with steel body-on-frame construction and rear-drive. The two cars were shown in January 1946 at the Waldorf-Astoria in New York and met with rave reviews, but soon after the front-drive car was scrapped as too complicated in favor of using the Kaiser name on entry-level versions of the more conventional Frazers. The cars came out in 1947 powered by 100 bhp 3.7-liter Continental sixes (Kaiser-Frazer later assembled engines in-house at a plant acquired from Hudson). Priced at $1,868 for the Kaiser and $2,053 for the Frazer, the cars' modern slab-sided styling proved quite popular. By 1948, sales exceeded 180,000 units and new models were added to the range—a Kaiser Custom and the Frazer Manhattan (which would later offer a supercharged six producing 140 bhp).

Although both cars shared the same mechanicals, the body designs were different and the Frazer was regarded as not as good-looking or innovative as its sibling. Kaiser was one of the first cars to offer hardtop styling on its Virginian and pioneered the hatchback in the Traveler, a 4-door sedan that had a rear window that would swing up and a wagon-like tailgate that would drop down.

As fresh as the Kaiser-Frazer line looked in 1947, by 1950 they looked dated when compared to the 1949 offerings from General Motors and Ford, which were their first all-new postwar designs. The "one white chip" cry had come back to haunt Kaiser-Frazer, for the firm was undercapitalized and unable to afford a new engine to replace the Continental, which was a prewar design. Joseph Frazer had departed a year earlier in a dispute with Kaiser over Frazer's plan to cut production and costs in order to conserve cash.

Meanwhile, Henry J. Kaiser returned to a dream he had during the war of building a modern Model T priced under $400. For the 1951 model year, he launched the Henry J, a small 2-door sedan riding on a 100-in. wheelbase. It was powered by a 68 bhp 134 cu.-in. four or an 80 bhp 161 cu.-in. six, acquired from Willys-Overland. The reality of the car's pricing didn't quite match the dream—the two models were priced at $1,363 and $1,499 respectively. One of Kaiser's weaknesses as a new entry to the auto industry was the lack of a large, healthy dealer body. One way he sought to increase volume was using non-traditional distribution, and he entered into an agreement to supply Sears, Roebuck & Co. with a car called the Allstate. Sporting a slightly modified grille, nicer upholstery and Sears branded tires, battery and spark plugs, the Allstate actually undercut the base price of the Henry J. Also in 1951, both the Kaiser and Frazer were redesigned, but sales never reached the heights of 1948. Even a 2-seat fiberglass sports car with unique doors that opened by dropping into the door sills failed to spark sales. That car was designed by Howard Darrin and called the Kaiser-Darrin, but it faired poorly against the Chevrolet Corvette and Ford Thunderbird. By 1953, the Frazer had been dropped and the company changed its name to simply Kaiser and acquired Willys-Overland. In the meantime, Willys had re-entered the car market for the first time since 1942 when it introduced the Aero series of compacts in 1952. Unfortunately, these cars were smaller and more expensive than the standard Ford and Chevrolet models of the day. After its acquisition by Kaiser and consolidation of all car building at Willys' Toledo works, the company decided in 1954 that it would give up on cars in order to concentrate on the Jeep business, although it did build the Kaiser Manhattan in Argentina for South American sales until 1962.

140 top Industrialist Henry J. Kaiser (center) welcomes his son Edgar (left) as vice president and general manager of Kaiser-Fraser, as company president Joseph Fraser looks on.

140-141 Despite being totally redesigned in 1939 with a new torpedo body shape, the LaSalle was dropped from GM's line after the 1940 model year. This 1940 LaSalle Special convertible, featured fender-mounted sealed-beam headlamps and a chrome grille treatment that featured auxiliary inlets between the headlamps. The LaSalle was replaced in 1941 by a new entry-level Cadillac called Series 61.

Tucker Torpedoed

While Kaiser met with limited success in the late 1940s, Preston Tucker was another dreamer who wanted to join the ranks of the established automakers. He may have built only 51 cars, but he earned notoriety as either a con man or a genius who was crushed by the automotive establishment. The truth is that he was neither, but instead just an ambitious soul who never had the wherewithal to make his dream come true.

Tucker had worked as a salesman for both Dodge and Studebaker, and during the war he made a tidy sum producing gun turrets that he designed. Working with designer Alex Tremulis (the former Auburn-Cord-Duesenberg designer who penned the Chrysler Thunderbolt), Tucker came up with the idea of a front-drive 6-passenger car with fenders that turned with the front wheels allowing the lights to shine around cor-

ners. The design, which included a huge 589 cu.-in. horizontally opposed engine, proved unworkable.

The prototype that debuted in 1948, called the Torpedo, was a rear-engine, rear-drive 6-passenger sedan with fixed fenders and three headlamps, including a center-mounted light that would swivel in the direction that the front wheels were turned.

Power in subsequent models of the Tucker came from a 166 hp 334 cu.-in. flat six based on an air-cooled prewar Franklin design used in helicopters and adapted for water cooling. Other advanced features included disc brakes and safety features such as a pop-out windshield, a padded dash and seat belts. Various models had a pre-war Cord gearbox, others some form of pre-selector transmission, while a few used the Tuckermatic, an automatic transmission with two torque converters and only 30 parts. The car was said to be capable of a top speed of 120 mph.

Tucker planned to build the car in a Chicago facto-

ry in which Dodge had built B-29 engines and fuselages during the war. Although Tucker had some of his own money in the venture, he primarily relied on a stock offering of $15 million and used some of the money for the first year's rent on the factory.

While folklore has it that Tucker's car was so good that the major manufacturers sought to stop him with investigations by the Securities and Exchange Commission, the truth is that Tucker's own hype may have been his undoing. He promised in late 1947 that by the spring of the following year, he would be producing 1,000 cars a day. When that didn't happen, an investigation by the SEC caused his stock to fall further and dealers began to sue him for not providing promised cars. Brought up on fraud charges in 1949, he was acquitted in 1950. It was too little, too late, for both the car and company were history. Preston Tucker tried unsuccessfully to build an economy car in Brazil, and in 1956 he died of lung cancer.

142 top Preston Tucker waves from behind the wheel of his controversial postwar cars. Tucker, a tireless promoter, hoped to build his car in an old Dodge factory in Chicago.

142-143 and 143 bottom Designed by Alex Tremulis, the Tucker Torpedo featured a center-mounted headlight attached to the steering system allowing it to swivel in the direction of a turn.

143 top Tucker's logo included the words "Symbol of Safety" to tout the Torpedo's massive bumpers, recessed controls and pop-out safety glass. Although it has a conventional grille in the bumper, the Tucker Torpedo actually used a rear-mounted engine, one version of which was an air-cooled Franklin flat six converted to liquid cooling. For all its talk of safety, the four-door Tucker still had so-called "Suicide Doors" that opened from the car's B-pillar.

Both Kaiser and Tucker had learned the hard way that auto making had matured into a complex industry in which the stakes were too high for entry. No longer could a tinkerer with a better idea set up shop, make cars and be successful.

First of all, auto manufacturers needed tremendous cash reserves in order to stay in business and ride out the lean sales cycles. As the 1930s had shown, many companies simply ran out of cash and had to close shop. The established companies that survived the 1930s and converted their facilities to war production regained their health, thanks to this infusion of government money. If it weren't for defense work, surely Packard, Willys-Overland, Hudson and Studebaker would not have survived beyond the early 1940s.

Secondly, by the late 1940s, cars had become much more technically sophisticated with the advent of air conditioning and automatic transmissions and required professional engineering staffs to design and build quality vehicles. A third factor was the economies of scale that established automakers enjoyed. With large production runs and multiple model lines, these companies had an edge in obtaining huge quantities of raw materials at favorable pricing, making it much more difficult for new manufacturers to break into the business at a competitive price point.

Finally, existing automakers had a tremendous advantage in distribution—customers were familiar with their brands and there were large, established dealer networks that made buying much easier.

As complex as the business had become, however, it all turned on one thing: product. General Motors, Ford and Chrysler were basically selling spiffed-up versions of their prewar offerings for nearly four years after hostilities had ended. In that period of high demand for cars with nothing much new from the major players, a window of opportunity was open to outsiders. In 1949, Detroit would unleash a flood of new products that would close that window for at least a decade.

146 top Henry Ford II met the challenge of rebuilding his grandfather's business by bringing together new management to introduce the company-saving 1949 Ford.

146 bottom left President Harry Truman rides in a Lincoln Cosmopolitan in this 1950 motorcade.

146 bottom right Lincolns are viewed as prestigious automobiles both at home and aborad. Here a 1951 bears Queen Elizabeth II and the Duke of Edinburgh.

147 This 1947 Ford, unchanged from its prewar design, reflects the trouble the company faced, having lost its president, Edsel, in 1943 and founder Henry in 1947, control of the company passed to an inexperienced grandson, Henry Ford II.

148-149 The 1947 Chevrolet Convertible Coupe used the same body stampings as the 1942 model and yet was eagerly snapped by buyers in a country that had no new cars for four years and now had the money to buy them.

Ford Rises Yet Again

During the War, Ford Motor Co. was in shambles. Edsel Ford, who had been given the title but not the authority to run his father's company, died on May 26, 1943 from a combination of cancer and undulant fever. Always in the background was an aging Henry Ford, now nearly 80, who relied on Harry Bennett, head of security, to run the company's day-to-day operations. According to Automotive News, Bennett was "an ex-boxer who, with Ford's blessing, had recruited a group of bullies, ex-cons and boxers to keep workers in line and the union out."

Ford, who by this time was suffering from the effects of two strokes, announced the day before Edsel's funeral that he would again run the company. This in effect gave Bennett and other senior Ford officials control over the company until Henry's grandchildren were 32 years old. Ford's wife Clara and daughter-in-law Eleanor (Edsel's widow) eventually convinced the pioneer automaker to give control of the company to 26-year-old Henry Ford II, who had been released by the Navy after his father Edsel's death.

Henry Ford II was named president on Sept. 21, 1945, and he promptly fired Bennett with the backing of John Bugas, an ex-FBI agent who had been hired by

the family to keep tabs on Bennett. Still, after years of intimidation and lack of direction, many talented managers and engineers had left Ford and the company sorely lacked the people and experience needed to compete with GM. Ford had grown into a large company comprised of small fiefdoms with no centralized control. In fact some stacks of invoices from suppliers reportedly were paid by weight.

In 1946, Henry Ford II made two key decisions that would save the company. He hired Ernest Breech, an experienced executive at both GM and Bendix Aviation, as well as 10 young Army Air Corps statistical control specialists who sold themselves as a team to Ford. Put together by Charles "Tex" Thorton, the so-called Whiz Kids studied every facet of Ford's opera-

tions and presented a reorganization plan and, more importantly, the centralized financial controls that the company lacked. They came up with the kind of organization Edsel Ford had sought and his father rejected nearly a decade earlier.

Meanwhile, Breech recruited veteran financial, sales and manufacturing executives from General Motors. But while the systems were being put in place to remake Ford into a modern company, what Ford desperately needed was new product.

Bob Gregorie, who designed the Continental, was in charge of Ford styling and developed a range of postwar cars based on the company's pre-war chassis. Breech decided to move the three designs up one level: The Ford became the Mercury, the Mercury became the Lincoln, and the Lincoln became a new model called the Cosmopolitan. Breech also decided that the company needed an all-new car from the ground up for the Ford range. He commissioned an outside designer, George Walker, to develop the shape and Harold Youngern, a former Olds and Borg-Warner engineer, to redo the mechanicals.

In a blind competition, Walker's design was selected over that of Bob Gregorie, who resigned soon after. Meanwhile, Youngern started with the existing 114-in. wheelbase but got rid of the car's front and rear transverse leaf springs in favor of an independent coil front end and twin longitudinal leaf springs with a live axle in the rear. The new car would be 2.4 in. shorter at 196.8 in. overall, 1.6 in. narrower at 71.7 in. and 3.4 in. lower with a 61.5 in. height. Engines were carried over—buyers were offered a choice of a 95-bhp 225 cu.-in. inline six or the 100 bhp 289 cu.-in. Flathead V-8. But the engine was moved 5 in. forward, allowing the rear seat to be put ahead of the rear axle instead of over it, improving the ride characteristics of the car.

Walker's design was a smooth, envelope body that is significant for being the first post-war car with fenders the same height as the beltline so that there was one continuous line from the front of the car to the rear. In June 1948 the '49 Ford was launched and was an immediate hit, with dealers booking orders for 100,000 vehicles.

Priced at $1,333 ($179 more than the '48), the '49 Ford would be sold through a new entity at the company, the Ford Motor Division, one of the organizational changes recommended by the Whiz Kids. Ford sales nearly doubled to 806,766 that year.

Just as the Model A helped Ford move beyond the Model T, so had the '49 Ford propelled the company into the future.

150-151 The tailfin fad started with this innocuous upturned tail lamps on the 1949 Cadillac Sedanette Coupe. Within a decade, fins would become gargantuan and then suddenly disappear by 1962.

100 top Buffalo-based Pierce-Arrow owned the patent on fender-mounted headlamps, as shown on this 1933 model. As a result, all other makers mounted their lights inboard of the fenders.

100-101 The Packard 120 derived its name from its 120-inch wheelbase and was priced just under $1,000. Purists blame the car for diluting Packard's prestige in the luxury market.

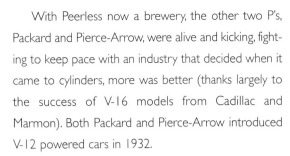

With Peerless now a brewery, the other two P's, Packard and Pierce-Arrow, were alive and kicking, fighting to keep pace with an industry that decided when it came to cylinders, more was better (thanks largely to the success of V-16 models from Cadillac and Marmon). Both Packard and Pierce-Arrow introduced V-12 powered cars in 1932.

The Packard rated at 160 horsepower and the Pierce at 150. Given their limited resources, both companies fitted the V-12s as options in the standard and long wheelbase cars powered by straight eights.

While most of the Pierce-Arrows tended to be factory bodied (the factory was one of the first to switch to all-steel bodies in 1929), the Packard was a favorite among coachbuilders such as Dietrich and LeBaron. But as the economy sunk to new depths, the V-12s didn't sell. Packard retailed only 549 and Pierce-Arrow 449. Packard embarked on a strategy to offer a more mainstream model called the 120 in 1935. With a base price just under $1,000, the car drew its name from its 120-in. wheelbase. A year later, the straight eight's output was bumped from 110 to 120 bhp, a number that also matched the model designation. In 1937 a 6-cylinder model, called the 115, debuted on a 115-in. wheelbase. The cars were popular and pushed Packard production to record levels in 1937 when nearly 110,000 cars were built. V-12 sales continued to lag and that engine was discontinued in 1939, while the

senior Packard Series 160 and 180 cars continued to be built with straight eights. But purists felt the 115 and 120 debased the marque and were ultimately responsible for the company's demise after World War II.

However, there's no doubt that if Packard had not offered the 120 and instead concentrated on the ultra luxury market, it would have suffered the same fate as Pierce-Arrow. At the time Packard was developing the 120, Pierce-Arrow had nearly gone that route with its lower priced Series 80/81.

These cars were poorly received and precipitated a 1928 merger with Studebaker. By 1933, Pierce-Arrow had regained its independence from Studebaker when a consortium of Buffalo businessmen purchased the company.

That year, Pierce-Arrow introduced the Silver Arrow show car at the Chicago World's Fair. Five of these stunning V-12 aerodynamic coupes were built (they were actually assembled at the Studebaker works in South Bend, Indiana) and retailed for $10,000 each. It was the second most expensive car on the American market, behind Duesenberg. The next year, a less radical coupe, still called the Silver Arrow, was built in Buffalo and retailed for a third of the cost of the original. Even though the Silver Arrow as well as the Series 1601 eight and 1602/1603 twelves, were well engineered and built, nothing could lift falling sales and by 1938, the factory ceased production.

Iconic Iconoclasts

Other iconoclastic makes, like the air-cooled Franklin and the steam-driven Doble, also failed to survive the 1930s. Franklin, an industry pioneer that traced its roots to 1902, tried to appeal to both the masses and the upper crust near the end of its run. Following Charles Lindbergh's solo flight across the Atlantic in 1927, it introduced its 6-cylinder Airman series, and in the late 1920s many Franklins sported custom bodywork by Dietrich. Franklin also built an air-cooled V-12 in 1933, which cost around $4,000. Only 200 were built and by 1934, Franklin was history.

Doble, which made an abortive start in Detroit before World War I, didn't begin building cars in earnest until 1924 at a plant in Emeryville, California. Abner Doble had literally perfected the steam car. His boiler was ready to produce steam for the 4-cylinder 125-horsepower engine in just 90 seconds, and the condenser was so efficient that the Model E could travel 1,500 miles on 24 gallons of water. A few cars based on the Model E sported bodies installed by Murphy in Pasadena. There followed a Model F, but by 1932 the company was driven out of business, the result of poor sales and stock manipulation.

The 1930s would also see experimentation with aerodynamics and vehicle form and function. All these

elements came together in two vehicles that shared a radical approach to moving people.

Futurist Buckminster Fuller, who developed the geodesic dome, decided to apply his concept to the automobile. Three of these vehicles, called Dymaxion, were built in 1933-34. Shaped like an aircraft fuselage and powered by a rear-mounted Ford V-8, the Dymaxion featured front wheels that were mounted amidship, while a single rear wheel provided steering. The vehicle could seat up to 11 passengers and the body was constructed of a combination of balsa wood and aluminum.

Unfortunately, the design proved to be too radical

103 bottom Futurist Buckminster Fuller tried his hand at automotive design with his Dymaxion, a rear-engine people mover that could carry up to 11 passengers.

for Fuller to find sufficient backing, and the Dymaxion was never built in volume.

More conventional-looking than the Dymaxion but no less innovative was the Stout Scarab, a car built by William B. Stout, an engineer who was an inventor, aviator and automotive journalist. Stout's first automotive venture was a 1913 cycle-car for which he was unable to find backers. He later edited Motor Age magazine and went on to work in Packard's aircraft division where he is credited with designing the internal braced cantilevered wing. Like Fuller's creation, Stout relied on a rear-mounted flathead Ford V-8 to power his rear-drive car, but the Scarab had four wheels each positioned at the far corners of the vehicle to provide maximum cabin space. With no running boards, the Scarab was one of the first designs to use flush, envelope body styling. The car featured coil-spring independent suspension, a flat cabin floor and seats that could be moved around or taken out of the vehicle, much like those found in a modern minivan. As many as nine were built between 1934 and 1939 and cost $5,000 each, or nearly 10 times the average automobile. The Scarab proved to be too far ahead of its time to find commercial success.

102-103 William B. Stout built only 9 Stout Scarabs between 1934 and 1936, a vehicle that accurately predicted the minivan, which would become popular 50 years later.

102 bottom Power for the Scarab came from a rear-mounted Ford flathead V-8. The design also featured removable seats, another feature common on modern minivans.

DYMAXION

The Big Three

While the 1930s were a difficult period for the independents, General Motors, Ford and Chrysler were able to turn adversity to their advantage. By offering a spectrum of cars across the market, these companies were able to not only enjoy certain economies of scale, but also make product improvements that would keep smaller companies, which were unable to sustain the same levels of investment, at a competitive disadvantage.

Collectors may prize Duesenbergs, Packards, Auburns, Pierce-Arrows and the like, but it was the advancements by Cadillac, Lincoln and Chrysler that kept raising the bar.

In 1930, Cadillac shocked the world with the introduction of the first production V-16, a mechanical marvel designed by chief engineer Ernest Seaholm. Called Model 452 after the engine's displacement of 452 cu.-in., the V-16 Cadillac produced 165 bhp. The bulk of the 2,800 cars were bodied by GM-owned Fleetwood.

Sales of the V-16 plunged to 364 in 1931 and less than 300 in 1932. The former sales slump was due to the recession and the latter because Cadillac introduced a twelve based on the V-16 that was considerably cheaper. The '32 sales dive also is attributed to the introduction of V-12s from Lincoln, Pierce-Arrow and Packard. Cadillac stuck with the V-16 through the 1930s despite sagging sales. Less than 100 V-16s were built annually from 1934-37, including the 1934 Series 452-D Fleetwood, a racy 2-door based on the stunning 1933 V-16 Fastback Coupe built specially for the Chicago World's Fair.

Cadillac offered an all-new V-16 for 1938, a short stroke engine displacing 431 cu.-in. rated at 185 bhp. This engine supplanted both the larger V-16 and the V-12 engines in the company's lineup. Cadillac used the new engine in the Series 90 bodywork that was already two years old and finally dropped the V-16 after the 1940 model year.

104 bottom and 105 Although General Motors had its own in-house design staff, bespoke body work from independent coachbuilders would appear on vehicles like this 1937 Hardmann-bodied V-16 Cadillac.

The Hardmann body, like most designs of the era, was not only influenced by aerodynamics, but also French design. Similar bodywork could be seen on Talbot-Lago and Delahaye cabriolets of similar vintage.

104 top During the 1930s, manufacturers began absorbing independent coachbuilders into their organizations, like Fleetwood, which specialized in building limousines for Cadillac.

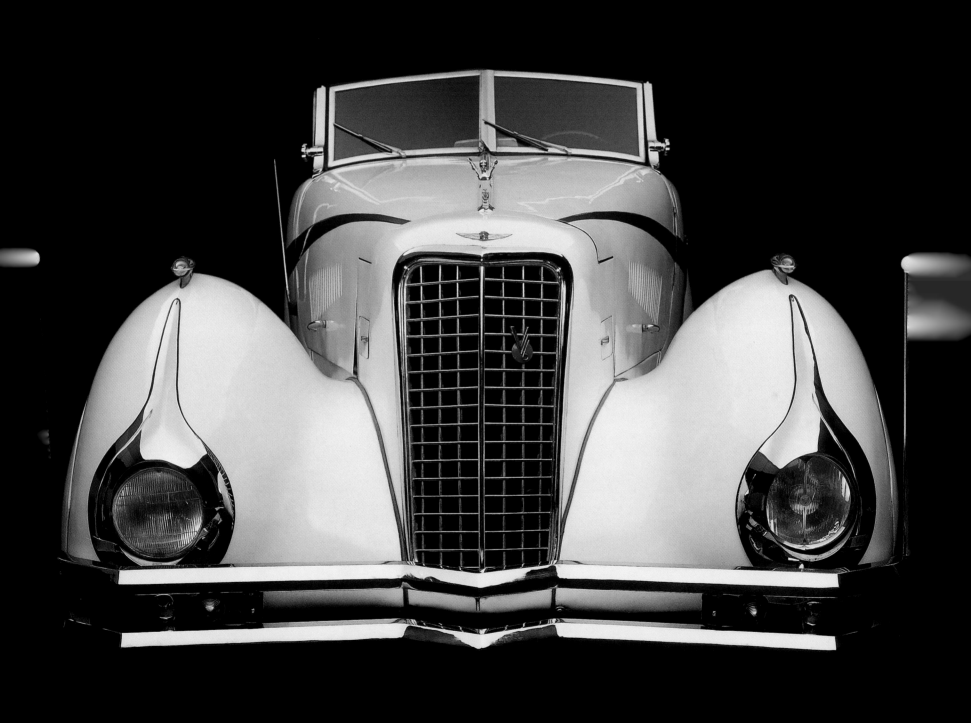

Lincoln's response to Cadillac was the V-12 powered KB model. Introduced in 1932, the KB was powered by a 448 cu.-in. L-head V-12 that produced 150 bhp. Unlike General Motors, which was increasingly relying on designs from Harley Earl's Art & Colour Section, Lincoln, under the tutelage of Edsel Ford, solicited designs from various coachworks like Willoughby, Dietrich, Brunn, LeBaron and Judkins and put them in a catalog for prospective clients. The KB was replaced in 1934 by Model K, which had a smaller displacement, higher compression V-12 with four instead of seven main bearings.

visit to the Briggs factory, was impressed by the prototype's layout, which might have influenced his design for the Volkswagen Beetle. Eugene "Bob" Gregorie would execute the final design for the Zephyr and would go on to style the Lincoln Continental.

The Mercury was similar in design to the '39 Ford when it was introduced in October of 1938. Riding on a 4-in.-longer wheelbase and powered by a beefier 239 cu.-in. V-8 rated at 95 bhp, the Mercury cost $165 more than the Ford and $430 less than the Zephyr.

Chrysler would take a different tack in competing with Cadillac at the top of the market and the rest of the GM divisions in midrange priced vehicles. In the luxury segment, Chrysler introduced the LeBaron-bodied CG Imperial in 1931, followed in 1932 by the CH and CL, which were built until 1934. Instead of a V-12, Chrysler relied on a 135 bhp 385 cu.-in. straight eight to power these masterpieces.

In the middle ranges, Chrysler was counting on advanced styling and unit body construction to revolutionize the family car market, only to stumble badly. In 1934, the company introduced the Airflow as both a Chrysler and DeSoto.

107 bottom The 1938 Lincoln Zephyr is significant for its use of a more horizontal grille theme at a time when most grilles were vertical in execution. It took some of its cues from the Cord.

108-109 Although a relative newcomer to the industry, Chrysler showed it could compete with the top luxury makers with its 1932 Imperial cabriolet. The CG model was powered by a 125 bhp inline eight. The 1932 Chrysler Imperial cabriolet seated two passengers in the main cabin and had a trunk-mounted rumble seat for two more riders.

The gap between these custom-bodied Lincolns and Ford's Model A was huge. A two-pronged response was formulated with the development of the V-12 Lincoln Zephyr, which would compete with the Packard 120 and LaSalle, while in 1938 a V-8 powered Ford Mercury would be introduced (the Ford preface was dropped in 1940). Designed by John Tjaarda of Briggs Body, the Lincoln Zephyr was not only sleek in design, but also unique in its unit body construction that combined both chassis and body. Tjaarda's original concept called for rear engine placement, an idea nixed by Edsel Ford. Reportedly, Dr. Ferdinand Porsche, in a

106-107 With V-12 power, the Lincoln Zephyr was positioned as a more affordable entry in the luxury car market in a bid to build volume.

106 bottom The large gap between Ford and Lincoln products was bridged by the creation of the Mercury brand in 1939. This cabrio offered a more powerful V-8 than the standard Ford.

THE AIRFLOW *Chrysler* FRAME
BUILT LIKE A BRIDGE

The new girder-trussed frame is designed like a bridge with longitudinal, vertical and diagonal girders extending from the front to the back of the body, up and over the top of the body. In the Airflow Chrysler you actually ride with part of the frame above your head. The result of this new construction is the safest and most rigid car built.

PART OF TH
IS ACTUALLY OV

RAME
OUR HEAD

YOU RIDE INSIDE THE FRAME

First shown at the 1933 Chicago World's Fair, along with a host of aerodynamic-inspired cars, the Chrysler Airflow was the only design that had any scientific grounding. Walter P. Chrysler had retained Orville Wright as a consultant on the Airflow and the car's body was tested in a wind tunnel.

In addition to its sleek shape, the Airflow was a unit body, which combined both body and frame. That construction allowed the car to ride lower and also helped position the wheels far out to the corners of the vehicle, maximizing cabin space. Unfortunately, the Airflow was too aerodynamic. The public thought the car was

110-111 and 112-113
The 1936 Chrysler Airflow not only introduced the concept of aerodynamic design to car styling, it was one of the first vehicles with unit body construction rather than the traditional body-on-frame approach to manufacturing.

ugly with its droopy snout and massive waterfall grille. According to Automotive News, Chrysler sold only 11,292 Airflows in 1934, while DeSoto, which had no other car to offer, sold 13,940. The carryover Chrysler CA and CB models provided nearly double the volume. Despite a quick fix in 1935 by Chrysler designer Oliver Clark to give the car a more conventional nose and grille treatment, sales continued to dwindle to 4,600 in 1937, the last year the car was on the market.

Offered as a 6-window sedan, 4-window town car or 2-door coupe, prices on the Airflow started at $995 for a 6-cylinder DeSoto version, while the straight-eight powered Chrysler Airflow started at $1,345. In 1935, Ray Dietrich was retained by Chrysler to create a new line of cars called the Airstream that would debut a year later. More conventional in appearance and priced lower, these cars further cut into Airflow sales and contributed to its eventual demise.

111 The 1934 Airflow, although a radical departure in automotive design, reflected an overall fascination with streamlining in industrial design, as shown by this train.

Chrysler wasn't the only manufacturer that tried to capture the fancy of car buyers with aerodynamic styling. Hupmobile, which was prosperous in 1928 with sales of over 65,000 cars and a profit of $8 million, had fallen on hard times in the depression.

In 1934 it introduced its take on the aerodynamic sedan, this one penned by noted designer Raymond Loewy. Powered by a 101 bhp 6-cylinder engine, the D618 sedan was sold until 1936, although Hupmobile had closed its factory for a year and a half between December 1935 and July 1937 because of financial entanglements with Archie Andrews of Ruxton fame. Hupmobile tried again in 1938 with a more traditional 4-door sedan powered by a choice of 6- or 8-cylinder engines, but less than 4,000 were sold. Hupp Motor Company then cast its lot with Graham, having purchased the tooling for the Cord 810/812. In exchange for the right to use the tooling, Graham assembled both the Hupmobile Skylark and its own version known as the Graham Hollywood. By America's entry into World War II, Hupp Motor Company had disappeared.

Graham was a relative newcomer to the industry, being formed in 1928 as Graham-Paige when three Graham brothers (Joseph, Robert, and Ray) took over the Paige-Detroit Motor Car Company. The Grahams, who made trucks for Dodge before selling out in 1926, sold over 73,000 cars in 1928.

114 top The 1938 Graham Special 6 Coupe is a body style as known as a "business coupe" for its single bench seat and large trunk area to carry sample cases.

114-115 Although it was called the "Sharknose" Graham, the real designation for this design of the 1939 model was "Spirit of Motion."

115 top Hupp, established in 1909, closed for 18 months in 1936 after launching the Eight Deluxe touring sedan. In 1942, it ceased car building altogether.

CHAPTER 5

1949 - 1960
The American
Automobile
Reinvented

152-153 Nothing epitomizes the flash of the 1950s more than the tailfin of the 1959 Cadillac Eldorado.

I

n 1948, small vestigial fins appeared on the rear of the Cadillac Series 60. Fifties styling had arrived. Fins would come to represent the best and worst of American culture—best in the sense that they reflected the boundless optimism of the times, worst in that by the decade's end, they would become a symbol of conspicuous consumption and planned obsolescence.

The work of Frank Hershey, the fins were inspired by his boss, Harley Earl, who admired the twin boom tail look of the P-38 fighter that had been so successful during World War II.

Earl's influence had been growing steadily since he became a GM vice president in 1938 (it was then that he changed his department's name from Art & Colour to Styling). But the war intervened and virtually all work on automobiles had ceased. It wasn't until the 1950s that Earl was truly at the height of his influence. By then, GM was the undisputed industry leader flush with cash and operating without constraint under the plan set down years earlier by chairman Alfred P. Sloan, Jr. That vision of a ladder of products arranged by division with no overlap provided a host of products for Earl's staff to design, but that wasn't all. Sloan insisted on annual model changes. "I am sure we realize how much appearance has to do with sales," Sloan wrote to a fellow executive. "The changes in the new model should be so novel and attractive as to create demand for the new value, so to speak, [to] create a certain amount of dissatisfaction with past models as compared with the new one." Styling, more than technical innovation or manufacturing processes, would drive the American auto industry in the 1950s.

Designers were given a free hand, which they exercised with impunity. Earl wasn't alone in his fascination with aviation; aircraft would provide many of the decade's styling themes.

154-155 The 1953 Buick Skylark was a limited edition of the Roadmaster built to commemorate the division's 50th anniversary. Only 1,690 were built.

remaining portion enough to support the door. Buick introduced the hardtop on its 1948 Roadmaster, and by 1950, with hardtops available on the Super and Special models, they accounted for a full third of Buick's 670,000 sales that year. By 1953, all manufacturers offered a hardtop.

156-157 One of the hallmarks of Buick styling as shown by this 1956 Century was the hardtop look.

158 top left The lens for the rear-view camera was positioned over the tail cone on the futuristic Buick Centurion.

158 top right Space age influences can be seen in the styling of the Buick Centurion, which features soft-edged fins, a pointed tail and rocket-like exhaust tips.

158-159 The Buick Centurion was a 1956 dream car that offered such

futuristic touches as a bubble glass roof and a review television monitor instead of a mirror.

159 top left Beneath the bubble glass roof, the interior at first blush looks fairly conventional in the Centurion. However, the steering wheel

is mounted on a cantilevered column that projects from the center of the dash.

159 top right Positioned just above the center-mounted steering column is the television monitor designed to replace the conventional rear view mirror.

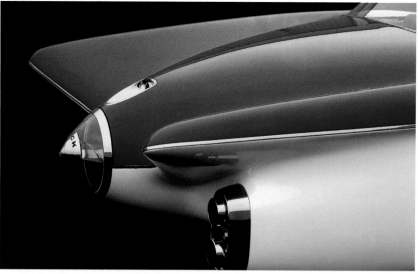

Just as he did with the 1938 Y-Job, Harley Earl again used Buick to reintroduce concept cars with the 1951 Buick LeSabre and XP-300. The LeSabre, which was more of a dream car than a precursor to an actual production model, was clearly inspired by the jet age. A nose resembling a fighter's intake nacelle dominated the front end, while the rear had large tail fins flanking a fuselage that tapered into a jet-like exhaust. All the controls and switches looked as if they had been lifted from an aircraft's cockpit. Conversely, the XP-300 was a roadster that sported a curved windshield, large chrome bumpers with integrated oval grille, and headlamps stacked over turn signals—a look that foretold the style of the 1954 Buicks.

160 top and 160-161 The jet-age influences on design first appeared on Harley Earl's 1951 Buick LeSabre dream car, his first since the 1938 Y-Job.

161 top left In addition to being used by Harley Earl as his personal transportation, the LeSabre also traveled around the world, making an appearance at the Paris Salon in 1951.

161 top right The LeSabre had a long life on the Motorama and auto show circuits, starring in New York City as late as 1953.

Although Ford had found success with its '49 model, and with rebodied Mercurys and Lincolns, it had little to compete with the flash and pizzazz that GM was serving up in the early '50s.

Likewise, Chrysler's cars were stodgy. Designers there slavishly followed the edict of chairman K.T. Keller that the company's entire product line offer sufficient headroom to enable a passenger to wear a hat while seated comfortably in the cabin. "We build cars to sit in, not piss over," Keller ordered.

It would be the smaller companies, like Studebaker

and Nash, which would provide stylish answers to the GM onslaught. Of particular interest was the 1953 Studebaker Starlight Coupe, designed by Robert E. Bourke of Raymond Loewy's industrial design firm. The Starlight Coupe featured a low nose, tapered body and the requisite tail fins.

Nash distinguished itself by offering a small compact car in 1950, at a time when the industry trend was towards larger, longer, lower and wider cars.

Called the Rambler, the bathtub-shaped economy car was priced at $1,800 and was the lowest priced car

by a mainstream manufacturer. The Rambler rode on a 100-in. wheelbase and was powered by a 173 cu.-in. straight six. In order to attract customers to the showroom, however, Nash—thanks to a chance meeting during a Trans Atlantic passage on the Queen Elizabeth between company president George Mason and Donald Healy—offered a 2-seat sports car in 1951 called the Nash-Healy.

Healy had been enroute to America to buy engines from Cadillac when he met Mason. When the Cadillac deal fell through, Healy and Mason struck an

162 The legendary "Loewy coupes" such as the 1954 Studebaker Regal Starlight, which were penned by noted industrial designer Raymond Loewy, were a clean, uncluttered

counterpoint to chromed and finned offerings from its larger competitors. The use of a horizontal grille theme gave the Studebaker a low and lean look that has withstood the test of time.

163 top Although the rear window treatment is conventions, the pillarless Regal Starliner had a smaller and more sharply raked backlight giving it a sportier appearance.

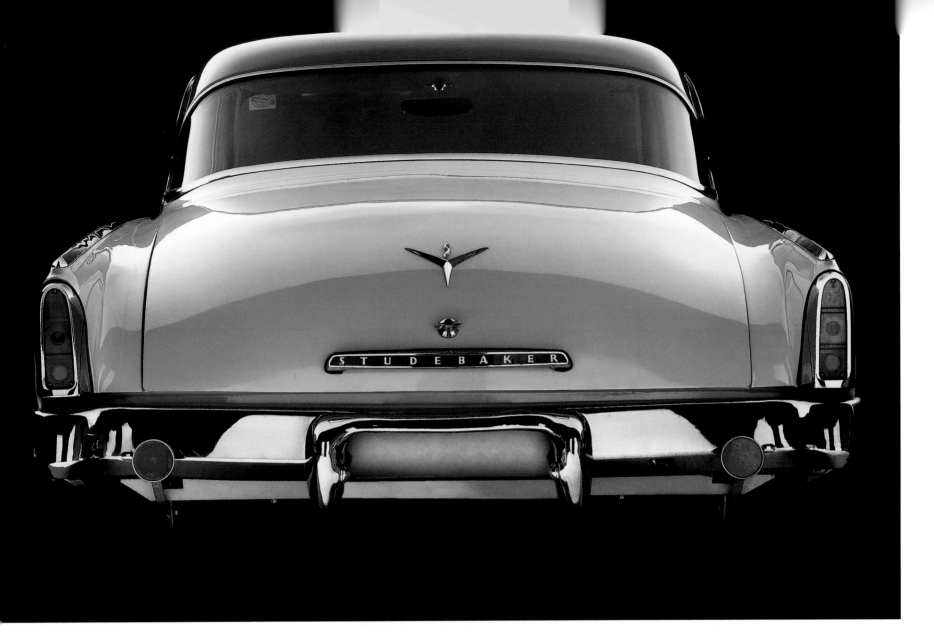

agreement to use a Nash drivetrain in a Healy chassis with bodywork by Italy's Pininfarina. It would be one of the first multi-country efforts to build a car specifically for the American market.

It's estimated that the transportation costs alone devoured any hopes of profit on the pricey Nash-Healy, which cost $5,128. Only 506 were made during the car's three years of production, but Nash felt it served its purpose as a showroom draw for potential customers.

163 bottom A chance encounter between Donald Healy and George Mason, president of Nash, on a trans-Atlantic crossing on the Queen Elizabeth resulted in the Pininfarina designed Nash Healy coupe and convertible in 1952-53. Here, Battista Pinin Farina (left) and his son Sergio inspect one of the two-door sport coupes at the company's Turin, Italy headquarters.

Another Italian-bodied car using Chrysler Hemis was the Dual-Ghia. Dual Motors, a Detroit-based cartage company headed by Gene Casaroll, commissioned the Turin-based Ghia design house to build a body on a Chrysler V-8 chassis. About 120 were built between 1955 and 1958 as 4-passenger hardtops or convertibles priced at $7,646.

Others using American V-8s in this era included Allard, which could be fitted with Cadillac, Mercury or Chrysler power, and home-grown Kurtis, a product of Indy racing legend Frank Kurtis, who produced his own road-going sports car in 1949.

After a 36-unit production run, he sold the tooling to Earl "Madman" Muntz, who had made a small fortune selling radios and televisions. Muntz moved the operation to Evansville, Indiana and later Chicago, where he converted the Kurtis into the Muntz Jet, a

A Taste for Power

With the introduction of high-compression overhead valve V-8s in 1949 by Oldsmobile and Cadillac, America's appetite for performance began to grow. The ohv V-8s—a 160 bhp 331 cu.-in. version for Cadillac and 135 bhp 303 cu.-in. Rocket V-8 for Oldsmobile—also gave GM a lift in stock-car racing, where Hudson's Hornet had been dominant. Oldsmobile made even greater inroads in 1951 when the new lightweight 88 body style was fitted with the Rocket V-8.

Sportsman Briggs Cunningham, who had successfully defended America's Cup, trained his sights on Le Mans. He entered the 1950 contest with a virtually stock Series 61 coupe (a lightweight entry-level model with a 3-speed column-mounted shift) and Le Monstre, a custom-bodied Series 61 chassis. The cars finished 10th and 11th respectively.

Cunningham would return to Le Mans a year later, but with a car of his own design powered by Chrysler's new powerful Hemi V-8 that was introduced in 1951. Starting with the C2R, Cunningham built a series of racers as well as a road car, the C3, bodied by the Italian coachbuilder Vignale.

It sold for $9,000 in 1953-54. Only 26 were built.

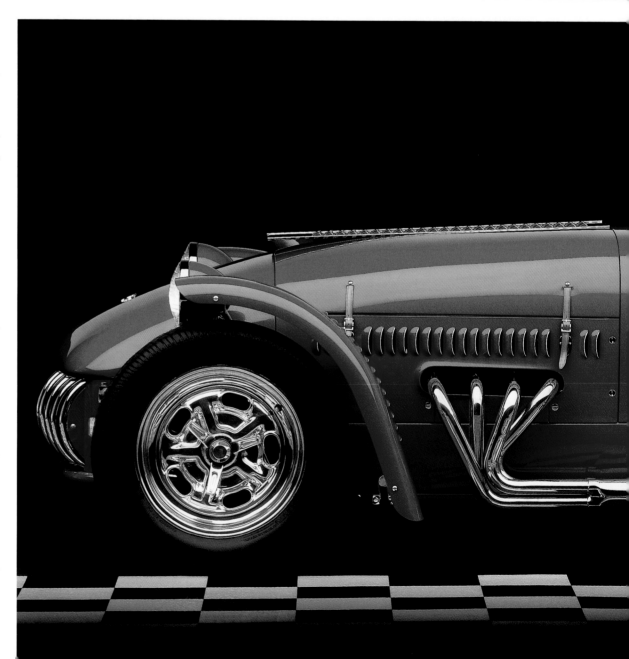

longer 4-passenger hardtop and convertible, which he sold at first with Cadillac power then switched to Lincoln V8s. Muntz produced just under 400 cars before going out of business in 1954, which was about the time Kurtis reentered the market with another road-going version of his successful Indy car. For two more years Kurtis sold three cars: the 500-S, which could be ordered with any engine; the 500KK tubular chassis, to which custom bodywork could be added; and the 500-M, which offered a supercharged 250 bhp Cadillac V-8.

Lincoln also developed a reputation for performance, winning the International Standard Class in the grueling Carrera Panamericana in 1952, '53 and '54. These Capri hardtop coupes were powered by a 285 bhp 368 cu.-in. overhead valve V-8 tuned to take the car to a top speed of 130 mph.

164 top Prior to racing on its purpose-built oval, which would open in 1959, the National Association of Stock Car Automobile Racing conducted speed events on the sands of Daytona Beach. Here a '57 Chevy starts a speed run.

164-165 Roadgoing versions of full race cars were common in the 1950s. Kurtis, which had made a name for itself at the Indy 500 issued a series of Kurtis-Craft 500-S Roadsters in 1954.

165 top The dream cars of the 1950s became much more futuristic and divorced from production cars, as evidenced by the Oldsmobile Golden Rocket shown at the 1957 Paris Salon.

Corvette: Concept to Reality

America's premiere sports car, the Corvette, actually started life as one of the many show cars dreamed up by Harley Earl's designers as they unleashed a flood of concepts to fill GM's new traveling auto shows called Motoramas. These self-promoting shows trace their origin back to the 1930s to the Parade of Progress, which essentially took GM's 1933 Chicago World's Fair exhibit on the road. Specially built trucks were used to haul the displays from town to town.

In 1949, GM re-engineered the concept by holding an exhibition called "Transportation Unlimited" at the Waldorf-Astoria Hotel in New York. After the second exhibition, in 1950, GM went back to the drawing board and in 1953 launched its first Motorama, which toured the country stopping in New York, Miami, Los Angeles,

166 top The 1953 Corvette was built in limited numbers in Flint, Michigan. Here a worker polishes a die used for the original tooling. Assembly was later moved to St. Louis, where it could be built in greater numbers.

166-167 Inspired by a Motorama concept car, the Corvette that debuted in 1953 was hardly a road-ripping sports car due to its anemic six-cylinder engine and two-speed automatic transmission.

San Francisco, Dallas and Kansas City. The Corvette, which was based on a Chevrolet station wagon chassis cut down to a 102-in. wheelbase, was powered by a 235 cu.-in. Blue Flame six with triple downdraft carburetors making 150 bhp. The transmission was a 2-speed automatic Powerglide. The car, codenamed EX-122, debuted in January 1953 at GM's first Motorama of the year, again at the Waldorf in New York. The car's reception convinced Chevy to put the roadster into production six months later. The Corvette's styling in production remained faithful to the concept, including the mesh covered headlamps, "twin cowl" dashboard and fiberglass body construction. The station wagon underpinnings were discarded in favor of a unique frame.

All the cars were Polo White with a red interior, and the car was equipped with a manual convertible top that stored under a hard tonneau cover. Snap-in side curtains were used instead of roll-up door glass. Only 300 were built that first year in Flint, Michigan. For 1954, production was shifted to St. Louis where larger volumes could be realized. Still, the 'Vette with its Blue Flame six and automatic transmission was more show than go. Priced at $3,523, the Corvette didn't sell as strongly as management had anticipated, although production of 3,640 was 10 times higher than 1953. Meanwhile at the Motorama, Chevy showed the Corvette with a lift-off hardtop, which would become available in later model years, and a Corvette Nomad, a 2-door station wagon that would be offered as a body style on the standard Chevrolet Bel Air in 1955.

167 top The Corvette was one of the first Detroit production cars to extensively use composite materials. A workman demonstrates the lightweight fiberglass tub.

168-169 Ford responded to the success of the Corvette with its own two-seater, the Thunderbird. This 1956 model featured a detachable hardtop with its signature porthole quarter window.

169 The Thunderbird was envisioned from the start as a personal luxury car as opposed to a pure sports car, although unlike the Corvette, it was introduced with V-8 power.

Ford, meanwhile, took note of the publicity that GM design had garnered with production cars like the Corvette. It promoted George Walker, the outside designer responsible for the '49 Ford, to vice president of design and began to counter GM with the Thunderbird. Noting the Spartan nature of the Corvette, designers envisioned the T-Bird as a personal luxury car with such features as power windows, air conditioning, power brakes and a more comfortable ride. The body would be steel instead of fiberglass, and one option at launch would be a lift-off hardtop complete with a porthole.

Unlike the Corvette's inline six, the Thunderbird was launched with V-8 power, a 292 cu.-in. 4-barrel V-8 producing 193 bhp when equipped with a 3-speed manual, or 198 bhp when equipped with the Fordomatic automatic transmission.

The Thunderbird was an instant hit, selling 16,155 units. Chevrolet's response for 1955 was a V-8 of its own, the small block or so-called "Turbo-Fire," which produced 195 bhp from 265 cu.-in. Still, the shortcomings in ride and comfort had taken its toll. Chevy could barely manage sales of 700 Corvettes that year. A redesign in 1956 that included conventional roll-up windows and even more performance (225 bhp) from Corvette chief engineer Zora Arkus-Duntov turned the corner for the car. It became a serious sports car and began to find its own market niche. By 1958, Ford had turned the Thunderbird from a 2-seat roadster into a 4-seat convertible and later, a coupe.

170 top The Thunderbird became an instant icon, being used to promote Marilyn Monroe's mid-'50s classic, The Seven Year Itch.

170-171 The 1956 T-Bird sports rear fender skirts, while the detachable hardtop is a rare model that lacks a porthole. The spare carrier, a so-called Continental kit that recalls an earlier era, is one of the signature design cues on the Thunderbird.

171 top Inspired by Indian lore, Thunderbird sported these elegant, turquoise-colored badges.

Chrysler's New Look

By mid-decade, design had become a higher priority at Chrysler as well. The company turned to Virgil Exner to breathe life into the company's moribund offerings. In 1955, he introduced the "$100 Million Look," which referred to the money invested in the overhaul of the stodgy lineup of Chrysler, Dodge, DeSoto and Plymouth cars.

This new design was cleaner, more muscular and, above all, lower than the previous generation cars. At the top of the range was the Imperial, which was marketed as a separate brand. It was distinguished by its split eggcrate grille and gun-sight taillamps mounted atop the fenders.

The real brute in the line was the new 300 series based on the New Yorker. Called the C300, it sported the Imperial's grille, and beneath the hood was a 300 bhp 331 cu.-in version of the Chrysler Hemi. The car boasted a top speed of 130 mph.

While Chrysler made a big impact with its new look, Ford design continued to evolve at a slower pace. In 1954, Ford's big news was the introduction of the Skyliner, which sported a large Plexiglas panel in the roof. The panel grew larger in the '55 and '56 models but was eventually dropped because of the material's difficult upkeep and propensity to scratch. In 1956 Ford began pushing the safety of its cars over styling.

Promoted under the "Lifeguard Design" theme, Ford touted such features as a padded dash, safety latches on the doors, a deep-dish wheel design that was said to lessen the seriousness of chest injuries, and optional seat belts. Sales were a disaster. According to Automotive News, in 1955 Ford trailed Chevy by 67,000 units; a year later that gap was 190,000. Henry Ford II reportedly said of his Ford Division manager, "[Robert] McNamara is selling safety, but Chevrolet is selling cars." Part of Chevy's appeal may have been design as well. The '55 and '56 Chevy Bel Air sported smooth, contemporary bodywork that is now considered classic.

172-173 Chrysler design chief Virgil Exner vaulted the automaker to the forefront of design with his lean, clean, Forward Look philosophy of design that blended large expressive fins and fenders with larger glass areas as demonstrated by this 1957 Imperial Crown Coupe.

173 top The 1957 Chrysler 300D blended raw performance from its 390 horsepower Hemi V-8 with Exner's cutting-edge look.

174-175 One of the most memorable convertibles of the 1950s is the 1957 Ford Skyliner which introduced the concept of the retractable hardtop to production vehicles.

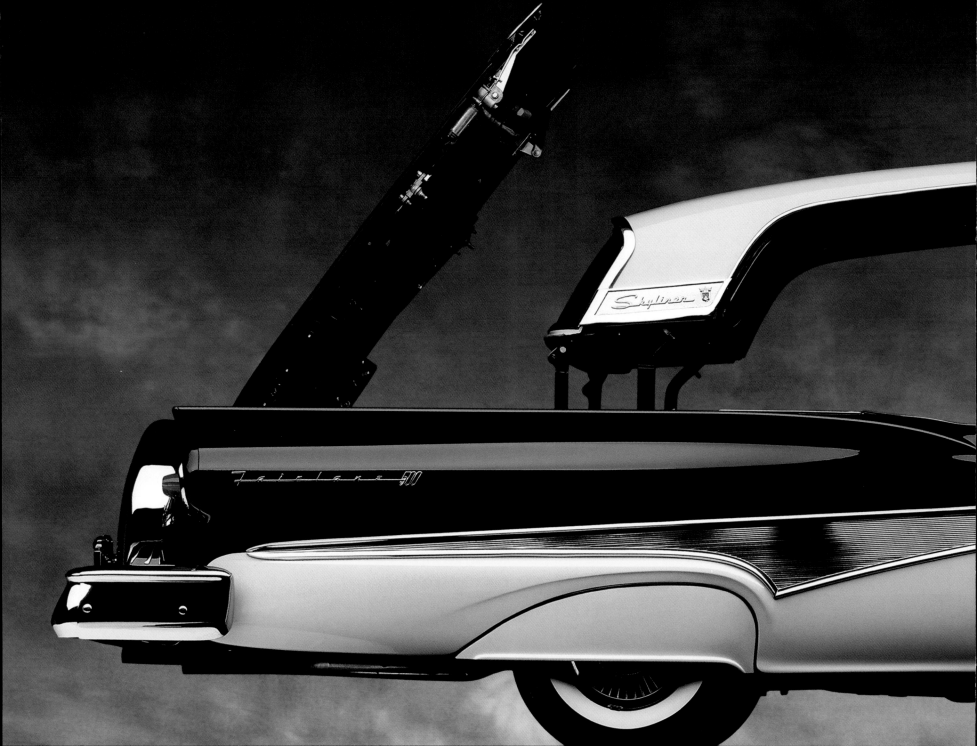

During this period, the pickup truck started to become more car-like. The 1955 Chevrolet Cameo Carrier sported a fiberglass-skinned flush cargo box and chromed bumpers. Later models added two-tone treatments and even fins.

Ford responded in 1957 by not only restyling the F-Series pickup, but also converting the Ford Ranch Wagon (a 2-door wagon similar to the Nomad) into a car-based pickup called the Ranchero.

Standing 16 inches shorter than the standard Ford pickup, the Ranchero offered the utility of a truck with the comfort of a car, with such features as air conditioning, power seats, power brakes and power steering. Chevrolet responded in 1959 with the car-based El Camino. Ford continued to sell the Ranchero until 1979, while Chevrolet ended El Camino production in 1989.

The Ranchero and El Camino were the first vehicles to bridge the gap between cars and trucks. Although they are no longer built, their influence is felt in the many car-like amenities as well as ride and handling attributes found in modern pickups, vans and sport-utility vehicles.

176 top Workers assemble a Chevrolet pickup truck front end in 1956. By the mid-1950s, car design was having an impact on truck styling.

176-177 The 1955 Ford F100 pickup was developed as a commercial vehicle, but in just two decades, the truck would find its way into personal use. Not only was the 1955 Ford F100 sold as a pickup, but its cab and chassis were adapted for a variety of uses from ice cream trucks to panel delivery vans.

177 top A Chevy pickup is tested in a heat booth in this 1956 image.

A Surfeit of Show Cars

The late '50s would be marked by excess—too much chrome, oversized fins and too much weight. These designs bordered on caricature and existed in part to spur the public's infatuation with show cars, which designers happily provided.

GM's roster of dream cars was extensive. Oldsmobile's first was the '53 Starfire, followed in short order by the F-88, sporting a 250 bhp 325 cu.-in V-8. Buick had its Wildcat series, which debuted in 1954 (strangely dubbed Wildcat II), followed by Wildcat III in 1955. Oldsmobile debuted a fastback in 1954 called the Cutlass, and Cadillac showed the El Camino, a fiberglass-bodied coupe with a brushed steel roof. A year later Cadillac resurrected the LaSalle name for an open-top show car that looked similar to the Buick Wildcat. In 1956, Buick offered up the Centurion, which looked more space age than jet age. It featured a rearview television camera and a cantilevered steering column that projected from the center tunnel, giving the driver more legroom. Pontiac's show car that year was the Club de Mer, a 2-place sports car that was said to inspire the Banshee, an aborted attempt to give the division a Corvette of its own. The Club de Mer had twin cockpit styling and a single rear-mounted dorsal fin. Chevrolet's Motorama property in 1956 was the Corvette Impala 4-seat coupe that foreshadowed the roof and grille treatment on the '58 Impala.

178 Cadillac, which had started the tailfin craze in 1949, saw this styling device reach its zenith on the 1959 models.

179 top The fin-mounted lights look like twin exhaust of a jet on full afterburner.

179 bottom If the two high mounted lights in the fin weren't enough to catch attention, the 1959 Cadillac had additional lights set in a bumper opening designed to mimic a jet exhaust.

180 The hood ornament or mascot is one design element that survived the transition from the Grand Classic era to the 1950s. Native American Chief Pontiac was a familiar fixture on the car bearing his name.

181 Perhaps one of the most bizarre taillamp treatments of the 1950s appeared on the 1959 Chevrolet Impala. The horizontal fins looked like brows above "Martian eyes."

182 Dream cars became more futuristic as shown by these three concepts developed for the 1964 New York World's Fair: the three-wheeled Runabout, the Firebird IV four-passenger coupe and the GM-I two-seat sports car.

183 top Harley Earl visits with test driver Murry Rose, who is at the controls of the turbine-powered Firebird I on GM's Desert Proving Grounds.

183 bottom left The 1959 Cadillac Cyclone show car was powered by a conventional V-12 engine, but experimented with radar braking.

183 bottom right Exploring alternatives to the internal combustion engine, GM built a series of turbine-powered cars including the 1956 Firebird II.

Outside the realm of production and show cars, GM also experimented with turbine power in a series of Firebird concepts, the first of which appeared in 1954 as the XP-21. The 370 hp turbine car looked like a jet fighter without wings. In 1954 GM built the Firebird II, a 4-seater with a 200 bhp turbine, titanium skin and self-leveling pneumatic suspension. The third and final turbine car was the Firebird III. Built in 1959, this car tested features like cruise control, anti-lock brakes and automatic air conditioning that would go into production vehicles. Similar in appearance was the '59 Cadillac Cyclone, which sported a huge retractable glass canopy, twin-boom styling and doors that slid outside along the body to provide access. Cyclone was powered by a V-12 that never made it into production.

Much of Ford's concept work, especially in the early '50s, was done in scale models. Examples are the 1950 Muroc, the 1953 Syrtis and the 1958 Nucleon, which purported to harness nuclear power. Ford's first concept car of note is the 1952 Continental Nineteen Fifty X, which featured a retractable clear glass targa roof. Among the practical features incorporated into this show car were automatic jacks for tire changing, a telephone and Dictaphone, and automatic hood and trunk releases. The barrel-shaped rear fenders of the car would later inspire the styling on the Thunderbird. The X was later freshened and rechristened the X-100 and sent to the Paris Auto Show in 1953. That car was followed by the Lincoln XL-500 that featured an all-glass roof, push-button automatic transmission and warning lights mounted in the windshield header.

Chrysler | 1956

Superbly styled for the Forward Look

In 1955, Ford would unveil the Futura, a twin-canopy show car powered by a 500 bhp Lincoln V-8 racing engine. The 19-foot-long car was eventually sold to California custom car builder George Barris, who converted it into the Batmobile for the 1960s Batman television show.

Also built the same year was the Mystere, which featured a rear engine bay designed to hold a conventional engine or a turbine powerplant. Inside, rear-seat passengers were treated to television, while up front, the steering wheel could be moved from right to left to accommodate right- and left-hand drive markets. The Mystere wasn't shown until 1956 for it was feared that the design would tip off the competition on styling cues featured in the company's 1957 models.

Chrysler, under Virgil Exner's influence, produced more subdued show cars, often in collaboration with Ghia. One of his earliest designs, the d' Elegance, actually made it into limited production. Others included the 1954 Fire Arrow, the Ghia Falcon in 1955 and the handsome 1957 Diablo Dart.

One of Exner's collaborations with Ghia, the Chrysler Norseman, had the dubious distinction of going down with the *Andrea Doria* when that Italian liner collided with the *Stockholm* off the eastern seaboard on July 25, 1956.

185 top Chrysler touted its new "Forward Look" design theme in ads promoting the 1956 lineup.

185 bottom The flair of Chrysler designer Virgil Exner was heavily influenced by the Italian design house of Ghia, which built this limited edition Chrysler d'Elegance, imported in 1953.

Packard Passes On

Even a fading marque like Packard offered up a dream car in 1956 that was called the Predictor. It predicted the shape of 1957 models that were never built.

Packard had done reasonably well with its Clipper, and the company sought to reclaim its luster by offering more upscale cars.

In 1953, the company sold some Derham-bodied Patricians as well as the Caribbean convertible, which was based on a show car. About 750 of the limited-edition Caribbean were built powered by Packard's 327 cu-in. 180 bhp straight eight, which was increased in displacement to 359 cu.-in. a year later and made 212 bhp.

James Nance, Packard's president, decided that he also needed another mass-market nameplate to support Packard re-entry into the luxury car business.

In the spring of 1954, the company merged with Studebaker and in the fall offered a new line of redesigned Packards that boasted a new 5.8-liter V-8, innovative "Torsion-level" suspension, and "Twin Ultramatic" automatic transmissions.

The cars were fairly well received, and production edged up towards 70,000, but the losses at Studebaker plunged the company into crisis.

This led to its purchase by the aerospace firm of Curtiss-Wright as a tax loss. Meanwhile, Packard's body maker, Briggs, was acquired by Chrysler and said it could no longer be a supplier.

The 1957 models were scrapped and in their place were Studebakers thinly disguised as Packards. After 1958, Packard ceased to exist. A sidelight to the Curtiss-Wright takeover is that Daimler-Benz, which had been talking to the company about aircraft engines, worked out an agreement whereby Studebaker would become the U.S. distributor for Mercedes-Benz. It was a short-lived arrangement, with the German firm buying out the distribution contract in 1964 when Studebaker closed its South Bend, Indiana works and moved its operations to Canada.

186-187 A fitting swan song for the legendary Packard line was the Caribbean convertible. The 1955 model featured a three-tone paint scheme.

187 top Acquired by Studebaker, 1956 would be the last year for genuine Packards. In 1957 and 1958, rebodied Studebakers were being passed off as Packards.

AMC Is Born

The other major merger of the mid-'50s was the creation of American Motors Co. when Nash and Hudson joined forces. Packard had figured briefly in the discussions but was dropped from consideration when Nance asked that he be made president of AMC. After the merger in January 1954, Hudsons became rebadged Nashes with altered grilles. Power came from Hudson's six as well as a V-8 from Packard, and the cars came to be known as Hashes. By 1957, both Nash and Hudson nameplates were dropped and AMC continued to capitalize on the success of the Rambler. The company also offered the Metropolitan, a small 42 bhp 4-cylinder car that actually was built in Britain by Austin. Riding on an 85-in. wheelbase, the diminutive car was offered until 1961.

As the smaller makes either consolidated or fell by the wayside, Detroit's Big Three were gearing up to send the 1950s out with a bang. The 1957, '58 and '59 model years would see even larger fins, ostentatious displays of chrome and one of the biggest flops in automotive history, the Edsel.

It was Virgil Exner who yet again stole GM's thunder in 1957 with his "Forward Look" designs for Chrysler, Dodge, Plymouth and DeSoto. Long, low and lean, these products sported large tailfins that accentuated both the length and width of the cars. The hardtops featured delicate thin pillars, curved windshields and a cowl that, when coupled with a slightly lowered rear end, made the car look as if it were moving forward even when standing still.

Chrysler's switch to torsion bar suspension allowed it to lower the bodies across the line, which gave all its products the lower, longer, wider look espoused by Harley Earl. And although the Chrysler products sported the usual complement of chrome bits, the European influence of the body contours gave the cars a sensuous, yet athletic, appearance that was different from some of the more ponderous designs of the time. The most coveted of these 1957 models was the 300C with a 392 cu.-in. Hemi making 390 bhp.

The late '50s was also the end of the line for DeSoto, which had served since 1928 as the bridge between the Dodge and Chrysler brands. After launching a limited edition Adventurer in 1956, the '57 mod-

els, which also boasted the Forward Look styling, included the FireFlite and the lower cost FireSweep series, powered by the 5.3-liter Hemi V-8. Sales peaked at a record 117,747 that year, but indifferent quality and the 1958 recession took a huge toll on the upper middle-class segment of the market in which DeSoto competed. Sales plunged to just over 35,000. By December 1960, less than four months into the '61 model year, Chrysler pulled the plug on DeSoto.

Plymouth had a good run during this period, again benefiting from the combination of Exner's styling and the muscle of the Hemi V-8. The "$100 Million Look" of 1955 helped Chrysler's entry-level division to record sales of 742,991, but it wasn't until the '57 models debuted that Plymouth returned to third place in

industry sales behind Chevrolet and Ford. The hot performer in Plymouth's line was the Fury, which offered an optional 290 bhp V-8.

Dodge, which didn't become a player in the performance car market until the muscle car wars of the 1960s, was definitely in touch with its more feminine side in the mid-1950s. As part of the 1955 makeover, Dodge introduced the La Femme, a special two-tone pink and white (the company referred to the colors as Heather Rose over Sapphire White) Royal Lancer. In addition to a matching interior, the car featured two compartments on the back of the front seat; in one side was a rain cape, hat and umbrella, and in the other a leather handbag complete with compact, lipstick, cigarette case and lighter.

188 and 189 bottom DeSotos, which were essentially rebadged Dodges, go through the final production process on the tried, but true moving assembly line.

189 top Smaller literally and figuratively than the Big Three, Rambler decided in the 1950s that time was ripe for the compact car, hence the 1959 Rambler American station wagon.

End of
the Earl Era

General Motors, not to be outdone by Exner's Forward Look, introduced a range of splashy models in 1957, '58 and '59 with big fins and even a more liberal use of chrome. Harley Earl was retiring in 1959 and wanted to go out with a bang by completely changing the look of each division's cars over this period.

The best looking models of 1957 were the Chevrolets, which sported rather modest fins for the time and new bodies that featured a slight dip in the beltline, similar to the Cadillac.

The look inspired Ruben Allender, a Detroit businessman, to build the El Morocco, an aftermarket conversion that gave Chevrolet's Two-Ten sport coupes, sport sedans and Bel Air convertibles the look of Cadillac's flagship Eldorado Brougham. Meanwhile, Corvette, which was restyled in 1956, became an even more serious performer with the addition of fuel injection.

In 1958, Chevrolet's headlight count doubled to four, the fins became more horizontal than vertical, and a new roof treatment with a reverse angle C-pillar debuted. New model designations included the Delray and Biscayne.

The '59 models saw these lateral fins grow in size, the rear taillamps reduced to slits that looked like Martian eyes, while the quad headlamps dropped down to flank a larger grille and were topped by eyebrows on the hood's leading edge. These new cars were two inches longer and wider, rode on a 119-in. wheelbase and weighed 150 lbs. more than the '58. The Delray designation was dropped and Impala added as a range-topping series.

Pontiac introduced the Bonneville for the first time in 1957 on a fuel-injected convertible that boasted a 315 bhp 347 cu.-in. V-8. In 1958 the Bonneville was expanded to cover an entire range of vehicles as the cars adopted the reverse pillar roof treatment of the Chevrolet while sporting taller and rounder tailfins. The '59 model sprouted fins on the top and bottom of the

rear fenders and the front featured the first split grille design that would become a division trademark.

Oldsmobiles received a minor facelift for 1957 and a major overhaul in 1958. The cars had larger fins, were more slab-sided and featured massive amounts of chrome, some estimates say as much as 44 pounds. In addition to broad chrome bumpers front and rear, the taillights were surrounded in chrome. Large chrome accents ran down the side of the car and rimmed the roof.

The 1959 model showed some improvement, with much of the chrome stripped off, smaller side sections and more modest tailfins.

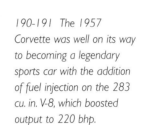

190-191 The 1957 Corvette was well on its way to becoming a legendary sports car with the addition of fuel injection on the 283 cu. in. V-8, which boosted output to 220 bhp.

191 top In an effort to keep sales rolling, auto styling changed virtually every year in the 1950s. While the 1957 Impala was wildly popular, the shift in 1958 to dual headlamps dampened enthusiasm for the car. The 1958 Impala also saw a shift from the sharp vertical tailfins to this softer edged horizontal treatment.

191 bottom Not only did the Corvette become a bona fide sports car, hot rodders flocked to it as a drag racer.

Buick's makeover for 1957 was more extensive than Oldsmobile's but it kept traditional cues like the "Sweep Spear" side styling and portholes.

In 1958, that distinctiveness disappeared along with the portholes. The "Sweep Spear" was now represented by a chrome strip and the car was more slab-sided with large fins. Again, the 1959 redesign resulted in a cleaner, lighter look, but the sweep spear had disappeared.

Cadillac reached new heights of ostentation during this period with its flagship Eldorado Brougham, a $13,074 car that featured suicide doors and a brushed stainless steel roof. Only 400 1957 models and 304 '58 cars were built. Tail fins, a Cadillac trademark, had grown to stupendous heights, culminating in the iconic '59 model that had twin rocket-shaped taillights projecting from each fin's trailing edge.

192 top The 1957 Cadillac Eldorado Brougham hardtop sedan featured suicide doors and an unpainted stainless steel roof. It retailed for the princely sum of $13,000.

192-193 Although custom coachwork had all but disappeared in the 1950s, there still were a few exceptions including this 1959 Cadillac Eldorado with its landau hardtop.

Cadillac

193 top Just as garish as the large tailfins was the huge chromed grille on this 1959 Cadillac Eldorado convertible. If you look closely above the wipers, you can see the Autronic eye that would automatically dim the high beams.

193 center The 1953 Cadillac Eldorado convertible looks understated in contrast to the heavily chromed and tall finned Cadillacs that would follow.

194 Note that the signature high-flying fin has been trimmed level with the car's beltline.

195 The tailfin of the 1959 Cadillac Eldorado may have been just another styling gimmick, but over time, it has become revered as a work of art.

196 top The 1957 Continental Mark II was the ultimate personal luxury car of its era. Sold exclusively through the Continental Division from 1956 to 1958, the operation was headed by William Clay Ford, the younger brother of Henry Ford II. The hand-built Mark II was large, yet not ostentatious. It was heavily influenced by European design standards that eschewed excessive chrome and tailfins.

196-197 The Mark II had frame rails that dipped low between the wheels giving the car a low ride height, as demonstrated by this profile shot of a 1956 model.

197 top The classic Continental kit for the spare tire was smoothly integrated into the trunk; a feature that all Mark models would carry into the 1990s.

Ford's passenger car offerings during this period were quite conservative by comparison. Instead, the company let its designers express themselves with Mercury, Lincoln and the newly formed Edsel Division.

The biggest development for Ford in 1957 was the introduction of the Skyliner, a convertible with a retractable hardtop. The power top featured a small foot-long section that would fold underneath the main part of the roof so that the entire mechanism could be stored in the oversized trunk. The hydraulic top was controlled by 10 solenoids, seven high-torque motors and over 600 feet of wiring. Skyliners could be equipped with an optional 300 bhp 352 cu.-in Interceptor V-8. The Thunderbird was freshened for 1957 and had a longer body that provided a useable trunk. A year later, the car was converted to a 4-passenger convertible on a longer 113-in. wheelbase. A 2-door car had also been ready to go as a carryover model, but it was axed by Ford Division chief Robert McNamara, who reasoned that Ford should make money on all its car lines. Although the Thunderbird outsold projections, it still wasn't profitable. McNamara's gamble paid off and by 1960, the company was selling 92,000 Thunderbirds annually, nearly three times as many as the 2-seat version's peak of 37,893 in 1955.

At the top end of the market, Ford introduced the Continental Mark II, a 2-door luxury coupe that was sold as its own brand, a departure from the original Continental, which was a Lincoln model. Henry Ford II's younger brother, William Clay Ford, headed the new Continental Division. The car featured hardtop styling, a Continental kit integrated into the rear deck lid and a long, low body with minimal chrome. It was powered by a Lincoln V8. Only 2,989 were built, including one convertible for William Clay Ford's wife.

While the Lincolns grew more ornate with the times, the real head-turner was Mercury's Turnpike Cruiser, which debuted as a 1957 model. With knife-edged V-shaped fins, headlights stacked on an angle and a reverse angle retractable rear window, Mercury boasted the Turnpike Cruiser went "from dream car to showroom in 10 months."

Unfortunately, the car was launched into the same recession that took its toll on other mid-market cars and also spelled doom for the Edsel.

The Edsel Experiment

In the mid-1950s, Ford management closely watched the success of GM's Pontiac, Oldsmobile and Buick divisions, and it came to the conclusion that a gap in the medium-priced segment existed between its Ford lineup and its Mercury offerings, which were looked upon as junior Lincolns.

Originally, the Edsel rode on its own 124-in. wheelbase and was offered with a choice of two V-8s: a 5.9-liter unit in the entry-level Pacer and Ranger, and a 6.7-liter V-8 in the upscale Citation and Corsair. The four model names were at one time each considered as a name for the division, but Ford president Ernie Breech insisted on calling the car Edsel in honor of Henry Ford's son, who had died in 1943.

Styling on the 1958 Edsel was controversial. It sported a horse-collar upright grille at a time when virtually all grilles were horizontal, and rear slit taillamps, along with a heavy dose of chrome accents all around the body. Launched during an economic downturn, the Edsel was also beset with quality problems. Sales of the

car, which had prices ranging from $2,519 for a 2-door Ranger to $3,801 for the Citation convertible, were disappointing at 60,000, given that the company expected to sell 200,000 per year. By January 1958, as a result of the poor launch, Ford abandoned the idea of a separate division for the car and merged operations with Lincoln-Mercury. In 1959 only 44,000 were sold. The next year only the Ranger model was offered and that was essentially a Ford with a different grille and badges. The death of the Edsel was symptomatic of the times. The recession had deeply hurt the middle class, causing consumers to question the need for bigger, larger, flashier new cars every year. Perhaps Detroit had gone too far, they reasoned, closing their pocketbooks to Sloan's ideal of a car for every purse and purpose. Imports were gaining in popularity; the Volkswagen Beetle had begun to make its presence felt. The retirement of Harley Earl, the passing of Packard, and Ford's monumental failure with the Edsel were signs that the times were changing.

198-199 The Edsel's "horsecollar" grille is most often cited as one of the reasons why the public rejected the car out of hand. Launching this new brand in the midst of a recession didn't help either.

CHAPTER 6

1961 - 1972
The Second
Golden Age

200-201 William "Bill"
Mitchell's Mako Shark
concept car points to a new
styling direction not only for
the Chevrolet Corvette, but
also for GM in the 1960s.

I f the 1950s were noted for excess in styling, then the 1960s are best remembered for excess in performance.

The bridge between the two, ironically, was the rise of the compact economy car. These small lightweight cars, which dispensed with the ostentatious ornamentation of the previous decade, proved to be the most potent form of what would be known as American Muscle when their thrifty 6-cylinder powerplants were replaced by large, strapping V-8s from Detroit's full-size offerings.

The 1960 model year marked the debut of this new generation of compacts from the Big Three—the Plymouth Valiant/Dodge Lancer, Ford Falcon and the Chevy Corvair—cars that were the very antithesis of the standard offerings just a year earlier.

While the new models seemed to appear out of nowhere, development of these smaller, lighter vehicles had begun even as Detroit was busy introducing the last of the longer, lower and wider cars bedecked with chrome and monstrous tailfins.

The success of the modestly priced and sized 1958 AMC Rambler American had gotten the atten-

tion of the executives at General Motors, Ford and Chrysler.

There also was the growing popularity of small imported cars: In 1959 Volkswagen sold 88,000 Beetles, while Renault, the import sales leader, posted 91,000 Dauphines on the books.

The crushing failure of the Edsel, the impact of the recession on average car buyers, and the outcry over conspicuous consumption as embodied in these so-called highway leviathans (a seminal work was John Keats' *The Insolent Chariots*) were responsible for this abrupt about-face by the Big Three.

It's a Small World

Although smaller than the standard Chrysler offerings, the Plymouth Valiant and Dodge Lancer were the most flamboyant of this new generation of small cars, sporting a large grille, quad headlamps, a fair amount of chrome strips, tailfins and a fake Continental kit molded into the rear trunklid.

Two significant mechanical improvements were the first use of an alternator rather than a generator to supply current and charge the battery and the debut of Chrysler's legendary slant-six powerplant.

The alternator not only was lighter in weight, but it also could provide current at much lower engine speeds than a generator, providing greater protection against run-down batteries.

The slant-six was so called for the 30-degree offset between the crankshaft and cylinder head that resulted in an engine that appeared to be lying partially on its side. It displaced 170 cu.-in. and produced 110 bhp.

When equipped with a 4-barrel carburetor, the slant-six was good for 148 bhp. An added benefit to the slant design was that it allowed for a lower hood height.

The Ford Falcon was much truer in spirit to the idea of an economy car. Its styling was spare, with single headlamps and a plain, slightly rounded body with minimal chrome.

The Falcon rode on a short 109.5-in wheelbase and was powered by a 90 bhp 144 cu.-in. inline six with a base price of under $2,000.

The car was an instant hit, selling more than 435,000 units, which accounted for almost half of Ford sales that year.

202-203 The 1961 Dodge lineup features radically different styling from the Lancer (foreground) to the fastback Dart Phoenix Coupe and the full-size Polara hardtop sedan (background).

Chevrolet's approach was more daring. Inspired by the rear-engine, air-cooled four of the Beetle, Chevy's engineers set about to create a rear-engine, air-cooled flat-six economy car designed to compete on equal terms with small imports and the more conventional domestic compacts.

The Corvair, which had unit body construction, also sported an independent suspension comprised of a rear swing-arm setup that would become the car's Achilles heel. Beneath the rear deck lid was a 140 cu.-in. horizontally opposed six that had an aluminum block. Depending on carburetor, the engine made 80 or 95 bhp and was mated to a 3-speed floor-mounted manual or a 2-speed automatic. A sportier 2-door coupe version of the Corvair launched midway through 1960 was equipped with bucket seats and a 4-speed manual.

The radically styled Corvair was much smaller and lower than other compacts, standing only 51.5 in. high. With a base price starting below $2,000, the Corvair was a moderate success with first year sales of over 250,000 units. Although it fell short of the popularity of the Falcon, it outsold the Valiant by nearly 80,000 units. It was offered in a complete range of body styles: 2-door coupe, 4-door sedan and station wagon, as well as a cab-forward pickup and van series called the Greenbriar. The pickup featured a unique side-access ramp on the cargo bed.

Consumer crusader Ralph Nader made the Corvair and its swing axle independent rear suspension a focal point of his book, *Unsafe At Any Speed*, in 1965 and helped launch a new era in vehicle safety regulations. Contending that under hard cornering the swing axle had a tendency to fold under and cause rollovers, Nader certainly helped to make Chevy's decision to ax the Corvair easier. Safety issues aside, sales of the

Corvair had been declining since their peak in 1961. Not only was the car complex with spotty quality, it also was redundant as an entry-level car for the brand in the wake of the 1962 launch of a conventional front-engine compact called the Chevy II. Patterned after Ford's successful Falcon, the Chevy II had simple, clean styling, weighed only 2,430 lbs. and was powered by a base 153 cu.-in. four making 90 bhp or an optional 194 cu.-in. inline six making 120 bhp.

After the launch of the Chevy II, Chevrolet decided to push the Corvair as a more expensive performance car aimed primarily at the enthusiast market, capitalizing on its Monza version with a turbocharged 150 bhp engine. Eventually, the conversion of the Corvair from import fighter to poor man's Corvette took its toll. Sales continued to decline and in 1966 the car was discontinued, despite having undergone a redesign that gave it a sleeker body and a more predictable suspension that addressed the shortcomings of the swing axle setup.

204 Workers install the front suspension and the rear engine/transaxle module in a 1960 Corvair. The rear independent swing-arm suspension was prone to oversteering.

205 Conceived as an import fighter, the Corvair didn't need a grille since the engine was in the back and the trunk under the front hood. The Chevrolet Corvair had a flat open floor thanks to the rear-mounting of the engine. When the Corvair was introduced in 1960, the compact represented a stark departure from the heavily chromed, big finned behemoths that marked the 1950s. The Corvair came it two versions, the 500 and 700, both with a three-speed manual transaxle, while a two-speed Powerglide automatic transmission was option.

End of the Trail for Studebaker

While Studebaker had foreseen the rise of compact cars and was ready a year earlier than the Big Three with its 1959 Lark, getting a jump on the competition wasn't enough to save this company that had a long tradition of teetering on financial ruin. The Lark was innovative because while it appeared to be an all-new vehicle, it actually carried over the Champion's midsection and used other bits and pieces of Studebaker models with a new squared off front and rear end treatment. Two models were offered: the Lark VI, which was powered by a 90 bhp 169 cu.-in. straight six, and the Lark VIII with its 180 bhp 259 cu.-in. V-8.

After selling more than 150,000 units in 1959, Studebaker found itself facing stiff competition from the Valiant/Lancer, Falcon and Corvair. By 1964, volume had plummeted to 44,000 vehicles. Even sexy new products like the Brooks Stevens designed GT Hawk Coupe in 1962 and the stunning 1963 Avanti from Raymond Loewy couldn't ignite Studebaker sales.

The GT Hawk Coupe was an update of the pillarless Hawk body style of the 1950s with a bolder grille and a more formal roofline. Powered by a 289 cu.-in. V-8 with output as high as 225 bhp, the GT Hawk was good for a top speed of 120 mph and a 0-60 mph capability of less than 10 seconds.

Even though it was sporty, the GT Hawk played a supporting role to the Avanti. Designed by Raymond Loewy, Studebaker's new flagship had clean, advanced styling and a 4-place bucket seat, aircraft-inspired cock-pit. The base engine of this fiberglass-bodied flier was a 240-bhp 289 cu.-in. V-8, while a supercharged version of the same powerplant provided 290 bhp. The car sold in limited numbers—3,834 in 1963 and 4,445 in 1964—but it struck such a chord among enthusiasts that the Avanti outlasted Studebaker itself.

By 1964, the South Bend works were closed, with all production shifted to the Hamilton, Canada plant for three years before the firm finally ceased operations. In 1965, Leo Newman and Nathan Altman had purchased

the tooling and a portion of the abandoned Studebaker works in South Bend, Indiana, and began continued production of the car, now called Avanti II. Instead of the Studebaker 289 cu.-in. V-8, however, the Avanti II used Chevrolet's 327 cu.-in. small block making 300 bhp. The car would remain in production for 30 years, with Newman and Altman's company changing hands several times. Avanti would spawn both convertible and 4-door sedan models, and in 1997, the Avanti AVX (for AVanti eXperimental) was launched using new body panels mounted on a Pontiac Firebird chassis.

The Avanti wasn't the only early 1960s car to become a design icon with sleek lines and minimal use of chrome. Lincoln's 1961 Continental set the aesthetic tone for the decade. Riding on a 123-in. wheelbase, the Lincoln was offered in a 4-door sedan and convertible models and sported rear hinged back doors (so-called suicide doors). Powered by a 403 cu.-in. V-8 producing 300 bhp, the Continental was compact yet stately looking with gently contoured body sides capped by a razor-sharp and chrome-covered fender line that ran fore to aft. Dual headlamps were recessed on either side of a horizontal grille and the thin A-pillars and the hardtop styling gave the car a light, airy feel to the greenhouse.

Sales of 25,000 in that first year helped propel Lincoln past Imperial in the luxury car race. The styling of this Lincoln was an instant classic and remained unchanged for much of the decade, other than the use of different grille textures and a longer 126-in. wheelbase from 1964 on. In 1966 a 2-door Continental rejoined the lineup, and the V-8 was enlarged to 462 cu.-in. and power increased to 340 bhp. The use of the Mark designation returned in 1968 when the Continental coupe took on the styling cues of the Mark II introduced over

a decade earlier. The Mark III, overseen by William Clay Ford, was based on the Thunderbird's 117.2-in. wheelbase (the Thunderbird had grown to receive its own set of suicide doors for 1968, making it a sedan for the first time). The Mark III sported hideaway headlamps and the signature Continental kit spare tire treatment on the rear deck lid. It was a sensation. Although it only sold 7,770 in 1968 (it was a late model year offering coming in April of that calendar year), by 1971 it was selling in volumes of over 25,000 units.

206 top Raymond Loewy again works his magic for a failing Studebaker by designing the Avanti sports coupe. The design is so good that car outlives the Studebaker brand.

206-207 The 1961 Lincoln Continental is considered one of the best-looking Lincolns ever. The hardtop sedan features center opening doors. A chrome strip that runs the entire length of the vehicle highlights the beltline.

207 top Lincolns have been the limousine of choice for many presidents. In 1969, a custom-built Continental was delivered to the White House and features a rear step bumper for Secret Service agents.

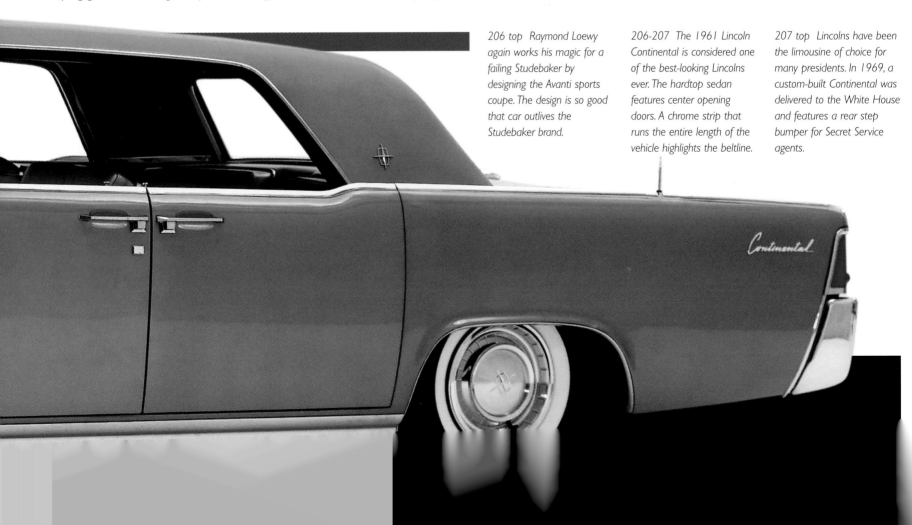

The Mitchell Era

The popularity of cars with clean designs had a huge impact across the industry. At GM, this change in design direction also can be attributed to the promotion of William Mitchell to head of GM styling in the wake of Harley Earl's retirement. Equally flamboyant in dress and management style as his predecessor, Mitchell had a much different approach. Less impressed with aviation themes, Mitchell had a keen appreciation for European design, both prewar classics as well as contemporary themes. Tighter body shapes, fewer fins and a more judicious application of chrome were Mitchell hallmarks. Although he subscribed to Earl's philosophy of longer, lower, wider, Mitchell also believed in larger glass areas with thinner, more elegant pillars. His designs were almost delicate in comparison to some of the ham-handed designs of the late 1950s.

This shift can be seen in the 1961-63 models as tailfins receded into the trunks and then disappeared across the board on full-size GM cars. And unlike the utilitarian Falcon and Chevy II, the new 1961 compacts from Buick, Olds and Pontiac were expressive without being overdone. The trio—Buick's Skylark, Olds' F-85 and Pontiac's Tempest—shared major body panels and yet managed to distinguish themselves from one another through different grille treatments and engine options. The Olds and Buicks relied on 155 bhp 215 cu.-in. V-8s, while the Tempest was equipped with a 195 cu.-in. four making 110 bhp. The Tempest was also noted for its rear-mounted transmission. The Skylark was further differentiated a year later by offering a V-6 option for the first time, while Olds turbocharged and fuel-injected its V-8, calling the new 215 bhp offering the Jetfire.

208 Cadillacs moved through a paint drying booth at their assembly plant.

209 top Bill Mitchell (left) was a protégé of Harley Earl, succeeding his mentor in 1958 as the second design chief in GM history. Between Earl and Mitchell, they ran GM design for 50 years, from 1927 to 1977.

Like Earl, Mitchell was fond of using show cars like the Make Shark for personal transportation.

209 bottom Bill Mitchell's Mako Shark concept for the Corvette featured a paint job that mimicked the coloring of a shark, fading from a dark upper to a light lower underbelly.

The cars that best represent Mitchell's approach to design include the 1963 Corvette Sting Ray, the 1963 Buick Riviera, the 1966 Oldsmobile Toronado and the 1967 Cadillac Eldorado.

The Sting Ray, upon closer examination, carries a lot of classic styling cues one would find on a 1930s French coupe like the Bugatti Atlantic or Talbot Lago, but presented in a fresh, contemporary way.

Like the Atlantic, the Corvette had a center spine running the length of the car, a split rear window treatment, doors cut into the roof, and a boattail rear end, although the split window feature was dropped in 1964. The Corvette would be restyled once more during the decade in 1968 with a voluptuous "Coke bottle" shaped design inspired by a show car called the Manta Ray.

210-211 The 1963 Corvette Sting Ray was a thoroughly modern design that carried design cues such as a split rear window and doors cut into the roof, pioneered by the 1937 Bugatti Atlantic.

211 top To this day, the Corvette's logo still features the crossed flags that include racing checkers.

Mitchell was a champion of the 2-door personal luxury car, the archetype of which is the long and lean 1963 Buick Riviera. The body hewed to Mitchell's philosophy of rounded contours punctuated by bold character lines. He likened the look to a rounded pant leg with a sharp crease in it.

The Riviera was followed in 1966 by the Olds Toronado, GM's first application of front-wheel drive. The Toronado featured hideaway headlamps and a smooth, flowing body with tension provided by well-defined character lines. It was powered by a 425 cu.-in. V-8. Sharing the same front-wheel-drive layout was the '67 Cadillac Eldorado, another 2-door personal luxury coupe. The Cadillac was much more slab-sided with knife-like fenders and pointy taillamps.

Mitchell, like Earl, was fond of building dream cars,

but unlike his predecessor, who seemed intent on building land-going aircraft, Mitchell's concepts for the 1960s were closer to pure racing machines. The best example was the Corvair-based Monza GT, which debuted at the 1962 New York Auto Show. The closed coupe with its fiberglass body used midship-mounting of the Corvair's flat-six engine. The windshield, roof and doors were one unit that swung forward to open the cockpit for entry and exit. A companion roadster, called the Monza SS, returned the flat-six engine to its original rear-mount position behind the axle. The SS rode on an 88-in. wheelbase, 4 in. shorter than the GT's. One unique feature was the fixed seating position, while the pedals were adjustable. Another significant concept car of the era was the Chrysler Turbine. Designed by Elwood Engel

and built by Ghia in Italy, the Turbine had a clean modern look with a front end and greenhouse treatment that was similar to the 1961 Thunderbird. A total of 50 were built and lent to various VIPs and customers around the country for three-month test drives. The turbine motor could spin as fast as 60,000 rpm, though it would operate primarily between 30,000 and 45,000 rpm. Engine temperature was between 1,500 and 1,700 degrees Fahrenheit. One of the reasons for the testing was to determine the acceptability of the turbine engine in production cars, specifically the problems of excessive heat and the tremendous lag in throttle response, although once rolling, the car could reach 60 mph in about 11 seconds. The 4,100-lb. car was also very thirsty, delivering only 11.5 mpg. The project was eventually abandoned.

212 left Nothing said America more than a Cadillac, with its large fins. Here Paul Newman poses with a Caddy on the set of Hud *in 1962.*

212 top right The 1967 Cadillac Eldorado was another landmark car for Bill Mitchell. The razor-sharp taillamps became an instant classic.

212-213 The 1967 Cadillac Eldorado was strictly a personal luxury coupe with limited rear seating. The front-drive coupe's design sported sharp character lines that looked like the creases in freshly pressed slacks.

ELDORADO

214 top and 215 bottom
Rebuffed when he tried to
buy Ferrari in 1963, Henry
Ford II commissioned the
Ford GT40 to beat the
Italian sports car at the
Le Mans 24 Hours. In 1966,
Ford GT40s swept the top
three spots in the Le Mans
classic. The cars would
dominate the race for the
next three consecutive years.

214 bottom Ford's GT40 is
here photographed in its
classic Gulf livery.

215 top The GT40 Mark II
prepares for Le Mans by
competing in the Sebring
12 Hours.

While GM and Chrysler were testing alternative technologies, like air-cooled 6-cylinder engines and turbines, Ford in the mid-1960s had a more pragmatic goal in mind: winning the 24 Hours at Le Mans. In 1963, Henry Ford II had been negotiating to buy Ferrari, but after Enzo Ferrari balked at the terms, Ford decided he wanted to compete toe-to-toe with the Italian exotic at the world's most prestigious race.

Work began on what was known as the Ford GT in Britain on a design loosely based on Eric Broadly's Lola GT. Introduced in April 1964, the cars failed to finish Le Mans that year.

Later in 1964, Carroll Shelby was hired to oversee the program and he installed a 427 cu.-in. stock car engine in the Mark II version of the car, which became known as the GT-40, a reference to the car's 40-in. height. In 1966 the car won its first Le Mans and would prove to be unbeatable four years in a row.

America Shows Its Muscle

The American muscle car can trace its roots back to the 1950s when V-8s became the universal powertrain of choice for Detroit's standard full-size models. These large cars, like the Cadillacs that Briggs Cunningham competed with at Le Mans and the Lincoln Capris that were victorious in the Carrera Panamericana in Mexico, were legendary for their strong, bulletproof V-8 powerplants. And Chrysler's use of the legendary Hemi in the 300 letter series car starting in 1955 is considered the beginning of the American muscle car.

In the early 1960s, as the chrome and fins were being stripped off the full-size standard sedans being offered by Ford, GM and Chrysler, astute teenagers discovered the value of helping their parents order the next family car. For just a few hundred dollars more, larger, more powerful V-8 engines could be had. Thus the term "sleeper" was born. It referred to a staid looking family sedan that could blow the doors off a hot rod. A perfect example is the 1961 Chevy Impala, which offered a 360 bhp 409 cu.-in. V-8 as a $425 option. The option list for the Pontiac Bonneville featured a heavy duty 421 cu.-in. 373 bhp V-8. Meanwhile, Ford's full-size Galaxie 500 in 1964 could be had with a 425 bhp 427 cu.-in. V-8, while the Dodge Polara 500 produced similar output from its optional 426 cu.-in. Hemi. While all these full-size family cars offered pavement-ripping performance and filled the field in NASCAR events, it was the introduction of the big block V-8 in the intermediate-sized Pontiac Tempest as the GTO that kicked off the serious performance war among American muscle cars.

The Tempest and its upscale sibling, Le Mans, along with the Buick Skylark/Special, Olds F-85/Cutlass and a new entry, the Chevy Chevelle, all designated A-bodies for 1964, had grown in size and changed from unit body to full body-on-frame construction.

Pete Estes, who would later become GM president, led Pontiac at the time and the division's chief engineer was John Z. DeLorean. At that time, GM's top brass had decided to enforce a racing and performance car ban adopted by the Automobile Manufacturers Association in 1957. By 1963, many of the divisions had covert racing programs and had introduced a number of high-performance models. GM Chairman Frederic Donner decided it should stop and issued a memo reinforcing GM's commitment to the ban. Ironically, at the same time, Henry Ford II renounced the agreement, stepped up Ford's presence in NASCAR and committed the company to its Le Mans effort.

Donner's memo decreed that a vehicle could not have more than 10 cu.-in. of engine displacement for every pound of curb weight. As a result, the theoretical maximum displacement that could go into the Tempest/Le Mans body shell was a 330 cu.-in. engine. Bill Collins, who headed Pontiac's advanced vehicle operations, wanted to equip the car with the 389 cu.-in V-8 from the Bonneville/Catalina line, an engine that produced, depending on carburetor, 325 or 348 bhp. The way Collins and DeLorean slipped the car into the system was to put the engine in an option package, W-62, rather than create a separate model.

In addition to the bigger motor, buyers would get a stiffer suspension, dual exhaust, and a Hurst floor-mounted shifter, all for $289. If you wanted the more powerful Tri-Power triple 2-barrel carburetors, it would cost an additional $115.

DeLorean decided to name the package GTO, which stood for Gran Turismo Omologato (Italian for Grand Touring Homologation), a name Ferrari used on its 250 GTO to designate the model as a homologation special for racing purposes.

While initial projections put GTO sales at 5,000 units, more than 32,000 rolled out of Pontiac showrooms in 1964. Sales more than doubled and by 1966, GTO was a separate model in the Pontiac line. Profitable sales of the GTO had shredded GM's ban on performance products.

216 In addition to clay, designers worked with wooden templates when developing new cars. Here the rear end of the 1963 Chevy Impala is being measured for production tooling.

217 top Muscle cars were not limited to intermediates. This full-size Chevy Impala SS came equipped with a 409 cu. in. V-8 packing 390 hp in 1961.

217 bottom The Pontiac GTO is credited with creating the American muscle car by putting a large engine in a lightweight intermediate body shell. This 1967 model was equipped with a 400 cu. in. V-8 producing more than 300 hp.

Pontiac caught the competition flatfooted in the intermediate segment. Ford was offering a relatively tame 210 bhp 289 cu.-in. V-8 Fairlane, while Mercury came out midyear 1964 with its Cyclone equipped with the same V-8 (although an optional version did put out 271 bhp). In the mid-'60s, Ford used its heavy, full-size Galaxie 427 to carry the company's banner in the muscle car wars and later turned to using higher output engines in its restyled Mustang/Cougar pony cars to compete in the category. The late '60s would see such intermediate entries such as the Torino Talladega and Fairlane Cobra.

It wasn't until the '65 model year that the competition began to heat up. Other GM divisions jumped headlong into the horsepower race: Chevy fitted its intermediate Malibu SS and Chevelle SS with the 375 bhp 396 cu.-in. V-8, while Oldsmobile countered with the Cutlass 4-4-2, which jumped from 290 bhp to 425 bhp by 1966. The Olds designation stood for 4-speed manual floor shift, 4-barrel carburetor and dual exhausts. Buick's muscle car took the form of the Skylark GS, a $200 option package that included a 401 cu.-in V-8. Buick would later add the more potent GS Stage I Gran Sport, which would grow from 400 cu.-in. in 1969 to 455 cu.-in. a year later.

Mercury pumped up its Cyclone GT in 1966 to boast 335 bhp from a 390 cu.-in. V-8, and a year later offered the 427 big block with output ranging from 410-425 bhp. Dodge responded in 1966 with the Charger, a fastback coupe based off the Coronet, powered by a 426 cu.-in. Street Hemi V-8 producing 425 bhp. Soon there was a proliferation of muscle cars from Chrysler, including Plymouth Road Runner/GTX, Dodge Super Bee, Dodge Challenger, and Plymouth's grown-up pony car, the Barracuda. Muscle car mania would reach down into the compacts, with Dodge offering a Hemi-powered version of the Dart, called GTS, by decade's end.

The most striking models of the muscle car era, however, are the Plymouth Super Bird and Dodge Charger Daytona, sold during 1969-70. The cars could be equipped with a choice of 440 cu.-in. V-8s with

218 AMC president George Romney (right) discusses a new compact car with styling chief Richard Teague (left). It's said that Teague could design a car for what it cost GM to do a door handle.

either a 4- or 6-barrel carburetor or a 426 cu.-in. Hemi. Both cars were fitted with aerodynamic noses with hideaway headlamps and a high rear wing. Sales of these street models allowed Chrysler to homologate the shape for its NASCAR stockers.

The last of the Chrysler "letter cars" would be the 1970 300-H, the H representing the Hurst performance package which included a rear spoiler, special gold and white paint job and a hood scoop on what was essentially an Imperial Coupe. Powered by a 440 cu.-in. V-8 making 375 bhp, the 300-H was built in limited numbers. Only 501 were sold.

AMC, which never had the resources of its crosstown rivals, did compete in the muscle car wars by offering the 1967 Rebel SST, which could be equipped with an optional 390 cu.-in. V-8 making 315 bhp. It was followed up in 1969 with the compact SC/Rambler, a Hurst-prepared Rambler American coupe fitted with the same 315 bhp V-8 and offered in a red, white and blue paint scheme.

218-219 The legendary Dodge Daytona sported a large rear wing and aerodynamic nose designed specifically to help the division's racing effort in NASCAR stock car racing.

219 top The 1969 Plymouth Road Runner was the Muscle Car of choice for the budget-minded. It was essentially a stock Belvedere coupe, complete with pie-plate hubcaps and steel wheels with a few stripes and 335-horsepower V-8 wedged beneath the hood.

219 center The 1969 Barracuda convertible was a compact, yet potent muscle car when it was equipped with either a 340 or 383 cu. in. V-8.

The Pony Car Revolution

While muscle cars were basically conventional full- and intermediate-sized family cars with large engines stuffed beneath the hood, Ford created a whole new segment of small, sporty, fun-to-own vehicles known as pony cars. In fact, it was the overwhelming success of the Mustang that kept Ford out of the muscle car wars of the mid-1960s.

But, why would Ford need another sporty 4-passenger car in the lineup when it had Thunderbird? The T-Bird had grown from a 2-seat GT into a 4-passenger convertible in 1958 and later into a coupe and even a sedan by 1968. The problem was the car never stopped growing, eventually settling on Ford's intermediate chassis.

Mustang was the creation of Ford division general manager Lee Iacocca and product planner Hal Sperlich. Originally, Ford was looking to compete with the then-popular rear-engined Corvair Monza, a 2-door, bucket seat model that had captured the fancy of the enthusiast market. At first, Ford experimented with a Mustang concept that featured a mid-engine Ford of Europe V-4 in a slick, open-top body.

While the Mustang would have made a great sports car, Iacocca was looking for a vehicle with wider appeal. He envisioned a compact sporty car that would share a great deal of components with the division's dull but successful Falcon economy car.

The Mustang would be a tidy design, 181.6 in. in overall length, weighing 2,572 lbs. and costing just $2,368. It was available in two body styles at launch, a notchback and convertible, with the fastback following in 1965. The sporty good looks—it had a

220 top Always with its eye on the future, General Motors has a long history of promoting its products at fairs and through its own traveling auto show called Motorama. For the 1964 New York Worlds Fair, GM constructed its own pavilion called Futurama. Futurama was also about the present as this display of a 1964 Oldsmobile Starfire Convertible shows.

long hood, short rear deck, large grille with a galloping pony emblem, bucket seats and floor-mounted shifter—captured the imagination of the youth market. When it was introduced in April 1964 at the New York World's Fair as a mid-year model (it was called the 1964 1/2 Mustang), it created a sensation and was featured on the cover of both Time and Newsweek. Although initial projections pegged sales at 100,000 annually, Ford sold 418,000. The base engine was a prosaic 101 bhp 171 cu.-in. inline six, while 260 or 289 cu.-in. V-8s were available as options. The smaller V-8 made 164 bhp, while the larger engine could be had in 210, 220 or 271 bhp, depending on tune.

220-221 The Ford Mustang created a sensation when it was launched in April 1964. Based on the Falcon economy car, the Mustang's styling created a whole new segment known as pony cars.

221 top GM used its World's Fair Pavilion as a jumping off point for this parade of Pontiac Bonnevilles that also featured Miss Universe.

222 top left The Cobra badge was the tip-off that the GT500 was a special KR model, which stood for King of the Road, thanks to the 400 hp V-8.

222 top right Even the Pony Car, which was conceived as a sporty economy car, got an infusion of muscle as the '60s drew to a close. This 1968 Ford Shelby Mustang Cobra GT500KR was equipped with the Cobra Jet 428 cu. in. V-8.

222-223 The Shelby Mustang Cobra GT500 in convertible trim featured a padded roll bar and rear spoiler.

224-225 Carroll Shelby started building Cobras by installing 289 cu. in. Ford V-8s under the hood of British-built AC sports cars. Eventually, he would add modified bodywork and a big block 427 cu. in. V-8s pictured on this 1964 Cobra.

COBRA

G.T. 500

The car proved so popular that Ford decided it needed to mollify its Lincoln-Mercury channel by offering the division a version of the car called the Cougar in 1967. Riding on a longer 111-in. wheelbase, the Cougar cost more (at $,2851, it was $200 more than Mustang) and used the 289 cu.-in. V-8 as its base engine instead of a six.

Meanwhile, Mustang got a huge infusion of performance from Carroll Shelby, an experienced racer who managed Ford's Le Mans GT-40 effort and established his own business of installing Ford V-8s in British-built AC sports cars. Shelby's Cobras beat the likes of Ferrari and Corvette in international competition. Applying the same magic to stock Mustangs, he created the Shelby GT350 (including 936 models that saw service as Hertz rental cars) and GT500 models. In SCCA Trans Am racing, the Mustang distinguished itself by winning the over 2.0-liter category in the first two seasons.

In addition to finding success on the track, the Mustang also became a movie star: A 1968 model was immortalized in a famous San Francisco chase scene in the Steve McQueen film "Bullitt."

Chrysler responded almost instantly to Ford's pony car with the 1964 Plymouth Barracuda, which it rushed along when it learned of Ford's plans. The Barracuda was a 2-door Valiant coupe fitted with an enormous rear fastback window. The Barracuda's power came from a choice of two sixes displacing 170 or 225 cu.-in. and a 273 cu.-in. V-8. By 1965 Barracuda began to grow larger and move out of the pony car category and into the muscle car realm with a 235 bhp V-8 engine option. In 1967 the car was restyled to include a convertible and notchback to compliment the original fastback. It later gained optional 383 and 426 cu.-in. high output V-8s. In 1970-71, it became the 'Cuda and shared the Challenger's swoopy design. The base engine was a 340 cu.-in. V-8 and the 383 and 426 Hemi were joined by a 440 cu.-in. V-8. One of the models, the AAR 'Cuda, was a street version of the car campaigned in Trans Am by Dan Gurney's All-American Racers.

AMX/3

AMC also rushed into the fray, remaking its Rambler Classic sedan into a fastback. Riding on a 112-in. wheelbase, this car was called the Marlin and offered with a choice of a 232 cu.-in. straight six or a 302 cu.-in. V-8. In 1967, the Marlin was moved to the longer Ambassador wheelbase, which helped its looks considerably. Meanwhile, AMC chief designer Dick Teague penned the AMX show car in 1966, a smart looking 2-door fiberglass-bodied coupe with a hatch-back rear window and pop-up rumble seat.

The next year, AMC replaced the Marlin with the Javelin, a 4-passenger sport coupe that carried a lot of the styling cues of the AMX show car. This model came with the base 232 cu.-in. inline six and the choice of a 290 or 343 cu.-in. V-8. AMC sold over 55,000 Javelins the first year. In 1970 a special red, white and blue SST model debuted to the mark AMC's entry into Trans Am racing. Team owner Roger Penske with driver Mark Donohue finished sec-ond overall and then took the crown in 1971 and '72.

Meanwhile, the AMX finally made it into production in 1968 as a steel-bodied 2-place coupe (sadly, the rumble seat failed to see production). Riding on a 97-in. wheelbase, the AMX offered an abundance of performance from its 225-bhp 290 cu. in .V-8 and optional 280-bhp 343 cu.-in. and 315 bhp 390 cu.-in. V-8s. Unfortunately, the car was only built until the end of 1970 when it was killed as part of a program to pare down AMC's product offerings. Only 19,134 were built. GM's response to the Mustang waited until the 1967 model year when the Chevrolet Camaro and Pontiac Firebird were introduced. The company followed Ford's strategy of offering 2-door coupes and convertibles with a base 6-cylinder engine and optional V8s. The Chevy offered a 140 bhp inline six and 327 and 396 cu.-in. V-8s making anywhere from 210 to 350 bhp. The Firebird's base six, an overhead cam unit, made 165 bhp, while its optional V-8 made 325 bhp. It's ironic that by giving Pontiac the Firebird, GM top management scotched that division's plans for a 2-seat sports car similar to the Corvette called the Banshee.

Both cars shared body shells with the Camaro, sporting a relatively flat front end flanked by single headlamps. Customers could order the Rally Sport appearance package that featured hideaway headlamps. The Pontiac had a more pronounced nose with a split grille and chrome shell and quad headlamps.

The Camaro was priced $5 more than the $2,461 Mustang and $200 less than the more upscale Firebird. In 1970 the cars were restyled again with longer, lower bodies and pontoon-style fenders with single headlamps. The grille treatments remained different, with Firebird carrying over the split grille theme while the Camaro had a large, square eggcrate grille design.

While the pony car lived on—Mustang is still a popular Ford entry, while Camaro and Firebird survived until the end of the 2002 model year—the fates weren't so kind to muscle cars. By the early 1970s, they had all but disappeared. Tightened emission requirements and the energy crises of the early 1970s are generally credited for the demise of this uniquely American phenomenon. In reality, the party was over even as it was starting in the mid-1960s. Just as the first Pontiac GTOs were being introduced, the government was becoming increasingly involved in automotive safety. And it didn't take long for insurance companies to discover that these smaller intermediate cars with the large engines were being snapped up by young people. Rates skyrocketed for the young buyers that were the prime market for these road rockets.

If the 1956 Fords established the conventional wisdom that "safety doesn't sell," Detroit's slavish devotion to that canard left it wide open for the government to step in and mandate safety equipment. The first step was requiring the use of seat belts as standard equipment in the front outboard seating positions in all new cars beginning with the '64 model year and for the outboard rear seating positions in '66. While the industry complied with little fuss, there was little serious thought given to safety issues.

It wasn't necessarily the industry's benign neglect of safety that spurred Congress to act, but rather the arrogance displayed by one of the last unregulated businesses in America that eventually turned the tide. Chief among these sins was GM's hiring of private investigators to dig up dirt on Corvair critic Ralph Nader, who also happened to be on the staff of U.S. Sen. Abraham Ribicoff.

When Nader sued for invasion of privacy, GM Chairman James Roche publicly apologized to Nader and the company reached an out-of-court settlement. However, the episode set the tenor for the adversarial relationship between Detroit, the safety lobby and government regulators for years to come. This affair, a rising traffic toll (over 50,000 were dying annually on American roads) and the disclosure that GM spent only $1 million on safety during a year when profits hit $1.7 billion, provided the impetus for Congress to pass the National Traffic and Motor Vehicle Safety Act in 1966. This act established a government agency, the National Highway Traffic Safety Agency (later changed to Administration), to develop safety standards and to monitor industry compliance.

In 1970 Congress again acted, this time to reduce air pollution. The hydrocarbon and carbon monoxide output of a car's exhaust would have to be reduced 90 percent by 1975, while a similar reduction in nitrous oxide would be required by 1976. The 1960s began with the industry introducing smaller, cheaper and more economical cars in response to market and societal pressure. As the times got better, the cars became larger, higher priced and more powerful. In satisfying this newfound need for speed, Detroit was again setting itself up for a fall. History would repeat itself in the 1970s as the industry would offer smaller and more economical cars, but this time not because it necessarily wanted to, but because it had to.

228 top Safety became a growing concern, especially after the passage of new auto safety laws in 1966. In 1967, Ford began experimenting with child restraints, this one was called "tot guard."

228 bottom Size does matter as this impact between a Ford Galaxie and a subcompact Ford Pinto demonstrated in 1972. The much larger, body-on-frame car obliterates the unit body Pinto.

229 top Col. John Stapp (left), demonstrates the efficacy of seatbelts with his Dynamic Research Sled. An unbelted dummy flies out of the same sled during the demonstration.

229 bottom Airbags, now taken for granted, were a risky proposition in the 1960s as this failed deployment shows. The dummy slams into the windshield and is pushed back by the force of the crash.

CHAPTER 7

1973 - 1981
Regression,
Regulation,
Recession

230-231 The excesses in
chrome and size from the
1950s reappeared during the
1970s as this customized
Cadillac Fleetwood
demonstrates. Many of these
creations sported padded vinyl
roofs, fake wire wheels and
huge hood ornaments.

The first observance of Earth Day, April 22, 1970, was the beginning of the end of the American muscle car as it was conceived six years earlier in the Pontiac GTO. Chief among environmental concerns was auto emissions. After nearly eight months of hearings, debates and legislation, President Richard M. Nixon signed the Clean Air Act of 1970, a law that would mandate a 90 percent reduction in exhaust pollution.

This law severely impacted the industry's ability to put large V-8s in lightweight cars. Clamping down on emissions meant throttling back the power. Cars that routinely produced 400 bhp were supplanted by models that produced half that. It wasn't long before cars like the Plymouth Road Runner would disappear and models like the Olds 442 and Pontiac GTO would be shadows of their former selves.

While the new regulations helped kill off the muscle car, even before the Clean Air Act became law Detroit had embarked on a program to produce small,

efficient subcompact cars. It wasn't a move to get ahead of the curve on social issues, but a response, yet again, to the threat of imports. A decade earlier, the industry built compact cars as an answer to the inroads made by imports and then promptly fell asleep at the switch. Mesmerized by muscle cars, Detroit allowed its compact offerings to grow into V-8 intermediates. It wasn't long before it was caught flat-footed without small, 4-

cylinder economical entry-level vehicles to compete with the Volkswagen Beetle and the Toyota Corolla. By 1970, Volkswagen sales had grown to 569,000 cars and upstart Toyota had cracked the 200,000-unit barrier.

As the new decade dawned, the industry was ready to act and each new domestic entry spoke volumes about the relative strength and market position of the company concerned.

Detroit Discovers Subcompacts

The first American subcompact was introduced on April 1, 1970, and it came from the smallest manufacturer, American Motors, which had made its mark at the end of the 1950s by being first with compacts. Its new Gremlin, with its hacked-off hatchback styling, was the largest of the domestically produced subcompacts and was powered by a base 199 cu.-in. six making 128 bhp, rather than a more economical four. Derived from the Hornet compact introduced in January, it was the best AMC could do given its limited capital. Both the cars also offered a Chevrolet-designed 232 cu.-in. inline six making 145 bhp. The Gremlin later dropped the 199 cu.-in. engine and offered optional 150 bhp 258 cu.-in. sixes and 210 bhp 304 cu.-in. V-8s, making it the muscle car of the subcompact set.

Chevrolet's entry, introduced on September 10, 1970, was a much more ambitious undertaking. The all-new Vega (also sold as the Pontiac Astre) was offered in a 2-door hatchback, 2-door wagon and unique Kammback panel wagon. It rode on a 97-in. wheelbase and was powered by an aluminum block 140 cu.-in. 4-cylinder engine with two levels of output, 90 or 110 bhp. In addition to creating a new car from the ground up, GM built a new factory at Lordstown, Ohio, then the largest auto assembly plant under one roof, to produce this import fighter.

Unfortunately for Chevy, both would prove costly in the long run: The all-new Vega suffered from mechanical and rust problems, while GM's newest assembly plant became a hotbed of labor unrest leading to several costly strikes.

Originally designed to be powered by a Wankel rotary engine, the Vega was switched to an all aluminum 4-cylinder powerplant, which was prone to warping heads, rough idling and oil leaks. A sportier version, powered by an engine designed by English race engine builder Cosworth, also proved to be a disappointment. The high output engine was detuned to meet increasingly stringent emission standards so that by the time the car was introduced in 1975, the Cosworth Vega produced only 110 bhp, or about the

232 top and 233 top The Chevrolet Vega was GM's response to the growing popularity of the VW Beetle and Japanese cars like the Toyota Corolla. Unfortunately, the Vega, which had an aluminum block four-cylinder engine, suffered from quality problems. On the left, the cars are stacked vertically for transportation from the car's Lordstown, Ohio, assembly plant.

232 bottom American Motors entry-level subcompact was the Gremlin, an oddly-shaped hatchback introduced in 1970 that sold for less than $2,000.

233 bottom The Lordstown assembly operation for the Vega was one of GM's first large-scale applications of using robots for welding operations. Of the 3,900 welds used, robots accounted for 95-percent.

same as the optional engine in 1970. The twin-cam Cosworth model was costly with a sticker just under $6,000 when most cars in its class sold for half that. It never met its sales goal of 5,000 units a year, and in 1975 nearly 1,500 of the engines were scrapped due to a lack of interest in the car.

In 1975 General Motors drew on its global resources to build its first subcompact global car, the T-body. It was a 4-cylinder rear-drive hatchback that sold as the Chevy Chevette in the United States, the Opel Kadett in Germany and the Isuzu Gemini in Japan. The Vega was quietly dropped in 1977.

Ford used a more global approach in 1970 when it developed the Pinto, a 2-door fastback coupe and wagon that rode on a diminutive 94.2-in. wheelbase. A version of the car was badged Bobcat for sale by Mercury dealers. Unlike Chevy, which experimented with a new all-aluminum engine, Ford opted for its tried-and-true 98.6 cu.-in. British-built 75 bhp pushrod four as a base engine and its German-developed sohc 122 cu.-in. 100 bhp four as the step-up powerplant. The Pinto outsold the Vega by nearly 100,000 units in its first year, but the car wasn't trouble-free. Early models were plagued by an unshielded gas tank that would cause fires in rear-end collisions.

Chrysler, like AMC, had limited capital to spend on new product programs and chose to compete against imports with imports. From 1971 until 1973, it brought in Hillman Avengers from Britain and rebadged them as Plymouth Crickets. At the same time Chrysler contracted with Mitsubishi to supply entry-level hatchbacks sold as Plymouth Arrow and Dodge Colt until 1978, when finally Chrysler became the first of the Big Three to develop U.S. designed and built front-drive 4-cylinder subcompacts known as the Dodge Omni and Plymouth Horizon. The 4-door hatchbacks were dead ringers for the Volkswagen Rabbit. Entry-level models used VW's 75 bhp 1.7-liter 4-cylinder engines and in

1984, a 64 bhp 1.6-liter four supplied by Peugeot.

Chrysler developed its own 84 bhp 2.2-liter four, which became an optional engine in 1981. The lineup was broadened with more distinctive 2-door fastback hatches called the Dodge O24 and Plymouth TC3 as well as a pickup version, sort of a diminutive front-drive El Camino.

In turn, Ford and GM would also play the captive import game, the former importing its European Capri subcompact, that it sold through Mercury, while GM brought in German Opel Kadetts and GTs (sometimes referred to as the poor man's Corvette), that it sold through Buick.

234 and 235 left The 1970s were marked by two energy crises. Left is the scene in California on May 9, 1979 when gas rationing began. During the energy crises, open gas stations (right) were difficult to find and limits on the amount of fuel purchased were common.

235 right, first photo Instead of developing its own subcompact, Chrysler relied on its partnership with Mitsubishi in Japan to supply the Plymouth Arrow in 1977.

235 right, second photo Mitsubishi also built the Colt, a small economy car.

235 right, third photo Chrysler developed its own small front-wheel-drive two- and four-door hatchbacks in 1979. This is the two-door Dodge Omni 024.

235 right, forth photo Henry Ford II promised to push imports back into the sea and counted on the Ford Pinto to do it.

235 right, fifth photo Chrysler imported the Plymouth Arrow Sport from Mitsubishi.

Even though the American manufacturers had new entries in the subcompact market, the 1973 Arab Oil Embargo unleashed economic and legislative forces that would forever change the industry. The first was an economic downturn that saw industry record sales of 11.2 million cars plunge over 22 percent to just 8.6 million in 1974. Further exacerbating poor sales was the lifting of temporary price controls used in an attempt to curb inflation. When automakers were able to pass through price increases from the new safety and emission systems, oftentimes the percent increases were double digits. The term "sticker shock" was used to describe the impact these price hikes had on buyers. The industry would have to resort to rebates to move the iron. Chrysler was the first to offer them in 1975.

John Naughton, then sales group vice president of Ford, told Automotive News: "Rebates are like dope. You've got to get off it. If something like that continues, it's an indication that something is basically wrong." Nearly 30 years later, rebates and incentives are still a fact of life in the American auto industry.

Just as manufacturers learned that they needed cash rebates or other incentives to sell their products, Congress learned that it did not want to pass laws that unnecessarily would rile car buyers, who also happen to be voters. In 1974, safety laws required that cars be equipped with seatbelt interlock systems that prevented a car from being started if the driver's seatbelt wasn't hooked up. The outcry from frustrated motorists forced Congress to retreat on the issue, the first auto safety advance that was undone by public pressure. It also taught the regulators that it was best to tackle these social problems with the manufacturers directly rather than try to effect social change at the retail level.

Washington Tightens Its Grip

So, instead of passing high gasoline taxes to discourage consumption in the wake of the first energy crisis, as had been the practice in Europe, in 1975 Congress passed the Energy Policy and Conservation Act, which required manufacturers to boost their average car fleet fuel economy. In other words, it was up to the manufacturers to save fuel by raising each company's average fleet fuel economy to 18 mpg by 1978 and 27.5 mpg by 1985. A loophole in the law provided for less stringent fuel economy requirements for light trucks, one that the industry would exploit later in the 1980s and 1990s. But in the '70s, this law would lead to downsizing and a massive switch to front-wheel drive, a trend helped along by the second oil crisis of the decade in 1979.

Further complicating matters were the industry's tasks at hand—meeting stricter emission requirements from the 1970 Clean Air Act while simultaneously adding weight to cars with mandated safety equipment like 5 mph bumpers. Meanwhile, 1974's recession, a result of the energy crisis, produced economic hardships not seen in the auto industry since the Great Depression. All these factors were like asking the industry to walk, talk, chew gum and perform brain surgery while its pockets were being picked.

On the technical front, there were some remarkable advances and abysmal failures, the most spectacular of all coming from the industry leader, General Motors. On the triumph side was the catalytic converter, a canister fitted to the exhaust system that traps exhaust gases and, through a chemical reaction, increases the temperature of emissions to incinerate unburned hydrocarbons, carbon monoxide and nitrogen oxides.

On the failure side of the ledger were GM's abandonment of the rotary engine after spending millions on development, Oldsmobile's diesel experiment, and Cadillac's variable displacement V-8-6-4.

GM's experiment with rotary engines led to the development of the GMRE (General Motors Rotary Engine), which, according to Automotive News, was an

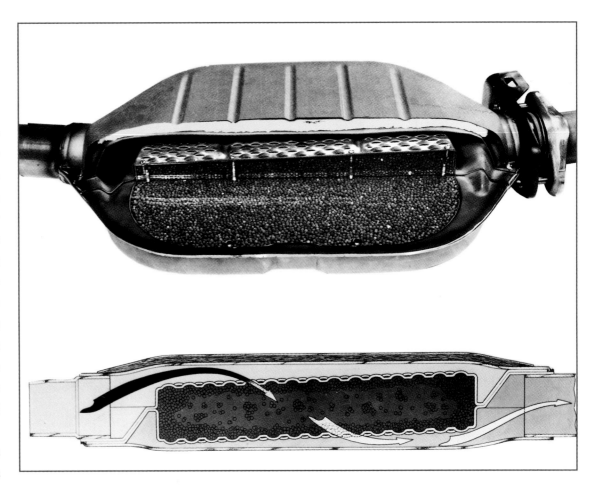

236 The catalytic converter, which was invented by GM, used precious metals to create a reaction that dramatically increased exhaust temperatures to oxidize hydrocarbons that weren't completely burned in engine combustion.

237 In an effort to increase fuel economy, Oldsmobile converted a 5.7-liter V-8 gasoline engine over to diesel power. Unfortunately, the engine could not handle the high compression stresses. As a result, the engine had severe quality problems.

all-iron design with an apex seal life of 100,000 miles. Oil changes were required only after 24,000 miles. Unfortunately, the engine wasn't as fuel-efficient or clean as conventional engines and was shelved after the 1973 oil crisis.

Olds introduced a 350 cu.-in. V-8 diesel in 1978, followed by a 260 cu.-in. V-8 in 1979 and even a V-6 version in 1982. These engines delivered about a 25-percent boost in fuel economy, but they were noisy, unreliable and poor performers. Once the gasoline lines disappeared after the '79 crisis, diesel sales plummeted.

The Cadillac variable displacement engine was designed to run on all eight, six or four cylinders depending on engine load and vehicle speed. Although the idea is making a comeback in current cars, thanks

to advanced engine electronics, the less sophisticated engine controls of the late 1970s led to poor reliability and drivability. The cars would often stall out completely only to run flawlessly for the mechanic after being towed in for service.

The reliability problems of the Olds diesel and Cadillac V-8-6-4 prompted GM to quit on the Wankel engine. This had a major impact on AMC, which had designed its 1975 Pacer around the rotary power plant. Perhaps the most innovative design of the decade, the Pacer, conceived by AMC design chief Richard Teague, was polarizing.

Designers loved the car, but the public criticized it as an aquarium on wheels, much like the Chrysler Airflow some 40 years earlier. The rounded shape, large glass area and low cowl and beltline gave excellent visibility throughout the car. Other innovative features included a passenger side door opening that was larger than the driver's side door to ease entry into the rear seat. The large glass area and hatchback configuration of the Pacer was said to have so impressed Dr. Ferry Porsche that it reportedly influenced the shape of the Porsche 928.

The compact size of the rotary engine allowed for a very low hood and a sleek nose, but when the powerplant wasn't forthcoming, the hood line had to be raised to accommodate AMC's workhorse 232 cu.-in. and 258 cu.-in. inline sixes and even later, the 304 cu.-in. V-8. The Pacer, which eventually was offered in both

2-door hatchback and station wagon, was dropped in 1980. Meanwhile, AMC continued to struggle. Its largest car, the Ambassador, looking old and stodgy, was dropped after 1974.

The backbone of AMC family sales was the Hornet, which ironically was one of the company's last muscle cars when a '71 SC/360 2-door model was introduced with a 285 bhp 360 cu.-in. V-8. After that bit of excess, the Hornet settled down and was offered in a variety of body styles including a 2-door fastback hatchback (with a performance version that resurrected the AMX designation), 2-door notchback, 4-door sedan and a wagon.

The Hornet compact soldiered on in relative anonymity, selling a total of 400,000 units before being supplanted by the Concord in 1978. A year later, Hornet's subcompact sibling, the Gremlin, would be lengthened slightly and given a more conventional fastback hatch and a new name, Spirit.

AMC tried to dress up its image in 1974 by replacing its mid-size Matador with a stylish fastback coupe to complement the rather staid 4-door sedan and wagon. This coupe would also take the place of the Javelin, which was dropped at the end of the model year. But Matador sales were uninspiring and the entire line was discontinued in 1978.

Downsizing Begins

As AMC struggled to survive, industry-leading GM embarked on a massive program to downsize its cars to meet the new fuel economy standards. The first product of this smaller-is-better mindset would come from the division that had forever operated on the philosophy that size does matter, namely Cadillac. In 1975 Cadillac launched the Seville, which was based on the Chevy Nova platform. The squared off, yet handsomely styled Seville was 27 in. shorter, 8 in. narrower and 1,000 lbs. lighter than the standard Cadillac Coupe de Ville. It was powered by a fuel-injected 180

bhp 5.7-liter V-8. The Seville wasn't the only sign of the times at Cadillac. Because of safety concerns, manufacturing complexity and a lack of customer interest, the convertible was becoming an endangered species. Chrysler was the first of the Big Three to drop the body style altogether in 1970 and by mid-decade it was apparent that factory-built convertibles were history. On April 21, 1976, what was thought to be the industry's last convertible, a Cadillac Eldorado, rolled off the assembly line of Cadillac's Clark Street plant in Detroit. But public demand for ragtops would see convertible production resume at the Big Three less than a decade later.

Following the Seville's launch and the convertible's

demise, GM's standard size B- and C-body cars were shortened and squared off in 1977. The B-bodies included Chevy Impala/Caprice, Pontiac Bonneville, Olds Delta 88 and Buick LeSabre, while the C-bodies were the Cadillac De Ville, Buick Park Avenue and Olds 98. A year later the mid-size A-bodies, still rear-drive, would be trimmed in size and weight. In addition to the 2-door coupes and conventional 4-door sedans in the Chevy Malibu/Monte Carlo, Olds Cutlass, Pontiac Grand Prix/Le Mans and Buick Regal/Century lines, the company introduced the "aerodeck" design, a fastback shape in 2- and 4-door models that looked like a hatchback, but wasn't. It proved unsuccessful.

GM began to ignore the tenets laid down by

Alfred P. Sloan regarding product overlap and pricing. This shift in philosophy was driven by two factors: the need for greater economies of scale on the manufacturing side and an insistence by dealers to offer the same kinds of products that the other divisions offered. Although some divisions, like Buick with its V-6s and turbochargers and Oldsmobile with its diesel experiment, would specialize in certain engine technologies, for the most part engines were being shared across divisional lines like never before.

With similar styling and as little as a few hundred dollars difference between cars like the Chevy Monte Carlo, Buick Regal, Pontiac Grand Prix and Oldsmobile Cutlass, the perceived value difference made a huge impact on sales. With its more upscale aura, Oldsmobile was able to sell over a million cars for the first time in its history in 1978.

This model sharing also continued across the lower product ranges. The Olds Omega and Buick Apollo joined the rear-drive Pontiac Ventura (a version of which was the last and quite forgettable GTO) and Chevy Nova in 1973-74. In 1975, a new generation of small cars designed to slot between Chevette and the dying Vega were given to all the divisions in the form of the Chevy Monza, Olds Starfire, Pontiac Sunbird and Buick Skyhawk, further blurring the distinctions among the divisions.

238 top Oldsmobile was on a roll in the 1970s, often ranking third in industry sales. Its top-line Delta 88 Royale Holiday hardtop coupe retailed for $3,964.

238-239 The first real effort at downsizing the traditional American sedan began in 1975 when Cadillac introduced the Seville, a car that was more than two feet shorter and 1,000 lbs lighter than the full-size Coupe de Ville.

239 top The Olds Cutlass, shown here as a 1970 Holiday Sedan, was the backbone of Oldsmobile's success in the 1970s, by the end of the decade, the GM division topped 1 million units in annual sales three years in a row.

A Fox and Panther for Ford

Ford wasn't as swift as GM to downsize its standard offerings, but going into the early 1970s, it did have a small, 6-cylinder heir to the original Falcon in the Maverick. Introduced in 1969, the Maverick was a mainstay until the Fairmont 4-door sedan and wagon and slightly swoopier Fairmont Futura 2-door would replace it in 1978. Over at Mercury, this new compact was called the Zephyr. The new platform, designated the Fox, would provide the basis for the next generation Mustang and Thunderbird. The Fairmont was a no-nonsense design—crisp, clean and boxlike. It had the Pinto's 200 cu.-in. four as its base engine and Ford's proven 302 cu.-in. V-8 as the step-up powerplant.

The Fox platform reinvigorated the Mustang, which had been downsized in 1974 and renamed the Mustang II. Based on Pinto components, the Mustang II rode on a 96.2-in. wheelbase and was powered by a choice of 88 bhp 140 cu.-in. four or a 105 bhp 170 cu.-in. V-6. The car came in a notchback coupe or fastback hatch, with the up-level notchback called a Ghia and the V-6 fastback a Mach I. In 1975, when the 302 cu.-in. V-8 was wedged in the car, Ford renamed these models the Cobra.

The compact Fox platform was much closer in concept to the Falcon, which provided the underpinnings for the original Mustang. With a wheelbase of 100.4 in., the 1979 Mustang was again offered in a choice of notch or hatchback styling and engines ranging from an 88 bhp 140 cu.-in. four up through the 140 bhp 302 cu.-in. V-8. In the mid-size range, the Ford Torino, a stylish 2-door and conventional looking 4-door sedan, saw sales fall after the first energy crisis, despite a total redesign for the 1972 model year. Ford would try again in 1977 with a minor facelift and some weight reduction. It renamed the car LTD II as sort of a downsized version of the full-size LTD. A more successful alternative was the 1975 Granada, a boxy 4-door sedan with styling cues inspired by the stand-up grille and slab-sided styling of Mercedes-Benz.

Built on a stretched Maverick platform with a wheelbase of 109.9 in. the Granada also spawned a Mercury version called the Monarch. In 1977, a gussied-up version of the car was given to Lincoln and called Versailles. Unlike the Seville, which had its own sheet metal, the Versailles had a Lincoln-style grille and deck lid with a Continental kit hump and a few more accessories than the standard Ford and Mercury offerings. Priced at $11,500, the Versailles was a failure, selling only 15,434

models when Cadillac sold 45,060. The full-size LTD, which measured 19 ft. in overall length wouldn't be downsized until the 1979 model year. Like the Fairmont before it, the LTD, which would bring back the Crown Victoria name from the 1950s, was based an all-new platform codenamed Panther. The Panther would prove so successful that it would remain the basis of the Crown Vic for the next quarter century. The car rode on a shorter 114.3-in. wheelbase and yet offered better passenger room and trunk space than the 1973-78 models. As Ford wrestled with the best ways to address the changing tastes of a volatile market, there were also changes coming in the upper reaches of company management. Henry Ford II, having run the company since the end of World War II, wanted to retire. At that time, the Mustang's creator, Lee Iacocca, had risen to become president of Ford Motor Co. However, Ford wasn't happy with the prospect of handing the company reins over to Iacocca and fired him on July 13, 1978. Ford

reportedly told Iacocca, "Sometimes, you just don't like somebody." By the end of the year Iacocca was at Chrysler, and Ford turned to Phillip Caldwell, whom he elevated to president and eventually chairman when Ford retired in 1980. Chrysler suffered from the same myopia as Ford, hoping to capture full-size vehicle market share when GM rolled the dice with its downsizing program in the mid-'70s. Instead of lopping inches off its full-size cars, Chrysler killed a number of muscle car models across the range, axing the Road Runner in 1971 and the Satellite and Barracuda by 1975. All large Plymouth offerings were dropped in 1979 and the division was repositioned as the entry-level range for the renamed Chrysler-Plymouth division. The full-size Chryslers remained intact through the first energy crisis. Imperial, New Yorker and Newport were the top Chrysler models, while the Monaco and Monaco Brougham were the Dodge versions and Plymouth had the Fury. In 1975 Chrysler jumped into the personal luxury coupe market with the Cordoba and branded the Dodge version of the car the Charger, which later begat the Magnum. In the compact range, the all-new Plymouth Volare and Dodge Aspen were introduced in 1976 on a 112.7-in. wheelbase. A year later that platform was used for the new mid-size Chrysler LeBaron and Dodge Diplomat. At this time, Dodge "downsized" its Monaco by using that name on its intermediate Coronet. True downsizing of Chrysler's large cars didn't happen until 1979, when a new generation New Yorker, Newport and Dodge St. Regis were introduced on a 118.5-in. wheelbase.

For the most part, the cars of the era reflected the fact that the industry wasn't having a very good time of it. Emissions and fuel economy laws were emasculating performance cars. The Corvette retained the same

basic body style throughout the 1970s and saw output from its 350 cu.-in. V-8 drop to a low of 165 bhp in 1975. While Ford offered the 351 cu.-in. Ford V-8 De Tomaso Pantera through its Lincoln-Mercury stores in the early 1970s, there were no new sports cars from the Big Threes between 1970. It would be up to imports to fill this niche from Datsun's 1970 240Z to Mazda's RX-7 in 1979.

Then there was the Bricklin, a plastic-bodied 2-seat gullwing sports car of which 2,897 were built between 1974-75. Malcolm Bricklin was an entrepreneur who helped establish Subaru's U.S. distributor. In the mid-1970s he built a 2-place "safety sports car" called the Bricklin SV-1. Using the chassis from AMC's Javelin, the Bricklin was powered by a 175 bhp AMC 360 cu.-in. V-8. In later models, that engine was supplanted by a 162 bhp Ford 351 cu.-in. V-8. The plastic-bodied car, which had its paint impregnated into the material, sold for $7,500-$10,000, although estimates had production costs at nearly double the base price.

Former GM exec and father of the GTO, John Z. DeLorean also had a dream to build what he called an "ethical sports car." His design also was a 2-seat mid-engine car with gullwing doors, but instead of plastic, the body was made of brushed stainless steel, which remained unpainted. Struggling during the late 1970s to secure financing, DeLorean set up shop in Belfast, Northern Ireland with a grant from the British government. The car, with a chassis designed by Lotus and a V-6 engine supplied by Renault finally rolled off the assembly line in 1981. In a bizarre bid to find more cash for his foundering company, DeLorean was ensnared in an FBI sting operation involving a cocaine deal. He was later acquitted, but his company went out of business in 1982 after producing almost 6,000 cars.

Imports
Set Up Shop

The 1970s were a time in which imports gained a significant foothold on the American market. While Volkswagen entered the decade as the undisputed import leader, by 1975 it was surpassed by Toyota which sold 337,409 vehicles to VW's 267,730. But, just as VW had prodded the domestic manufacturers into recognizing the subcompact segment, the German automaker would pave the way for its Japanese rivals in setting up U.S. transplant assembly operations.

In 1975, VW launched the Rabbit, the U.S. version of its European Golf, a small, boxy front-drive hatchback that would become the new template for the economy car worldwide. As noted earlier, Chrysler patterned its Omni/Horizon after the Rabbit. Chrysler also provided VW the means to produce the Rabbit in America when it sold an unfinished assembly plant in Westmoreland, Pennsylvania to the Germans. On April 10, 1978 Rabbits began rolling off the assembly line—the first foreign cars built on American soil since Rolls-Royce closed up shop its Springfield, Massachusetts in the 1930s. VW would later add the notchback Jetta model as well as a pickup version to the plant. However, high prices, quality problems and a chassis that enthusiasts complained didn't ride or handle as well as German-built models hurt sales. Just over 10 years later, on June 15, 1988, the last VW was built at the plant. VW consolidated all its North American car building at its Puebla, Mexico factory.

When Volkswagen opened its assembly plant in 1978, the U.S. industry was enjoying one of its best years ever with sales of 11.1 million cars. But the second oil crisis of the decade in 1979 would start the roller coaster ride downward yet again. Sales would drop to 10.5 million in '79 and spiral downward to 7.9 million by 1982.

The fact that the industry wasn't having any fun was also reflected in the dearth of dream cars from this era. With money being poured into engineering to improve safety, boost fuel economy and reduce emissions, there were precious few resources to devote to show cars. While this new generation of boxier, downsized cars was beginning to come off the drawing boards in response to the Corporate Average Fuel Economy law, the 1970s were also marked in design with a yearning for the classical elegance of the 1930s. Many of the pioneering automotive designers of the 1930s were nearing the end of their careers and it seemed as if they were trying to recapture some of the magic of their youth.

242 top and bottom left Volkswagen, which had opened the door for imports with its Beetle, called its replacement the Golf in Europe and the Rabbit in the U.S., as this cartoon shows the evolution of the VW badge.

242 bottom right Three years after the Rabbit's 1975 launch, VW began assembling the cars at a U.S. factory outside Pittsburgh, Pennsylvania. It was the first foreign-owned factory to produce cars since Rolls-Royce closed its U.S. operation in the 1930s.

243 top The late 1970s saw a spate of cars that sought to recapture the elegance of the classics from the 1930s. Alain Clenet based his car on the running gear of a Lincoln Mark V.

243 bottom Noted industrial designer Brooks Stevens actually created the first neoclassic, the Excalibur in the 1960s, modeling his car after the Mercedes SSK. Brooks Stevens stands between Bill Kimberly (left) and Huschke von Hanstein. Seated in the car is auto journalist Denise McCluggage.

The Rise of Neoclassics

Brooks Stevens, a famous industrial designer responsible for such vehicles as the Jeep Grand Wagoneer, is the father of this so-called neoclassic movement. In 1964 he designed a 2-seat open roadster built on a Studebaker chassis that resembled the legendary Mercedes SSK roadsters of the 1930s. The Excalibur used a 327 cu.-in. Chevy V-8 and was later redesigned from a 2-seat roadster into a 4-place phaeton with running boards and the car was built throughout the 1970s and into the early 1980s.

From 1967 through 1981, the Glenn Pray Co. of Auburn, Indiana built high-quality replicas of the Cord 810 called the 866. The fiberglass-bodied car road on a modified Ford chassis powered by a 365 bhp 428 cu.-in. V-8. Later the firm built the Model 874, a modern interpretation of a classic dual-cowl phaeton as well as an Auburn 851 Boattail speedster.

Alain Clenet, who was a designer at AMC, introduced his take on a classic '30s roadster in 1976. The 2-seat steel-bodied Clenet used a Lincoln Continental Mark IV chassis and a Ford 351 cu.-in. V-8. A longer Series II 4-passenger model, powered by a 302 cu.-in. V-8, was introduced in 1979.

Newer neoclassics that weren't copies included a Pontiac Grand Prix-based car restyled in Italy called the Stutz Blackhawk and the Florida-produced Zimmer Golden Spirit. The major manufacturers weren't immune to the allure of the neoclassic style. William Mitchell, who succeeded Harley Earl as head of GM design, went from subtle to overt references to the grand classics as his designs evolved from the 1960s into the 1970s. While there were mere hints of the Bugatti Atlantic in the 1963 Corvette Stingray, the 1971 Buick Boattail Riviera proclaimed Auburn.

This retro styling is particularly evident in the personal luxury coupes of the 1970s, the archetype being the Monte Carlo, which began life as a tasteful, understated 2-door coupe in 1970. By 1973, the car, along with the Olds Cutlass, Buick Regal and Pontiac Grand Prix grew in size and sported opera windows (called Colonnade styling), vinyl roofs and wire wheel covers. Fenders and headlamps began to develop as separate forms from the body. The 1973 Pontiac Grand Am featured louvered opera windows, and 4-door models could be ordered with rear fender skirts. One of the last cars heavily influenced by Mitchell, who retired in 1977, was the front-drive 1980 Cadillac Seville, which featured "bustle back" styling, a shortened rear trunk that recalled classic Bentleys of the 1930s. The car also sported a two-tone paint scheme, whitewall tires and wire wheel covers. While Chrysler had its share of padded vinyl roofs and opera windows, Ford design, headed by Eugene Bordinat was not to be outdone by Mitchell. In the late 1960s, the Thunderbird had grown in size and featured a padded vinyl roof with signature landau bars. This trend toward larger and more ostentatious Thunderbirds would continue into the 1970s. In 1972, the Thunderbird's wheelbase grew from 115 in. to 120.4. The next year landau bars gave way to opera windows and the Thunderbird, which began life as a tidy 2-seater, was now looked upon as a junior Continental Mark, a belief reinforced by the fact that a Lincoln 460 cu.-in. V-8 was an available option on the T-Bird. Although the Thunderbird was downsized in 1977 to a 114-in. wheelbase, it still sported an opera window in the B-pillar, a massive stand-up grille and hideaway headlamps.

Lincoln was equally heavy handed in its neoclassic treatment of the Mark IV and Mark V, the last of the really large 2-door coupes. The Mark V in particular is noted for its two-tone paint schemes and special designer editions from Bill Blass, Givenchy, Cartier and Pucci. Many of the styling devices from the classic era, such as fender skirts, opera windows, padded vinyl tops and wire wheel treatments, were used to dress up even the most ordinary cars during the 1970s. The fact that many of these accessories are dealer rather than factory installed also means that even today, somewhere out there is a new car sporting a fake convertible top.

CHAPTER 8

1982 - 1989
Renaissance

244-245 In 1982, Chevrolet totally redesigned the Camaro, its first major overhaul since 1970. The new car retained its solid rear axle and V-8 power Z-28 version.

The 1980s would prove to be the most challenging decade in the history of the American automobile industry. Unlike the depths of the Great Depression in the 1930s, when there were more than 30 viable marques and little import competition, subsequent consolidation had left the country with only four U.S. manufacturers that now had to vie for market share with competitors from Europe and Asia.

Import penetration from the Japanese alone skyrocketed during the 1970s from 297,000 to 1.8 million cars by 1980, or about 20 percent of the market. It wasn't just competition from Japan, Germany, Britain, France, Sweden and Italy, but also newcomers from Korea and even Yugoslavia.

In addition, the business cycle became more compressed with huge swings between bust and boom. It was a time when learning to manage success became just as important as being able to reverse losses.

Each of the manufacturers coped with crisis in different ways. AMC sought capital from its French partner Renault, which by 1982 owned a 46.9 percent stake in the firm. Chrysler, with former Ford president Lee Iacocca at the helm, appealed to the government for loan guarantees. Ford dug into its cash reserves and embarked on a strategy of using aerodynamic styling to give its vehicles unique appeal. General Motors announced not only a joint venture with Toyota to build subcompact Corollas and Chevy Novas in California but also a long-term project called Saturn, which would reinvent the small car in order to compete with imports. Another significant development in this decade would be a wholesale shift to front-wheel drive as a means of making cars more efficient. Having one set of wheels steering and driving the car created a lighter weight package. According to Automotive News, only 1.1 percent of American cars were front-drive in 1975. Twenty years later that number would stand at 85.9 percent. The 1980s would also see the introduction of two new vehicles—the minivan and the compact sport-utility—which would transform the types of vehicles that average Americans parked in their driveways.

Alphabet Soup

The trend to consolidate platforms and seek even higher levels of common components, thereby achieving larger economies of scale, resulted in similar models being spread across divisional lines with minimal changes. The term for this approach was called "badge engineering." In other words, the major differences between car lines were merely in the badges they wore. These cars were more often identified by their platform designation than specific model name.

Although GM letter-body designations were used as far back as the 1930s, company officials rarely referred to these codenames in public. That all changed when the company consolidated engineering and manufacturing operations, taking many of these responsibilities away from individual divisions. This eventually led to the formation of the B-O-C Group (for Buick, Olds and Cadillac), that had responsibility for large cars and the C-P-C Group (Chevy, Pontiac and Canada), that developed small

246-247 The last car Bill Mitchell designed was the "bustle back" Seville, which was introduced in 1980, reflected the trend to pick up styling cues from the 1930s. This 1983 model is a two-tone Elegance model.

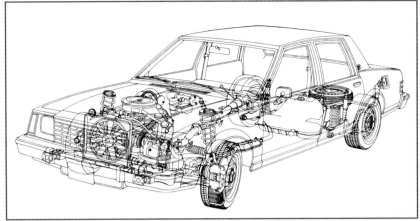

cars. From that point on, cars were more often than not identified inside and outside the corporation by their platform letter designation.

GM launched its first full-scale front-wheel drive program for family cars in early 1979. They were called the X-cars and were offered in all divisions except Cadillac. These models included the Chevy Citation, Pontiac Phoenix, Olds Omega and Buick Skylark. The X-cars featured a transverse mounting of either a 90 bhp 2.5-liter 4-cylinder engine or a 115 bhp 2.8-liter V-6. Body styles ranges from a 2-door

coupe or 2-door hatchback to a 4-door hatch. Chevrolet sold more 811,540 units in its first year, thanks in part to an early April 1979 launch of this 1980 model.

The X was followed in 1982 by the subcompact J-car and the mid-size A, which was basically a stretched X-body. The J-car was an ambitious program to compete with imports like Honda and Toyota. It was the first front-drive car that had a version for all five GM divisions—the Chevy Cavalier, Pontiac J2000 (later renamed Sunfire), Oldsmobile

247 top left GM decided that all its cars needed to be switched over to front-wheel drive. The first of this series was the X-car line that included the Buick Skylark (above), Chevy Citation and Pontiac Phoenix.

247 top right As this cutaway of the 1980 Buick Skylark shows, the engine is transversely mounted in order to drive the front wheels. The base engine was a 2.5-liter 4-cylinder powerplant, while a 2.8-liter V-6 was optional.

Firenza, Buick Skyhawk and even a Cadillac called Cimarron. Powered by a transversely mounted 88 bhp 1.8-liter four, the J-car, which rode on a 101.2-in. wheelbase, was offered in a number of body styles including a 2-door hatch, 2- and 4-door sedans and a wagon.

The larger A-body cars, sold as the Chevy Celebrity, Pontiac 6000, Olds Ciera and Buick Century, used a 90 bhp 2.5-liter four as its base engine with a 112 bhp 2.8-liter V-6 as an option. The previous rear-drive A-cars, the Chevy Malibu, Olds Cutlass, Pontiac Le Mans and Buick Regal, were rechristened the G-body and continued to be sold alongside the new front-drive versions for several more model years.

In 1985 GM would again downsize its full-size offerings, the Oldsmobile 98, Buick Electra and Cadillac De Ville, switching them over to front-drive and calling this platform the C-body.

The rear-drive B-body cars were retained as the Chevy Caprice, Cadillac Brougham, Pontiac Parisienne and Buick Roadmaster. In 1986 a shortened version of the C-body called the H was launched as the Pontiac Bonneville, Oldsmobile 88 and Buick LeSabre. Specialty front-drive platforms included the E-body, which was used for the Buick Riviera, Olds Toronado and Cadillac Eldorado, while the 4-door version, called the K, was used for the Seville. While GM was criticized for building cars that were difficult to distinguish between divisions, what it lacked in individuality it more than made up in distribution muscle. Its sheer size and economies of scale made it hugely profitable when industry sales began their climb to record levels in 1986.

Aerodynamics Gives Ford a Lift

At first, Ford's response to meeting the demand for fuel-efficient cars in a country wracked by recession was similar to its competition. It downsized its standard offerings and plunged into the development of a front-drive subcompact to replace the ill-fated Pinto. For most of its history, Ford had been a global player. But instead of exporting its technology as it did with the Model T, this time around it relied on the resources of its overseas units, which had a longer history of building smaller, more fuel efficient cars, to help develop a new world car to meet U.S. needs.

The car was called the Escort (Lynx in Mercury stores), a 3- and 5-door hatchback powered by a 1.9-liter 4-cylinder engine. However, by the time the U.S. unit changed the interior, tweaked the suspension, hung on 5-mph bumpers and tuned the car for American emissions, the Escort was far different than the ones sold in Europe. The idea of the world car may have failed, but the Escort proved to be a hit for Ford and even spawned a sporty 2-seat version known as the Ford EXP or Mercury LN7. In 1987 and 1988, it was the best selling car in the industry, retailing nearly 400,000 units. Besides reducing mass and switching to more efficient front-drive packaging, Ford decided that another way to improve fuel economy was through improved aerodynamics. But this would have a huge impact on styling, a risk in an industry that still remembered the failure of the Chrysler Airflow. This time, Ford would use

the aero look but with a European flair. Under the direction of chief designer Jack Telnack, the company would begin to build a series of cars that had wind tunnel influenced shapes that were softer and more rounded than the boxy styling that dominated the industry. The first of these vehicles was the Thunderbird, a stunning departure from the razor-edged car that preceded it. With rounded corners, exposed quad headlamps instead of hideaway lights, and a conventional quarter glass instead of an opera window and no vinyl top, the new car was the antithesis of its predecessor. In addition to its 232 cu.-in. V-6 or 140 bhp 302 cu.-in. V-8, the Thunderbird also offered a sporty turbo coupe at midyear with the 142 bhp 2.3-liter turbo four from the Mustang. Not only did the car look different from the boxy GM cars it competed with, the slick shape gave it a decided advantage in NASCAR stock racing, which further gave the Thunderbird a boost in retail sales.

In 1987 Thunderbird would receive a facelift that included flush headlamps and a new grille-less snout for the Turbo Coupe. Two years later both the Thunderbird

248-249 Chrysler discovered that it could build many different models off one platform, the so-called K-car. This component set was used beneath this sporty looking Dodge Daytona Turbo Z.

and Cougar would be totally redesigned, riding on a new platform called MN-12.

The no-grille look of the Turbo Coupe would be used across the line, and that high-performance model would be replaced by the Super Coupe, which was powered by a 210 bhp supercharged V-6. Right on the heels of Thunderbird came the 1984 Ford Tempo/Mercury Topaz, essentially lengthened Escorts that were offered in 2-door coupes and 4-door sedans. Telnack's "jellybean" styling featured soft contours to the body, doors cut into the roof, and headlamps, though not quite flush, that were squared off.

The Tempo sold over 400,000 units in its first year. In 1985 Ford took an even larger gamble: It would redesign its mid-size rear-drive Ford LTD and Mercury Marquis replacing them with the radically styled front-drive Ford Taurus and Mercury Sable. Now all its cars in the heart of the market would sport this new look. The public was ready for a change. "We made the aerodynamic look not just palatable, but desirable," Telnack told Automotive News. "Taurus was a break-

249 top Ford's venerable Thunderbird grew from its two-seat origins into a personal luxury coupe. By the 1983, it was totally redesigned using aerodynamic influences for a rounder body.

249 center The workhorse of Chrysler's 1980s lineup was the family-sized compact K-car, sold as the Dodge Aries (above), Plymouth Reliant and Chrysler Le Baron.

through for the industry. Other automakers had no choice but to follow our lead." Riding on a 106-in. wheelbase, the Ford Taurus and Mercury Sable shared the same sleek body shell but with differences in detailing. Both cars dispensed with grille work, but the Taurus had Ford's blue oval floating in the middle of its front, while the Mercury had a light bar that extended from headlamp to headlamp. Instead of the Taurus' traditional C-pillar, the Mercury wrapped its glass around the back into the rear window.

The Taurus was offered with a base 4-cylinder engine and an optional Vulcan 3.0-liter V-6, while the Mercury came as a V-6 only. The sales of both cars combined were more than 400,000 units a year and, by 1992, Taurus was the best selling car in America.

Give Me a K

Styling was not Chrysler's forte; instead the company relied on GM's strategy of letter cars, but over far fewer platforms. From the subcompact L-body Omni/Horizon would come the larger K-car, an architecture that would provide the basis for literally every Chrysler product from its compact to full-size entries. Flexible in wheelbase, it was stretched from its base configuration of 100.1 in. to more 124.3 in. for its Executive sedan and 131.3 for the Executive Limousine. The first K-cars were introduced in 1982 as the Chrysler Le Baron, Dodge Aries and Plymouth Reliant. In addition to offering the car as a 4-door sedan, Chrysler was the first to get back into the convertible market in 1984 with the Le Baron. The K-car was powered by a transversely mounted 2.2-liter four made by Chrysler or an optional 2.4-liter four from Japanese partner Mitsubishi.

What the boxy 4-door sedans lacked in style they more than made up in low purchase price and dependable operation. Chrysler continued to evolve the platform, spawning 2-door hatchback sporty coupes called the Chrysler Laser and Dodge Daytona in 1984. A smaller 4-door hatch, basically a modified K that was called the H-body and dubbed the Chrysler GTS and Dodge Lancer, was introduced in 1985. In 1986 the first evolution of the L-body Omni/Horizon, the new P-body Dodge Shadow and Plymouth Sundance, were launched. In 1987 full-size versions of the K-car were introduced in the Dodge Dynasty and Chrysler New Yorker.

My Other Car Is a Truck

In 1977 Hal Sperlich was vice president of market planning and research at Ford Motor Co. and had unsuccessfully tried to get the company to develop a car-based van to replace station wagons. The concept, known as Mini-Maxi (for minimum overall size, maximum interior volume), didn't appeal to Henry Ford II and he ordered then Ford president Lee Iacocca to fire the pugnacious Sperlich, who landed at Chrysler. A year later, Iacocca was turned out by Ford and turned up at Chrysler, where the pair revived the Mini-Maxi concept, based on the K-car mechanicals. Codenamed the T-115, this all-new vehicle was basically a box on wheels with two conventional front doors, a right-side sliding door and a rear lift gate. Offered with the same 2.2-liter and 2.4-liter in-line fours offered in the K-car lineup, the T-115 was an instant hit for families seeking the roominess of a traditional full-size station wagon that would easily fit in a garage while delivering the fuel economy of a compact car.

The Dodge Caravan and Plymouth Voyager rode on a 112-in. wheelbase and, because of their flat floors and removable seats, were classified by the government as trucks, which also subjected them to less stringent fuel economy, emission and safety standards than passenger cars. It was the perfect medicine for Chrysler, which was teetering on the brink of bankruptcy, saved only by government guaranteed loans. Using K-car components, the minivan was a low-cost way (about $660 million at a time new product programs routinely ran closer to $1 billion) to create a whole new segment.

Launched in November 1983, the minivan was an instant hit, selling more than 500,000 units and providing the cash needed to turn around the company's fortunes and pay back its loans ahead of schedule. In 1988, a long wheelbase version of the van was launched. Called the Grand Caravan and Grand Voyager, they were 14 in. longer in overall length and rode on a stretched 119.1-in. wheelbase. The extra length provided the additional cargo space families needed when all three rows were filled with kids.

Both Chevrolet and Ford reacted to the minivan but misfired on their first attempts. Instead of copying Chrysler's car-based concept with a transverse-mounted engine and front drive (which severely limited towing capability), Chevy and Ford responded with truck-based, front-engine rear-drive compact vans, the Chevy Astro and Ford Aerostar. These two vehicles were never as popular as the Chrysler minivans, and both companies would later return with front-drive packages similar to Chrysler's. By the end of the decade, minivans as a category would account for 1 million in industry sales, of which Chrysler's share was 60 percent. The success of minivans was proof that Americans still prized personal space, something that was being lost with each successive round of downsizing in the passenger car fleet as manufacturers scrambled to meet an average car fleet fuel economy of 27.5 mpg mandated by law. Trucks, however, had to meet only 17.2 mpg if they were 2-wheel drive and 15.8 for 4-wheel drive. By 1992, all trucks were required to have a fleet average of 20.6 mpg, still well below the level set for cars.

As a result, buyers flocked to trucks, where they still could find plenty of space in solid body-on-frame vehicles powered by big V-8 engines. Manufacturers also caught on to the fact that more car-like creature comforts in full-size vans and sport-utility vehicles meant big profits for little investment with minimal risk in violating overall corporate fuel economy standards. Full-size cars began to disappear, while pickup and sport-utility sales began to soar. New vehicles, like the minivan, were built to conform to truck standards as a means of minimizing the investment needed to comply with the more stringent car emissions, fuel economy and safety regulations. But for every buyer content with a full-size truck or van in lieu of a car, there were others who liked smaller vehicles. Compact pickups, a segment pioneered by Japanese imports, had become quite popular, and Ford and Chevy rushed the smaller Ranger and S-10 to market as an answer. Then in 1983, Chevrolet introduced the S-10 Blazer, a 2-door sport-utility based off its small truck. A year later, AMC/Jeep, which had been selling the full-size Grand Wagoneer SUV, as well as 4-wheel versions of its

250-251 *Before being acquired by Chrysler in 1987, American Motors, through its Jeep division, made a huge contribution to the industry's future by* *introducing the first four-door compact sport-utility vehicle, creating a segment that would eventually grow to more than 2 million units annually.*

Spirit and Eagle, introduced the first 4-door compact SUV. Like the minivan, the 4-door Cherokee would provide the template for a whole new segment that would become pervasive in the U.S. market. The vehicle virtually doubled Jeep sales from 82,140 to 153,801 and eventually pushed the brand's sales to over 200,000 trucks a year. While the Cherokee would prove to be a masterstroke, the car side of AMC was still struggling, bumping along in its relationship with partner Renault. In 1983 the company would retool its Kenosha, Wisconsin assembly plant to produce the front-drive Alliance 2- and 4-door sedan and Encore hatchback, a variant of Renault's European-designed R9. A larger car, the Medallion, based on the Renault R11 would be imported from France and a full-size entry, the R-25 based Premier, would be built at an all-new assembly plant in Brompton, Ontario, Canada. Eventually, the 4-wheel drive cars would be dropped from AMC's line. A sporty 2-door hatchback called Fuego would also come and go. AMC car sales fell steadily from the decade's peak of 193,351 to 72,853 by 1986.

Quota Quandary

As imports began to take a larger share of the U.S. market, the domestic manufacturers were eager to seek protection, just as Japan protected its home market from imports. In 1980, the combined loss of the Big 4 was $4.2 billion, with over half that amount attributed to Ford and Chrysler alone. And the auto companies had furloughed over 200,000 workers.

As U.S. manufacturers pressed for protection, the government sought to open the Japanese market to American cars and electronics and eventually worked out a voluntary restraint agreement (VRA) that capped Japanese car imports at 1.68 million units for 1982. Trucks were not included in that limit but were subject to an existing 25 percent tariff, a holdover from a U.S.-Europe trade war in the 1960s. That duty was the so-called "Chicken Tax" that was enacted when Europe banned poultry imports from the U.S. and then was met with a retaliatory tax aimed at the Volkswagen Bus. It stayed on the books and was used effectively against the Japanese, causing some of the makers to move pickup bed production to the U.S. These companies avoided most of the duty by importing lower-tax cab/chassis units and installed the American-built beds at the port.

Just as the American makers were asking for restrictions, they also were in bed with the enemy. Chrysler was importing Dodge Colts and Plymouth Champs

from Mitsubishi, and Chevrolet brought in the Suzuki-built Sprint and Isuzu-built Spectrum. In 1985 Chevy received its first Novas (a version of the Corolla) built at New United Motor Manufacturing, Inc. (NUMMI), the GM-Toyota joint venture at an old GM assembly plant in Fremont, California.

While the VRA, which moved up to 1.81 million in 1983 and 1.85 million in 1984, held down Japanese market share, it had some unintended consequences that would permanently change the U.S. auto industry. First, by limiting the availability of high demand Japanese imports, it created larger profit margins for the Japanese makers and their dealers, who charged additional mark-ups. It also hastened Japanese plans to build U.S. assembly plants. While Volkswagen was the first foreign auto company since World War II to establish a transplant operation in the United States in 1978, Honda followed in 1982, building its first Accord sedan in Marysville, Ohio and later adding Civic production. The company was followed in short order by Nissan, which built a plant in Smyrna, Tennessee for its Sentra subcompact and then Toyota, which chose Georgetown, Kentucky as a base to build Camry sedans. When the original VRA agreement expired in 1984, the U.S. government did not seek to renew the limits, but Japan's Ministry of International Trade and Industry (MITI) thought it would be politically expedient to continue the program to head off protectionist legislation in the U.S. Congress.

Now called the Voluntary Export Restraints, the limit was set at 2.3 million units in 1985. While the restraints continued to help the established makes in the U.S. market, it severely hampered relative newcomers like Isuzu, Suzuki and Daihatsu and prevented them from gaining a large foothold in the American market. Daihatsu eventually quit the U.S. because its allotment under VER was miniscule. Further playing politics, MITI began to tighten VER down to 1.65 million units in 1992 as U.S. production by Japanese manufacturers increased. Eventually the program was scrapped altogether in 1994. By the end of the 1980s, Honda, Nissan and Toyota operations were joined by assembly plants from Mazda in Michigan, Mitsubishi in Illinois and Subaru-Isuzu in Indiana. Of the 6.8 million cars produced in the United States in 1989, Japanese companies built 1.2 million of them. Like the NUMMI joint venture that produced the Nova for Chevy, the Mazda operation supplied Ford with front-drive Probes, a car that was supposed to be a replacement for the rear-drive Mustang. The Probe, based off Mazda's 626, featured a transversely mounted 110 bhp 3.0-liter V-6. The Mitsubishi transplant, known as Diamond-Star Motors, built the Eclipse for Mitsubishi as well as the Plymouth Laser and Eagle Talon for Chrysler. As successful as the Japanese were in penetrating the U.S. market, the European experience was much more mixed. Volkswagen's imports steadily declined and output from its Pennsylvania production plant fell until the facility was shuttered in 1988.

But the Europeans would return less than a decade later: BMW opened an assembly plant in Spartanburg, South Carolina to build the Z3 roadster and Mercedes-Benz opened its Vance, Alabama plant to build the M-Class SUV. The U.S. auto industry had a banner year in 1986 with sales of nearly 11.5 million cars. The strong dollar helped all imports, including European luxury cars, reach an all-time record level of 3.2 million units. But as the U.S. trade deficit ballooned, the government moved to devalue the dollar, and import sales, particularly among luxury marques, began a long, slow decline.

An Itch to Niche

Companies that had been scrounging for cash for new car programs soon found themselves awash in profits as the market rebounded from its 1982 low point. The invention of the catalytic converter and further advances in on-board electronics that allowed the widespread use of fuel injection enabled the manufacturers to keep pace or exceed tightening emission standards. On the safety front, manufacturers were able to buy time in the development of airbags by using passive belt systems, while the shift to front-drive made meeting fuel economy standards less of a burden.

With resources previously committed to meeting these regulations now freed, the American industry was prepared to have a little fun again. The first order of business was bringing back the convertible.

Chrysler, which was the first of the major makers to abandon the drop top, was also the first to bring it back with the Le Baron in 1982. GM soon followed with the Buick Riviera ragtop in 1983 and a Cadillac Eldorado convertible in 1984. Ford countered with its convertible version of the Mustang in 1985.

Ford had redesigned the Mustang in 1984 and while it shared the same platform as the '79 model, significant upgrades included a new high-performance version called the SVO Mustang, a vehicle developed by a small performance engineering team within the company. Using resources from Europe, the SVO Mustang sported a bi-plane rear wing and a turbocharged 2.3-liter four that made 175 bhp, the same as the optional 5.0-liter V-8.

General Motors wasn't about to give up the pony car market to Ford or the Japanese. It, too, worked on a front-drive replacement to the Camaro and Firebird but abandoned the project in favor of a slick 2+2 hatchback that retained a traditional front-engine rear-drive layout with a live rear axle. Riding on a 101-in. wheelbase, the new Camaro/Firebird was 7 in. shorter than the previous car. The base engine was an anemic 90 bhp 2.5-liter cast iron four called the Iron Duke. Upgrades included a 112 bhp 2.8-liter V-6, a 150 bhp 5.0-liter V-8 and a fuel-injected 5.0-liter V-8 that made 165 bhp.

Corvette was ready for its first major makeover since 1968. Called the C-4 for fourth generation Corvette, this car was had a delayed launch as a 1984 model due to production difficulties and as a result there was no 1983 version. Powered by a 350 cu.-in. V-8, the new Corvette had a sleek modern shape with unique front-hinged clamshell-opening hood. It produced 205 bhp and was offered with a choice of 4-speed automatic or 4-speed manual with a base price of $23,360, the most expensive Chevrolet yet. More than 50,000 Corvettes were sold in the '84 model year. Pontiac finally got a 2-seater it could call its own in 1984 in the plastic-bodied Fiero, although it was sold to upper management as a fuel-sipping commuter car instead of a full-on sports car. Powered by a 90 bhp 2.5-liter Iron Duke four, the Fiero sold more than 130,000 units in its first year. However, engine prob-

252-253 The 1989 Corvette ZR-1 was a limited-run model distinguished by its rectangular taillamps. That design would be used on all Corvettes starting in 1991. The heart of the ZR-1 model was the LT5 engine option, a 380-bhp 5.7-liter V-8 actually built by Mercury Marine in Oklahoma.

253 top An all-new Chevrolet Corvette debuted in the 1984 model year and two years later, reintroduced a convertible version, which cost $32,032.

lems and other quality issues dogged the car in its early years and sales suffered. Second-year sales were cut in half and by 1988, its last year of production, it sold only 34,000 units. Still, the last Fieros, in particular the GT, that sported new bodywork and a 135 bhp 2.8-liter V-6, were the best ever.

Pontiac wasn't the only division to get a new 2-seater during this period. Buick developed the Reatta, personal luxury coupe riding on a shortened 98.6-in. wheelbase derived from the Riviera platform. A trans-

versely mounted 245 bhp 3.8-liter V-6 engine drove the front wheels. Eventually a convertible edition was added. A noteworthy feature was the use of a CRT touch screen panel for the radio and the climate controls, a feature that wouldn't be common on luxury cars for at least another decade.

The car, which was expected to sell in annual volumes of 40,000 units, sold only a tenth of that number and was dropped in 1992. Cadillac sought to compete with the Mercedes-Benz SL 2-seat roadster with an

Italian designed front-drive 2-seater called the Allante, which was introduced in 1987. Designed by Pininfarina, the Allante is said to have had the world's longest assembly line. Frames made in Detroit were sent via 747 to Turin, Italy, where Pininfarina would assemble and paint the body, sending cars back on the return flight.

The cars were trucked over to the final assembly line at Cadillac's Hamtramck, Michigan plant where the engine would be installed. It was a costly system that was reflected in the Allante's $65,000 sticker price. The car rode on a 98.4-in. wheelbase and was powered by a 4.1-liter V-8 making 175 bhp. In its last year of production, 1993, the car was equipped with Cadillac's 295 bhp 4.6-liter Northstar V-8.

GM wasn't alone with an Italian connection. Chrysler's Lee Iacocca worked with Alessandro De Tomaso, who at the time controlled Maserati, to develop an Italian-built version of the LeBaron convertible called the TC Coupe.

The car featured a removable hardtop, a leather interior installed by Italian craftsmen, and a 2.2-liter 4-cylinder engine specially tuned by Maserati to produce 200 bhp when equipped with a manual or 160 bhp with a 3-speed automatic. Riding on a shortened 93.3-in. wheelbase and costing over $30,000, the TC was a flop, since buyers could get virtually the same equipment in a LeBaron convertible (save for a removable hardtop with Thunderbird-inspired portholes) for thousands less. Introduced in 1989, the TC was dropped by the end of the '90 model year.

Too Much Money

The mid-1980s were halcyon days for the U.S. industry. Profits soared to unheard-of heights during the years around 1986 when the market peaked. In 1986-87 Ford's profit was $10 billion and previously sick Chrysler banked nearly $5 billion. GM raked in around $8 billion. With all this money, the carmakers went on a buying spree. Some of the purchases were auto related, while others were outside the industry. During the previous downturn, the conventional wisdom developed that losses in the auto sector could be offset by profitable non-auto holdings. Ford, always the Eurocentric, looked to add a prestige make to its portfolio and in 1985 took a run at Alfa-Romeo, losing out to Fiat. A year later it bought Jaguar for $2 billion.

Chrysler used its money to buy AMC in 1987 primarily for the company's Jeep operations. It kept AMC cars alive in the newly formed Eagle Division, but it dropped the Alliance/Encore and shifted its Omni/Horizon production to the newly acquired Kenosha, Wisconsin assembly plant. It gave Eagle a version of the Mitsubishi Eclipse and kept the Eagle Premiere in Canadian production and gave a version to Dodge, reviving the Monaco nameplate.

In 1987 the company also bought Lamborghini, the Italian maker of exotics and invested the money needed to develop a successor to the Countach—the Diablo, which was introduced at the Chicago Auto Show in 1990. Iacocca was a firm believer in diversification and also bought business jet maker Gulfstream Aviation and increased Chrysler's holdings among defense contractors. By far the most ambitious of all executives when it came to spending and diversification was General Motors chairman Roger B. Smith. During the 1980s he purchased data processing giant Electronic Data Services, founded by the mercurial Ross Perot. When Perot butted heads with Smith over how GM ran its automotive business, Smith sent the Texan packing with a $750 million buyout. During this period GM also purchased Hughes Corp., which built satellites, helicopters and other defense-related technology, and invested $5 billion in a new automobile company called Saturn. Saturn was an all-new import fighter that would be sold differently than traditional GM cars. In order to do this, GM set Saturn up as a separate corporation, giving it a new assembly plant and dedicated engineers.

At a time when GM was consolidating its product development and manufacturing operations across divisional lines, Saturn was allowed to develop its own car, distribution network and corporate culture in a bold experiment to reinvent the American car. This expensive bet diverted product development money that could have been used by the other divisions and caused friction between Saturn and the rest of the corporation. While Saturn set up dealerships through the traditional franchise system, it had far fewer stores and allowed individual dealers to control large market areas, promising a low-pressure sales environment with "no-dicker stickers." In other words, the list price was the selling price—no incentives and no discounts.

Announced with much fanfare in 1983, Smith drove a prototype Saturn in 1985 and promised to drive the first car off the assembly line in 1987. But the car wouldn't be launched until 1990, just in time for Smith to take that inaugural spin just before he retired. The rocky start of Smith's pet project was just one sign of troubled times ahead.

254-255 In 1987, Chrysler bought the Italian company Lamborghini and invested money in order to develop the successor of the famous Countach, the Diablo, here in the photographs. The Lamborghini Diablo was first presented at the Chicago show in 1990.

CHAPTER 9

The Roaring '90s

256-257 *The fifth-generation Corvette, which bowed in 1998, was offered in both coupe (above) and convertible models right from the start. A hardtop coupe was added two years later.*

I f the 1990s held any lessons for the Big Three, they were that business was as volatile as ever and that diversification into non-automotive businesses was not the key to long-term success.

Although the mid- to late-1980s was very good to the domestic manufacturers, the barrels of black ink evaporated in the downturn that followed the 1991 Gulf War. In 1992, GM lost $4.5 billion, Ford $2.3 billion and Chrysler $1 billion.

Even though Chrysler's loss was much less than its rivals, the red ink devastated the smaller company, which had seen sales plummet from 2.3 million cars in 1987 to 1.5 million by 1991. And many of the architects of the early 1980s government-backed loan and product strategy had left the com-

pany. Chief among them were Hal Sperlich, father of the minivan, and the financial wizard Gerald Greenwald. This time Chrysler's turnaround would be purely product-based with no government safety net. It would also fall to an unlikely trio, sort of a latter day version of the Three Musketeers. Heading the effort would be Robert A. Lutz, Chrysler's new president, whom Lee Iacocca recruited from Ford. Engineering came under the direction of François Castaing, a former head of Renault's Formula One racing effort, who later worked at AMC/Renault and stayed on after Chrysler acquired the AMC portion. The third member of this product team was chief designer Tom Gale, who had joined Chrysler in 1967 after graduating from college.

There was no question that Chrysler needed new product. Even the groundbreaking minivan was

looking tired as the 1980s drew to a close. But the ingenuity in this turnaround plan wasn't so much what kinds of cars Chrysler built, but rather how they built them and presented them to the public.

At the time, product development at the Big Three consisted mainly of chimneys—vertical hierarchies organized by discipline. An idea would work its way up the design chimney where it would be tossed over to engineering, where it would work its way through the system before being handed off to manufacturing and then to the marketing and sales chimney. The platform team concept tore down those chimneys and created a cross-functional organization that had design, engineering, manufacturing, and sales and marketing working together from the ground up.

While the platform team concept was revolu-

tionary, Chrysler took a page from automotive history by using show cars as a way to whip up public enthusiasm and to let Wall Street know that there was new product in the pipeline. Dream cars had all but disappeared during the turbulent 1970s, making a bit of a comeback when times got better in the 1980s. However, many of these cars were aerodynamic studies like the Ford Probe series or the Buick Wildcat. Others would test wild ideas like GM's 3-wheeled Lean Machine in which the body would actually lean into the corner providing greater stability. Oldsmobile used its sleek Aerotech mid-engine car to set closed-course speed records. The kinds of concept car Detroit wasn't doing were the kinds that you would see on the show stand and hope to drive home someday, just like the original Corvette.

The Viper Strikes

At the 1989 North American International Auto Show in Detroit, the Dodge Viper, a 2-seat roadster with side pipes and an 8.0-liter V-10 engine boasting 400 bhp, debuted. Within six months, the green light was given for its production, and Chrysler's first platform team went to work to put out the car in less than 36 months in an industry that typically took four or more years to develop a car. While the Dodge Viper garnered all kinds of favorable publicity for Chrysler, it was a limited-production vehicle that even with a sticker of $50,000 would contribute little to the company's bottom line.

258-259 The Dodge Viper concept car drew rave reviews when it was unveiled at the North American International Auto show in January 1989. The two-seat, 400-bhp show car was designed to generate positive press for the cash-strapped company.

260 top The Dodge Intrepid is positioned as a lower priced family car and yet the LH body, with its clean, aerodynamic shape, gives it an upscale aura. The front end of the Dodge Intrepid carries some of the Viper's styling cues, especially in the headlamp area and the cross-hair grille anchored by driving lights.

260-261 Dodge returned to NASCAR racing in 2001 using a silhouette body on the rear-drive race car that looks like its front-drive Intrepid sedan.

261 top The LH cars were redesigned again in 1998 becoming even rounder and more modern looking. Note the short overhangs and that much of the Concorde's body is devoted to the passenger cabin.

261 bottom The Chrysler New Yorker was totally redesigned from its boxy shape into a rounder and more elegant look that Chrysler design vice president Tom Gale called "Cab Forward." These cars based on the LH platform were introduced in 1992.

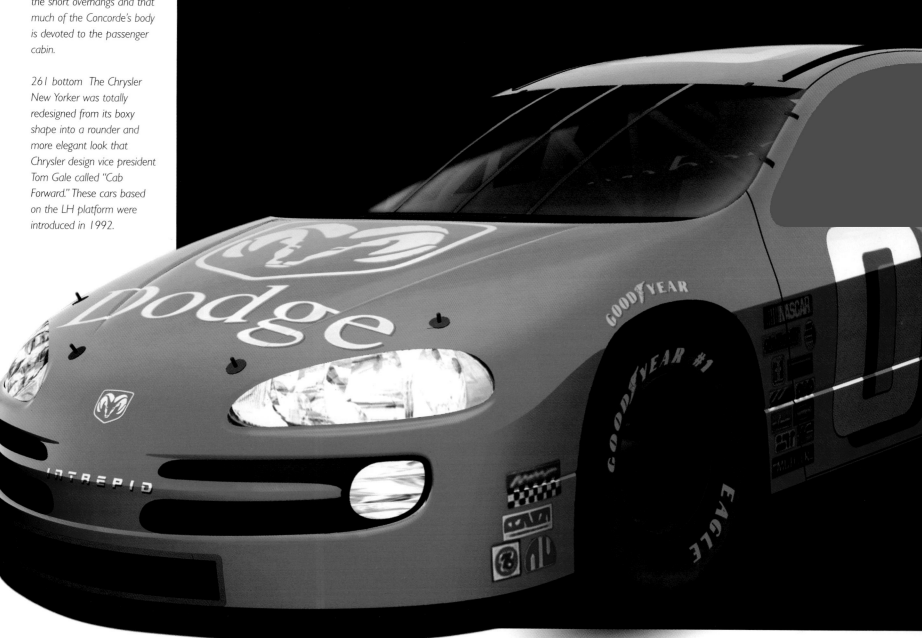

Chrysler set out to rebuild its business with a new full-size family car, the LH, which would have groundbreaking styling. Chrysler hoped the LH would do for it what the Taurus had done for Ford in 1986.

The LH, which Chrysler cynics derisively referred to as Last Hope, featured "cab forward" design, in which the touchdown point of the rakish front windshield would be almost at the centerline of the front wheels. With short front and rear overhangs, the design maximized the cabin space, giving the car full-size interior room in something a touch larger than a traditional mid-size car. And of course, there would be a

concept car to herald the LH's coming. It was the 1990 Eagle Optima, which rode on a 112-in. wheelbase. Although the shape was true to the new LH form, the powertrain was a 4.0-liter V-8 driving the rear wheels. In production, the 1993 LH cars—branded the Dodge Intrepid, Eagle Vision and Chrysler Concorde—would be powered by a choice of a 161 bhp 3.3-liter ohv or 214 bhp 3.5-liter sohc V-6 longitudinally mounted and driving the front wheels. A slightly longer version of the LH, the 207 in.-long Chrysler New Yorker and LHS were added to the lineup in 1994. Five years later, Chrysler resurrected

the famed letter car by introducing the LH-based 300M, which was powered by a 3.5-liter dohc V-6 making 253 bhp.

The LHs were the hit Chrysler needed, selling 175,000 in 1993 and 254,000 in 1994 with the addition of the New Yorker and LHS. While the Eagle Vision sold around 30,000 per year, the division had only one other product, the Mitsubishi-built Talon sports coupe, which sold in only half that volume. By 1998, Chrysler pulled the plug on Eagle, ending a car lineage that extended back through AMC to Hudson and Nash.

Chrysler was on a roll and hoping to use design to assert itself in segments where it previously was just a bit player. One of these targets was the pickup truck market where the company was an also-ran to Ford and Chevrolet.

The new Ram broke through with its bold grille and step-down hood and fender look of a long-distance semi-tractor. The public either hated or loved the look, which Lutz described as "polarizing." Those who loved the Ram's bold styling helped propel the company's market share in this key segment from 5 to 20 percent.

Chrysler also sought to infuse this newfound sense of style into the subcompact market, where the Dodge Omni/Plymouth Horizon and then the Dodge Shadow/Plymouth Sundance, soldiered on in relative anonymity. Again, the idea of a new subcompact was foreshadowed in the Neon concept, a cute bug-eyed 2-stroke- powered sedan that featured sliding front and rear doors. The production Neon (a car that had the same name while being sold as either a Dodge or a Plymouth), was much more conventional in appearance with rectangular headlamps and a traditional grille.

The public loved the 1991 show car's round headlights so much (huggable was the adjective used to describe the front end), the Iacocca ordered that the

262-263 Never a major factor in the full-size pickup market, Dodge used bold, semi-truck styling on its new Ram, which it launched in 1994, in an effort to win sales from Ford and GM.

263 top Special show cars that highlight Dodge's

reputation for high-performance cars is one way the division hopes to draw attention to its mid-size Stratus. The Stratus sports Dodge's trademark cross-hair grille and horizontal headlamp treatments similar to those of the larger Intrepid.

front end be restyled to incorporate the bug-eyed look. The Neon was launched in 1995 with two body styles, a coupe and sedan, and between Dodge and Plymouth sold nearly 300,000 units.

A year later, Chrysler used the same cab-forward philosophy on its mid-size Dodge Spirit and Plymouth Acclaim, replacing them with the so-called "cloud" cars—the Chrysler Cirrus, Dodge Stratus and Plymouth Breeze. Riding on a 108-in. wheelbase, the Plymouth Breeze was sold as an entry-level vehicle with a 132 bhp 2.0-liter four, while the Stratus and Cirrus offered step-up models powered by base 150 bhp 2.4-liter 4-cylinder engines or an optional 168 bhp 2.5-liter V-6 engine.

Also in 1996, Chrysler did a complete redesign of the minivan since its introduction in 1984 (although the company did update the original with a slight re-skin and new dash in 1991). This new generation "NS" minivan had a much sleeker shape and, for the first time, a rear driver's side sliding door.

The improvements allowed Chrysler to keep its grip on a lion's share of minivan sales with annual volumes topping 600,000 units. In just four short years, the company had remade its entire product line (company officials would boast that the oldest car in the line at that time was the '92 Viper), reintroduced the practice of using concept cars and returned the company to profitability.

In fact, Chrysler's performance caught the eye of Daimler-Benz chairman Jürgen Schrempp, who was interested in merging companies. Bob Eaton, Iacocca's handpicked successor, had recently fended off a 1996 hostile takeover bid by investor Kirk Kerkorian.

Not coincidentally, Kerkorian was being helped by Iacocca, who wanted to return to the helm of the company.

Not wanting to face yet another financial crisis like the 1991-92 downturn, Eaton agreed to Schrempp's overture and in May 1999, Chrysler ceased to exist—it was now part of DaimlerChrysler AG. Although billed as a merger of equals, it soon became apparent that the German company had acquired the American firm.

Eaton retired and was replaced by Tom Stallkamp, who still clung to the merger-of-equals concept. He was soon forced out and replaced by another American, Jim Holden. The downturn Eaton had feared finally arrived, and when Holden used incentives on the company's newly redesigned 2001 minivans, he was out. Schrempp installed a trusted aide, Dieter Zetsche, a veteran of Mercedes-Benz and Freightliner, to run the American unit.

264 top and 264-265
In 1983, GM Chairman Roger
B. Smith announced the
formation of a new division
called Saturn, which would build
cars to rival imports. The first
Saturns were launched in

1990 as a two-door coupe
(below, a 1992 model) and a
sedan. Saturn would later add
a wagon version (above) to its
lineup of small import fighters
built at an all-new plant near
Nashville, Tennessee.

Crisis at GM

Meanwhile, across town, chaos reigned. General Motors, which had weathered the 1981 downturn with moderate losses compared to those of Ford and Chrysler, was facing its first true financial crisis since founder Billy Durant's second ouster back in 1920. Roger Smith's reorganization of engineering and manufacturing, costly acquisitions like EDS and Hughes, and the huge investment in Saturn had yet to pay off.

While Saturn's intent was laudable—to find a way to beat the Japanese at their own game with a clean sheet operation—in practice it turned out to be a far more daunting and costly task to build a new brand from the ground up. With its greenfield

production plant in Tennessee and separate corporate culture designed to embrace the world's best practices while leaving behind the worst habits from GM, Saturn did benefit from this fresh approach, designing a stylish car that had scratch-resistant plastic body panels and state-of-the-art spaceframe construction.

At the same time, Saturn was isolated. There was no way for its team approach to filter back into the GM system, which was already suspicious and envious of this corporate fair-haired child that was consuming product development money. Not helping matters was the fact that the goals for Saturn's success were being changed, with initial volume forecasts lowered from 500,000 to 250,000 units annually and a development program that took 7 years, far longer than the industry average of 48 months. Introduced as a '91 model, the Saturn was an interesting car but didn't give Honda or Toyota pause to worry. It was launched as a 2-door coupe riding on a 99.2-in. wheelbase and a 4-door sedan on a 102.4-in. wheelbase. Power came from a 1.9-liter four-cylinder engine that made 85 bhp with the base sohc head and 123 bhp with optional dual overhead cams. The lower output models were called the SL Coupe and SL-1 Sedan, while the more powerful versions were the SC Coupe and SL-2 Sedan. Production ramp up was slow with only 48,629 built in 1991, 169,959 in '92 and 244,621 in '93. Sales would peak at just over 310,000 units in 1997.

Although Saturn didn't send imports packing, it did offer a refreshing change in how domestic cars were sold with a low-pressure environment, "nodicker" stickers and no rebates or lease deals. Unfortunately, lagging sales in the late 1990s helped draw Saturn back into GM's orbit. Its product development staff was re-integrated into corporate platform teams and a second model, the L-Series, was introduced in 2000. It was a re-bodied Opel Vectra built at a GM plant in Wilmington, Delaware rather than at Saturn's Spring Hill, Tennessee factory. Later models, the VUE sport/utility and ION subcompact, shared the same architecture as Chevrolet models. And in 2003 the company began offering rebates for the first time.

As Saturn was getting off to its slow start, the rest of GM's business was struggling. In 1988 the new generation of W-body/GM10 intermediates bowed to replace the aging Olds Cutlass, Buick Regal and Pontiac Grand Prix. Two-door coupes had always been the most successful variants of these mid-market cars, but market researchers had missed a significant shift to sedans. When the GM10 bowed, the new models were coupes precisely at the time when 4-door models were in demand. It wouldn't be until almost two years later that the 4-door versions would bow along with a Chevy entrant called Lumina.

Just as Chrysler design was beginning to turn heads, GM design was causing others to scratch theirs. Chuck Jordan, who was GM's fourth design vice president, replacing Bill Mitchell's successor, Irv Rybicki. One of Jordan's first efforts was the full-size Chevy Caprice in 1991. Its rounded shape and semi-skirted rear wheels was reminiscent of the step-down Hudson. The Caprice was nicknamed by some "the whale." It would take a performance version of the car called the Impala SS, with conventional rear wheel wells, a lower ride height and a more potent 250 bhp 5.7-liter V-8 in 1994 to set the car's looks right.

Another styling misfire came in the booming mini-van market. While the rear-drive Chevy Astro van had met with some success, especially with those who needed towing capability, the taller truck-based van didn't appeal to buyers of the car-based Chrysler mini-van. Looking to leapfrog Chrysler, GM developed a space-age looking minivan that featured aluminum spaceframe construction and plastic body panels. These "Dust Buster" minivans, which earned the nickname because they resembled Black & Decker's hand-held vacuum cleaner, were launched as the Chevy Lumina APV, Pontiac Trans Sport and Oldsmobile Silhouette. Riding on a 109.8-in. wheelbase, GM's minivan was powered by a rather anemic 3.1-liter V-6 making 120 bhp. In 1992, a 165 bhp 3.8-liter V-6 was added as an optional engine.

The long pointy nose and steeply raked A-pillars of the new minivan compromised front visibility. It

266 top and 266-267 Trucks and minivans became important moneymakers for the auto industry. Oldsmobile, which had sold cars exclusively for most of its 100-year history,

offered the Silhouette minivan (above) and the Bravada sport-utility vehicle. Interiors on minivans offer limousine-like refinement with such features as leather-clad Captain's chairs.

266 bottom The Olds Silhouette pioneered the on-board entertainment system for rear-seat passengers, first offering a video-cassette player and eventually moving to videodisk systems.

turned out that people didn't buy minivans for their styling, but rather practicality. In 1994 GM shortened the nose to improve visibility, but the front-drive APVs never seriously contended with Chrysler's offerings in this segment. In 1996 a more conventional front-drive minivan with a metal body was introduced to replace the APV.

When Smith retired as chairman in 1990 he was succeeded by Robert Stempel, one of the engineers who helped create the catalytic converter in the 1970s and who later served as general manager of Pontiac, Opel and Chevrolet. Second in command was another engineer, Lloyd Reuss, who was president. It was the only time in the company's history that the top two spots were filled by "car guys"—traditionally the top job was held by someone from the finance staff, while the president was usually from the product side. When Stempel was only a little over a year into

his tenure, the product miscues coupled with a $4.5 billion loss caught up with him, and roused the GM board of directors to demand quick fixes.

At first he was reluctant, forecasting stronger sales in 1992, but it wasn't enough to mollify investors. GM's stock tumbled to $27 a share, a four-year low. He later announced a plan in which GM would shed 80,000 workers and close 21 plants. Reuss, who was head of North American Operations, fell afoul of board member John Smale, the former chairman of Procter & Gamble.

By April, the board demoted Reuss, who took early retirement, and by October, Stempel was forced to resign. Jack Smith, a finance staffer who was vice-chairman of international operations replaced Reuss and then was named Stempel's replacement. Smale would exert tremendous influence over GM's day-to-day management for the balance of the

decade, shifting Sloan's vision of marketing through divisional identities to a packaged-goods approach that emphasized individual models as brands to be managed. During this period, product development responsibilities were shifted away from the divisions, and the once powerful heads of those units, who were traditionally corporate vice presidents, would now be mere managers. With Smale's blessing, Jack Smith hired Ron Zarrella, a top marketing executive with Bausch & Lomb to run GM's North American Operations. Using Procter & Gamble as a model, Zarrella sought to market individual car lines with little or no attention paid to divisional identity. He also hired brand managers with consumer product rather than automotive experience to market GM cars. During this period, GM's market share fell to under 30 percent for the first time in the company's modern history.

Oldsmobile's Slide to Oblivion

One of the indirect results of this change was the eventual demise of Oldsmobile, the oldest surviving American marque. From a record high of 1,066,122 sales in 1985, Oldsmobile had imploded to 389,173 by 1992. During the Stempel affair, Olds' new general manager, John Rock, had sought assurances from the board that Olds wouldn't be scrapped. He never received them. Nonetheless, that didn't stop Rock and the product development team at GM from putting together a survival program for Oldsmobile called the Centennial Plan, which was expected to hit its stride during the division's centennial celebration in 1997.

Oldsmobile was seen as an old man's car, a perception reinforced rather than dispelled by a series of ads touting the company's new lineup as "Not Your Father's Oldsmobile." Even though Olds had a broad product range, it included some misfires including the Silhouette minivan and the Achieva (sister car to the even uglier Buick Skylark and the much better received Pontiac Grand Am, Chevy Corsica and Beretta).

The division's comeback hopes were pinned on the Aurora, a sleek V-8 front-drive 4-door sedan in which the only divisional badging was the name Oldsmobile etched discreetly on the radio faceplate. The Aurora was about as unique as a car could be for GM, sharing the same G-body architecture as the swoopy Buick Riviera, which was a coupe. From there, the two cars couldn't be more different in character. The Buick featured V-6 power, while the Olds used a 4.0-liter variant of Cadillac's 4.6-liter dohc V-8 Northstar engine. The Olds produced 250 bhp, giving it the ability to crack the 9-second mark in 0-60 mph acceleration. It was a strong out of the block with about 48,000 sales in its first year, but the number dropped in half almost immediately and stayed there, the victim of a $35,000 sticker price.

The Aurora was followed by the Intrigue, a W-body replacement for the many Cutlass variants that had sprung up over the years. Powered initially by the ohv 3.8-liter V-6 with 200 bhp, Intrigue eventually got an exclusive 215 bhp 3.5-liter dohc V-6. It was followed in 1999 by the Alero, a more handsomely styled replacement for the Achieva. Even though Olds was given the Bravada, a version of GM's mid-size SUV, Olds sales continued to stagnate. The 98 was dropped, the 88 restyled and then eventually, an all-new V-8 Aurora was introduced in 2001 with an additional V-6 version to replace the 88. Olds' car lines had been reduced to three models. In December 2000, GM announced that it would phase out the division by the end of the 2004 model year.

268 As part of Oldsmobile's failed revival plan, it developed three very modern sedans, the flagship Aurora (top), the mid-size Intrigue (center) and the compact Alero (bottom). Unfortunately, the cars failed to turn sales around for the division.

269 top Large sport-utility vehicles, like this Ford Expedition, have replaced the station wagon as the family vehicle of choice.

With three-row seating, V-8 power and all-wheel drive, these vehicles have changed the face of American motoring.

269 bottom Ford set the industry standard for design with its aerodynamically styled Taurus in 1986. A decade later, it tried to repeat history with an even more radical look that failed to capture the public's imagination.

Ford Sticks to Business

Even though Ford suffered heavy losses at the beginning of the 1990s, it had stuck closer to its core business of building cars during the 1980s and decided to hang onto cash as a way to ride out the business cycle.

This conservative approach was reflected in the company's product program in the early part of the decade. It had the best selling vehicle in the business since 1982 with its F-Series pickup. The radical shift to aero styling with the Thunderbird and Taurus had now become the industry standard. Rather than mess with success, the 1992 Taurus was an evolutionary rather than a revolutionary redesign. A performance model of the Taurus, the Super High Output or SHO had a 220 bhp 3.0-liter V-6 and a 5-speed manual, a combination that helped it achieve cult status among car enthusiasts.

Taurus also influenced the facelifts of the Tempo and Escort, both cars received grille-free front fascias and flush headlamps. Ford also relied on its European-designed Mondeo to replace its aging Ford Tempo/Mercury Topaz. The new cars were called Contour and Mystique and were launched in 1995. Unfortunately, these compacts were smaller than traditional American models, especially in rear-seat room, and never became big sellers. Eventually Ford converted the factory that built these mid-size cars over to building the Escape, a compact SUV based on Mazda 626 mechanicals.

The biggest miscalculation by far, though, was the 1996 redesign of the Ford Taurus. Tom Gale's cab-forward LH models had eclipsed Jack Telnack's swoopy design for the original Taurus. In an attempt to recapture the design lead, Telnack introduced an even rounder, more aero Taurus and Sable that sported oval headlamps, an oval backlight and oval shapes throughout the dash. Although the company continued to sell in excess of 400,000 of the cars per year, the design was thoroughly panned by auto critics and Ford had to rely heavily on fleet sales to move the iron. The car was redesigned in 2000 to give it a more conventional backlight and front-end treatment.

Ford's full-size Crown Victoria and Mercury Grand Marquis retained their traditional American styling and actually prospered when Chevrolet radically restyled the Caprice in 1991 and later when GM dropped all its full-size rear-drive cars in favor of SUVs. That left the fleet market, particularly among law enforcement and taxis, almost exclusively to Ford.

In the minivan market, Ford had a false start with its rear-drive truck-based Aerostar. On its second try, rather than trying to break new ground in the segment, it did what any good Japanese company would do. It took apart Chrysler's minivan, studied it and built its own new, improved version. Based on the Taurus platform, the Windstar was introduced in the 1995 model year. Meanwhile, Ford collaborated with Nissan to develop a minivan for Mercury called the Villager, a sibling to the Japanese company's Quest. That van was actually built in Ford's Avon Lake, Ohio assembly plant using Nissan engines.

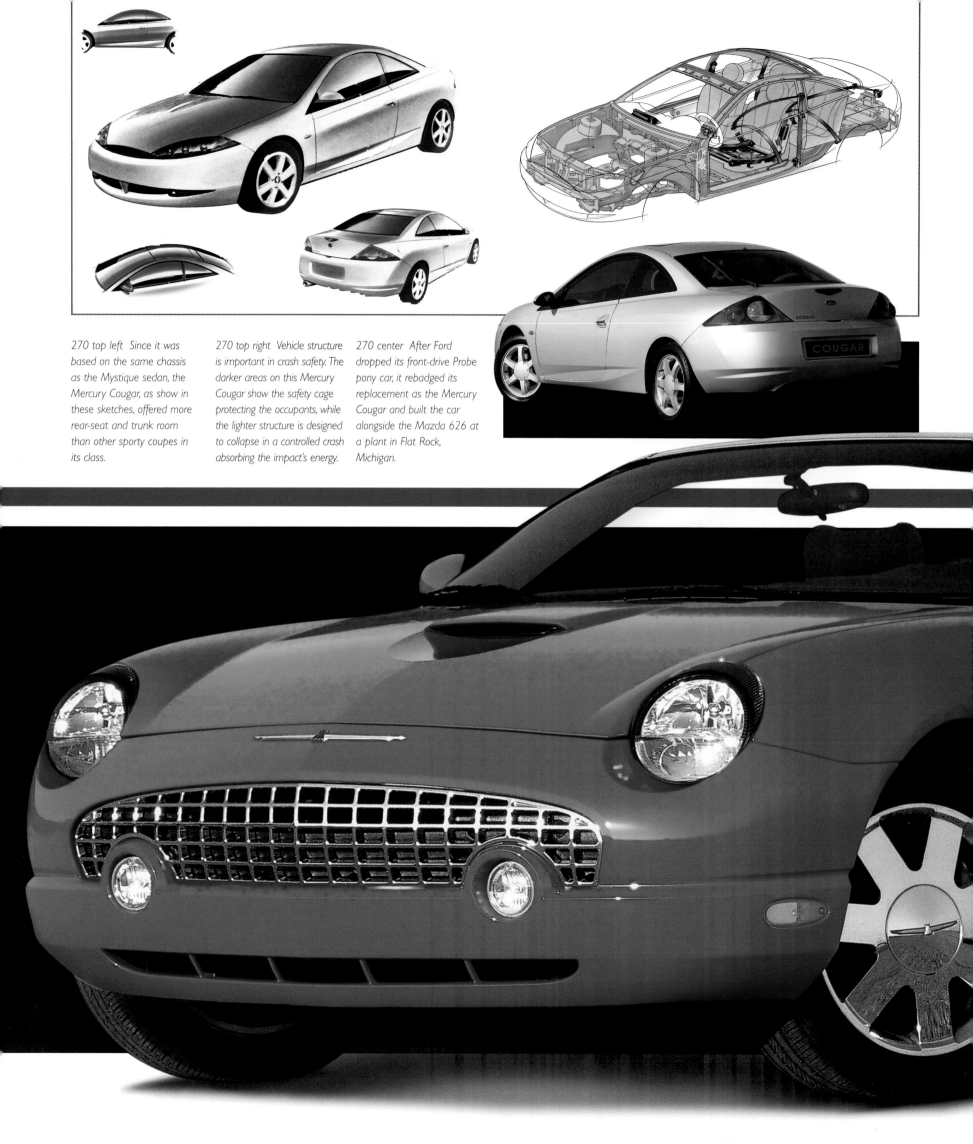

270 top left Since it was based on the same chassis as the Mystique sedan, the Mercury Cougar, as show in these sketches, offered more rear-seat and trunk room than other sporty coupes in its class.

270 top right Vehicle structure is important in crash safety. The darker areas on this Mercury Cougar show the safety cage protecting the occupants, while the lighter structure is designed to collapse in a controlled crash absorbing the impact's energy.

270 center After Ford dropped its front-drive Probe pony car, it rebadged its replacement as the Mercury Cougar and built the car alongside the Mazda 626 at a plant in Flat Rock, Michigan.

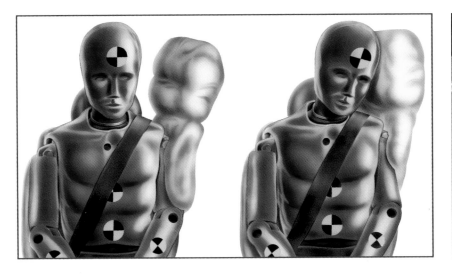

270-271 After having the Thunderbird grow from a two-seater to a five-passenger coupe, Ford decided to return to the car's two-seater roots. More cruiser than performer, it's offered only with an automatic transmission. The Thunderbird carries a lot of styling flavor of the 1955 original, including the turquoise-colored badges and egg-crate grille.

271 top left Safety has become a major selling point, even with sporty cars like the Mercury Cougar, which offered seat-mounted side-impact airbags.

271 top right Although the Cougar was a sporty car, it relied on the same MacPherson strut front suspension as the more mundane Mercury Mystique and Ford Contour sedans.

Another joint venture of note was the Ford's tie-up with Mazda to produce the Probe, originally designed as a front-drive replacement for the Mustang. However, the outcry over the changeover of America's iconic rear-drive pony car to front-drive was too much, so the Probe name (which had been used on a series of aerodynamic studies) was dusted off and given to the new car. Probe was never able to surpass Mustang in sales and as was dropped by 1998.

In the hope of developing a new niche by playing off the same nostalgia that saved the rear-drive Mustang, Ford re-introduced the Thunderbird in 2000 as a two-place, V-8 rear-drive convertible. Built off the Lincoln LS platform, the retro-styled T-Bird met with mixed reviews. Failing to sell to its projected annual volume of 25,000 units per year, Ford announced plans to phase the Thunderbird out by 2006. Mercury was equally conservative with the Grand Marquis and Sable, the heart of its franchise. In the small car market, it sold the Tracer, its version of the Ford Escort/Mazda 323, but only as a 4-door sedan and wagon.

Mercury attempted to import a front-drive 2-seat sports car called Capri from Australia from 1991-94, but the anemic performance from the 100 bhp 1.6-liter four, poor quality and the availability of the Miata, a real rear-drive sports car from Mazda, doomed the project.

By the mid-'90s the Thunderbird-based Cougar was also getting long in the tooth. Rather than restyle the car, Mercury dropped it in favor of a Mystique-based 2-door Cougar coupe built at Mazda's Flat Rock, Michigan assembly plant.

By now, the European influence on Ford's design was being felt, especially at Lincoln. In 1993 an all-new Mark VIII was introduced with a sleek aero shape that still managed to pay homage to its lineage thanks to a vertical bar grille treatment and ever-so-slight Continental kit hump in the rear decklid. Riding on the Thunderbird/Cougar 113-in. wheelbase, the Mark VIII was 4 in. longer and more than 3 in. wider than its siblings. Under the hood was a 4.6-liter V-8 making 280 bhp. A sporty version called the LSC was offered in 1996 and, thanks to dual exhausts, made 290 bhp.

The Continental, which changed over to front-drive with V-6 power in 1988, was overhauled for the 1995 model year. In addition to its clean, sleek, design, it was fitted with a 260 bhp 4.6-liter V-8 driving the front wheels. Eventually the car would be deemed redundant and dropped at the end of the 2002 model year. Lincoln also set its sights on the BMW 5-Series with a new mid-size rear-drive entry called the LS. Introduced in 2000, the European-inspired sport sedan rode on a 114.5-in. wheelbase; it was initially offered with a choice of 210 bhp 3.6-liter V-6 with 5-speed manual or automatic, or a 250 bhp 3.9-liter V-8 automatic. Its chief competitor in the American ranks was the Cadillac Catera, a version of the German-built Opel Omega introduced in 1997. It offered a 200 bhp 3.0-liter V-6 as its only engine. The car was replaced in 2003 by the U.S.-built rear-drive CTS which boasts a 220 bhp 3.2-liter V-6. Ford's strategy of hunkering down and tweaking its product line paid huge dividends. In the process, the company went on a buying binge, acquiring Aston Martin, Volvo and Land Rover, as well as a controlling interest in Mazda. But Ford wasn't immune to boardroom intrigue. There was a smooth transition from Donald Petersen to Red Poling at the beginning of the decade and then the company was handed over to Alex Trotman, who came to Detroit through Ford of Europe. Trotman decided to reorganize all of Ford product development into a

global operation called Ford 2000. However, the reorganization proved unwieldy and when Trotman handed the reins over to Jacques Nasser, his successor set about reorganizing the company yet again. The fast-moving 51-year-old Australian-born executive envisioned Ford as a global transportation provider with interests in new cars, rentals, aftermarket service and even dealerships. Nasser, who was behind the acquisitions of both Volvo and Land Rover, overreached and the company's fortunes reversed. In late 2001, Nasser was removed and William Ford, Jr., the son of William Clay Ford and great-grandson of Henry Ford, became chairman and chief executive officer.

272-273 and 273 top
Lincoln hoped to appeal to
a younger set of buyers with
a front-drive, V-8 powered
Continental, which had more
contemporary styling and
advanced technology than
the larger and more
traditional rear-drive Town
Car. Even though the
Continental had smart styling
and a roomy cabin, Lincoln
found greater success in
selling SUVs like its full-size
Navigator. The Continental
was eventually dropped
when the Town Car was
redesigned in 2003.

Performance Rules

The introduction of the Dodge Viper in 1992 was a not-so-subtle way of saying that performance was back again. While the 1980s saw a resurgence of performance models, many of them were turbocharged fours and sixes. The 1990s would be about the wholesale return of V-8s and the introduction of a V-10 in the Viper.

The Viper continued to evolve during the 1990s. Its original premise was not high-tech but "yestertech" a word coined by Bob Lutz to describe the raw nature of this 400 bhp beast. In addition to side pipes, the original Viper had side curtains instead of roll-up windows, did not have exterior door handles and, if it rained, a makeshift top called a toupee had to be fashioned out of canvas and aluminum tubes. In 1996 a coupe version of the Viper called the

GTS debuted. The exhaust was now routed through the back of the car and there were power windows, exterior door handles and creature comforts like air conditioning. A year later the roadster was reintroduced with roll-up windows and all the amenities of the GTS. The GTS became an FIA racer, winning the GTS class at Le Mans for three years running, from 1998-2000. Viper was redesigned completely for the 2003 model year, returned to its original roadster

roots with a conventional manual top, side exhausts and 500 bhp. Although not as extreme as the Viper, the Corvette had been making steady gains in performance and refinement. In 1992 it offered the LT1, a 5.7-liter pushrod V-8 that boasted 300 bhp. That engine soon made its way into the Camaro and Firebird tuned to produce 275 bhp. The next big step up would be the C5 or fifth-generation Corvette launched in 1997. This all-new car rode on a 104.5-in.

wheelbase, 8.3-in. longer than that of the car it replaced. Best of all was its new LS1 5.7-liter V-8 that made 345 bhp. Introduced as a coupe and convertible, the Corvette soon added an entry-level hardtop coupe. That latter model formed the basis of the 2001 Z06, a lighter and more powerful model fitted with the LS6 V-8, producing at first 385 bhp and then 405 bhp a year later. In addition, power of the base LS1 Corvette had climbed to 350 bhp.

274-275 The original Viper roadster lacked such amenities as exterior door handles and side windows. That was remedied when the Viper GTS coupe was introduced in 1996. The coupe went on to dominate GT racing at Le Mans.

Meanwhile, the Mustang would outlive both the Probe and Cougar front-drive entries thanks to a major rework of the car in 1994 that kept the aging Fox platform fresh. In addition to an all-new skin, the Mustang benefited from numerous improvements that reduced noise, vibration and harshness. Still, the car retained its live-axle setup and the 5.0-liter pushrod V-8, while output remained the same at 215 bhp in the GT and 305 bhp for the Cobra. In 1999 the Cobra got an independent rear suspension and a power boost to a claimed 320 bhp, though subsequent testing revealed much lower output and the cars were recalled for modifications to boost them to the advertised horsepower. As a result of this snafu, there was no 2000 model year Mustang Cobra. Meanwhile, the stock GT saw its output rise to 260 bhp. For the 2003 model year, the Cobra returned with a supercharged 4.6-liter V-8 boasting 390 bhp.

276 top With no Corvette or Viper in its stable, Ford decided to take the performance of the Mustang Cobra up a notch in 2000 with a special R or racing version. Note the side exhaust.

276-277 After 25 years based on the Fox platform, Ford redesigned the Mustang for the 2005 model year. Using an all-new chassis, the car retains its traditional solid rear-axle suspension. Note the rear quarter glass, last seen in 1967.

277 top The Mustang Cobra R features large aerodynamic add-ons such as the rear wing, sill extensions and a front air dam with an integrated splitter. The Cobra R was powered by a 5.4-liter V-8 making 385 bhp.

A Retro Revolution

As the 20th century drew to a close, it seemed that automakers were intent on looking backwards as much as they had looked forward 50 years earlier.

While German automakers had begun the retro trend with the VW New Beetle and the Porsche Boxster, which was heavily influenced by the 550 Spyder, Chrysler was one of the first on the retro bandwagon on this side of the Atlantic. The company's premiere retro ride was the 1997 Prowler, a modern take on the classic American hot rod. With huge 20-in. rear wheels and fendered 19-in. front wheels, the Prowler was powered by a 215 bhp 3.5-liter V-6 mated to an automatic transmission, not really the stuff of true hot rodders. But the outrageous styling, limited production numbers and relatively affordable $40,000 sticker made a huge impression on boulevard cruisers. Prowler would also have the distinction of being the last Plymouth and actually lived for a model year beyond the division's 2001 demise as a Chrysler.

278-279 The Plymouth Prowler has the distinction of being a hot rod built by a major manufacturer. After Plymouth was phased out following the 1999 model year, Prowlers were sold as Chryslers.

279 top Although it looked cool, the V-6 Prowler lacked both performance and practicality and never was able to rise above being merely a curiosity.

A much more practical application of retro styling came with the 2001 Chrysler PT Cruiser. Based on a modified Neon platform, the PT Cruiser was a tall wagon powered by a 150 bhp 2.4-liter four-cylinder engine. While hatchbacks have had a spotty track record in America, the retro hot-rod looks of the PT Cruiser hid its functionality. The vehicle's tall roof and high seating position also gave the driver a much more secure feeling when surrounded by pickups, vans and SUVs. With base prices starting at $16,000

and well-equipped versions listed at just under $20,000, the PT Cruiser sold out its first-year production run of 130,000 units and had a waiting list for 2002 units. Chevrolet launched its own retro-styled vehicle, the SSR, a 2-seat convertible pickup. Powered by a 6.0-liter V-8 making over 300 bhp, the SSR represented the blending of two major influences on American vehicles, nostalgic styling and trucks. It then followed with its own take on the PT Cruiser, the Chevy HHR.

280 Chrysler created a breakthrough vehicle in the small car market with its retro-styled PT Cruiser, an entry that combined the utility of a minivan with the efficiency of a compact sedan. The PT in the PT Cruiser name was said to stand for Personal Transportation. Its retro looks were said to have been inspired by the 1937 Ford.

281 top The first new model to come off the PT Cruiser platform is something completely unexpected, a convertible. The four-door hatchback has become a two-door drop top.

281 bottom With its bulging fenders and panel van greenhouse, the PT Cruiser created a sensation when it was introduced in 2001.

PT CRUISER

Keep On Truckin'

If the 1990s were a golden age for performance vehicles, then it was a platinum age for trucks. During the 1990s, the sport-utility vehicle market has exploded. More than 2 million SUVs were being sold annually by the turn of the century and manufacturers offered a full range of these vehicles from the compact-sized Ford Escape and Jeep Liberty to full-size monsters like the Ford Excursion and Hummer H2. Some were car-based, like the Escape or Saturn VUE, which used transversely mounted four or V-6 powerplants. Others were more traditional body-on-frame truck construction like GM's mid-size Chevy Trailerblazer and GMC Envoy or Ford Explorer and Mercury Mountaineer.

Much of GM's success in the late 1990s was based on the huge bet it made on trucks. In 1997 it converted its last plant that built full-size rear-drive sedans and wagons in Arlington, Texas over to full-size Chevy Tahoes and GMC Yukons. GM has since expanded its SUV lines to include a Cadillac SUV called Escalade, and introduced two new sport-utility trucks that had 4-door cabs and small cargo beds. Both the Chevy Avalanche and the Cadillac Escalade EXT were huge hits.

282 and 283 bottom Looking to cater to macho off-roaders, Chevy created the Avalanche SUT, a sport-utility truck that has a rear bulkhead that opens to expand the cargo bed's carrying capacity. The

series of photos on the left shows the flexibility of the Avalanche's cargo area. In addition to storage bins in the bed itself, the cargo area is covered by a lockable tonneau.

283 top The Chevy Avalanche also spawned a Cadillac sibling called the Escalade EXT. The Escalade incorporates the division's new sharp-edged styling theme that sets it apart from

the Chevy. The Cadillac Escalade EXT has the same flexible cargo bed and opening bulkhead, called a mid-gate that allows long objects to be carried partially inside the vehicle.

284 top In 2000, Jeep introduced the Commander, a full-size SUV powered by a fuel cell. The Commander project was abandoned since the fuel cell and its on-board reformer to convert gasoline to hydrogen was considered to be too complex and expensive to put into production.

284 bottom Dodge developed the Power Wagon concept for the 2000 North American International Auto Show to test a bolder design theme for future Dodge Trucks, including the Ram and Dakota, and to test a new diesel engine that burned a synthetic fuel.

284-285 The Jeep Commander has the traditional seven-slat grille design of all Jeeps. Despite being as big as a Hummer, Jeep touted the fuel cell powerplant as being environmentally friendly.

Eye on the Environment

For the most part, the American manufacturers kept pace with ever-tightening emission requirements and were given a break on Corporate Average Fuel Economy, which remained fairly stable. The only curveball tossed the industry's way was a California mandate that 2 percent of all major manufacturers fleet include zero-emission cars (essentially electrics) by 1998. A court challenge put the requirement on hold, although GM did attempt to reinvent the electric car with the EV1. Introduced as the Impact concept vehicle at the 1991 Detroit show, the EV1 was leased through Saturn dealers to California residents, beginning in December 1996. The purpose-built 2-seater had one of the slickest body shapes of a production vehicle (its coefficient of drag was 0.29) and was powered by 26 lead acid batteries that drove a traction motor connected to the front wheels. The EV1's rear track was actually narrower than the front, to help improve aerodynamics. Even though the cars were relatively quick, capable of 0-60 mph acceleration in less than 8 sec., the lead acid batteries had limited range of about 60 to 70 miles. A switch in later models to nickel hydride batteries improved that distance slightly, to about 100 miles between recharges.

Building just under 1000 units, GM kept the cars in service until announcing in late 2002 that it would end the lease program and take back all the cars. The company then unveiled an ambitious program of building hybrids, as many as 1 million gasoline/electric combines annually by 2007, in order to meet these zero emission requirements.

Ford introduced its first hybrid vehicle in 2004, applying the technology to its Escape SUV. Daimler-Chrysler, after first announcing a hybrid Dodge Durango SUV, shelved the program in favor of clean diesel technology to deliver higher fuel economy in its truck fleet.

DaimlerChrysler's approach to alternative fuels was showcased in a trio of concept cars unveiled at the 1999 Detroit auto show. These concepts included a natural gas Dodge Charger, a 4-door sedan with retro styling inspired by the original muscle car; the Dodge Power Wagon, a diesel-powered 4x4 retro pickup; and the Jeep Commander, a full-sized SUV powered by an electric fuel cell.

Long term, all three automakers looked to fuel cells to replace the internal combustion engine. Ford developed a version of its Focus subcompact powered by the technology for use in vehicle fleets, while DaimlerChrysler concentrated its research in Germany with Mercedes-Benz, developing a fuel cell for the A-Class car. GM has gone through two iterations of its Autonomy project, which fit all the fuel cell components into the chassis of the car. This so-called skateboard wore a variety of bodies—the first was a 2-seat sports car; the second, called Hy-Wire, which incorporated an advanced drive-by-wire system, was a 4-passenger cross between a station wagon and minivan. GM has hopes of building as many as 1 million fuel-cell vehicles by 2010.

Just as the 20th century began with many different technologies, from gas to steam to electric, competing to become the dominant force, it seemed that the 21st century would begin much the same way with the dominance of the internal combustion gasoline engine being challenged by hybrids, diesels and fuel cells.

286 Dodge spokesman Edward Hermann is followed up a flight of stairs by the Dodge Durango, a mid-size SUV based off the division's Dakota pickup truck. The Durango was one of the first SUVs in its class to offer three-row seating.

287 top left GM was one of the first manufacturers to get back into producing electric vehicles since the early days of the industry. As part of its EV1 test, it leased rather than sold the vehicles to customers.

287 top right The EV1 originally was equipped with lead acid batteries, which gave the car a range of 70-80 miles between charges. Later, nickel metal hydride batteries increased the range to about 100 miles.

287 bottom Although Toyota and Honda were the first to offer hybrid gas/electric cars to the American public, Ford offered the first hybrid SUV in this 2005 Ford Escape. In Ford's system, the vehicle's 4-cylinder engine powers the front wheels, while the rear is driven by an electric motor fed by a battery pack.

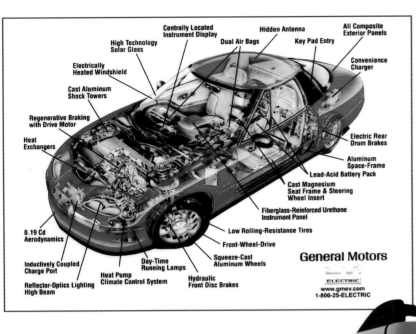

Centrally Located
Instrument Display
High Technology
Solar Glass
Dual Air Bags
Hidden Antenna
Key Pad Entry
All Composite
Exterior Panels
Electrically
Heated Windshield
Convenience
Charger
Cast Aluminum
Shock Towers
Regenerative Braking
with Drive Motor
Electric Rear
Drum Brakes
Heat
Exchangers
Aluminum
Space-Frame
Lead-Acid Battery Pack
Cast Magnesium
Seat Frame & Steering
Wheel Insert
Fiberglass-Reinforced Urethane
Instrument Panel
0.19 Cd
Aerodynamics
Low Rolling-Resistance Tires
Front-Wheel-Drive
Inductively Coupled
Charge Port
Day-Time
Running Lamps
Squeeze-Cast
Aluminum Wheels
Reflector-Optics Lighting
High Beam
Heat Pump
Climate Control System
Hydraulic
Front Disc Brakes

General Motors
EV ELECTRIC
www.gmev.com
1-800-25-ELECTRIC

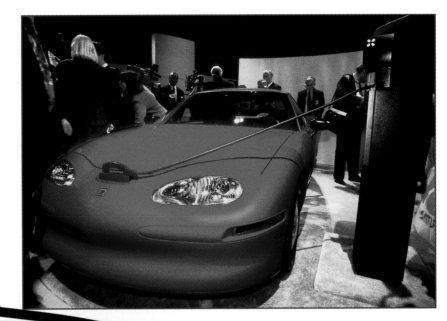

CHAPTER 10

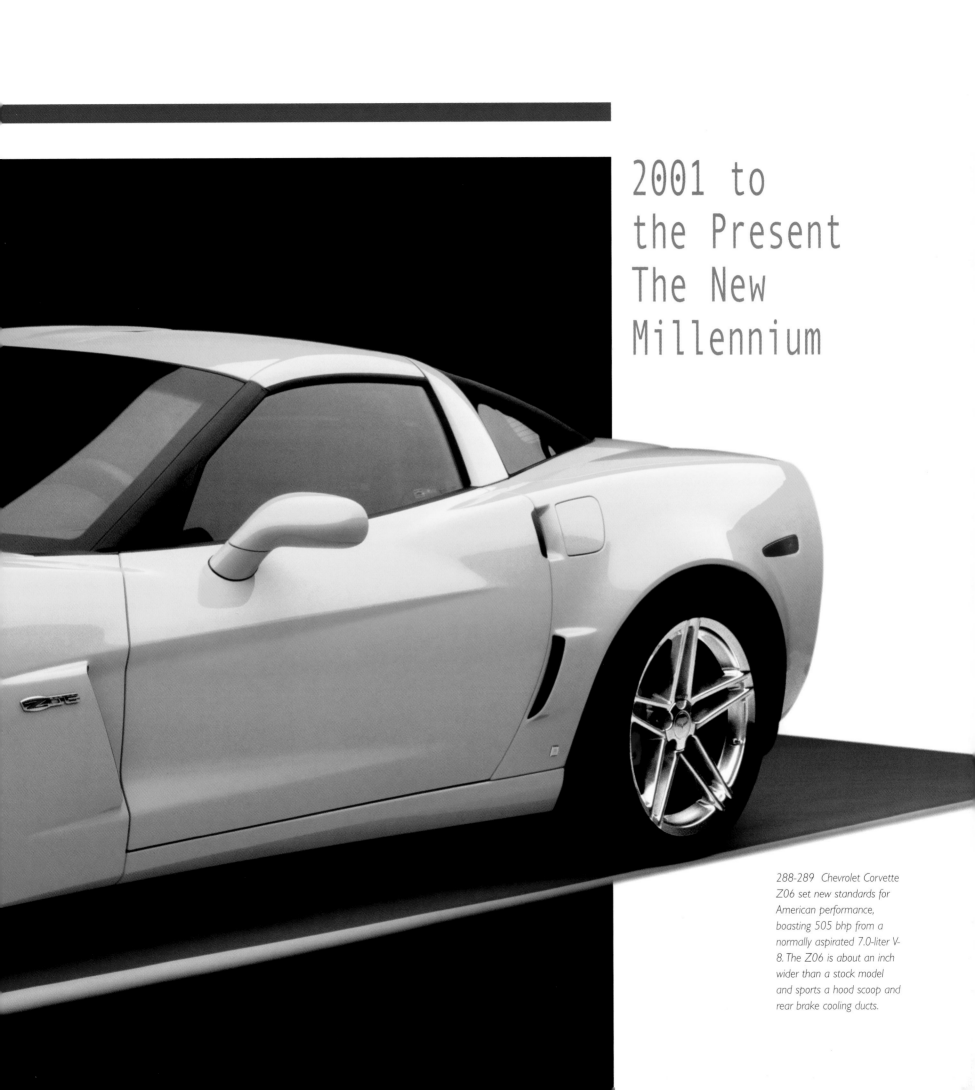

2001 to
the Present
The New
Millennium

288-289 *Chevrolet Corvette Z06 set new standards for American performance, boasting 505 bhp from a normally aspirated 7.0-liter V-8. The Z06 is about an inch wider than a stock model and sports a hood scoop and rear brake cooling ducts.*

The Rebirth of Rear Drive

The dawning of a new century brought with it a myriad of challenges—economic recession, higher oil prices and continuing shifts in consumer preferences due rising gas prices.

While some legendary names like Plymouth and Oldsmobile faded off into oblivion, others like Cadillac and Chrysler retooled their images with bold styling and a return to rear-wheel drive. Existing icons like Mustang and Corvette were reinvigorated with head-turning designs. Trucks remain popular, but their hold over fickle customers began to loosen as high gas prices fueled a shift back to conventional passenger cars.

Cadillac, hoping not to become irrelevant in a luxury market dominated by traditional European marques and upstart Japanese makes like Lexus and Infiniti, took a huge gamble in developing a new rear-drive platform codenamed Sigma, from which it retooled almost its entire lineup.

Key to Cadillac's success was styling that was uniquely American, rather than cloned European design. Under GM Design Vice President Wayne Cherry, a new design form called "Art & Science" was born. The look was edgy, with sharp creases, a large shield-shaped grille, stacked headlights and vertical taillights. This new look was introduced in the 2003 model year on the CTS sedan, which replaced the European-built Catera. Inspired by the F-117 Swallow stealth fighter, the CTS had a high-tech look that wasn't like anything coming from Europe. Its look was distinctly American and echoed the jet-age styling of 1950s Cadillacs. As Chrysler had discov-

ered with its Ram pickup, the look was polarizing. Either you liked it or you didn't. Fortunately, enough people loved it to make the CTS an unqualified hit, even though the rear-drive car, which rode on a 113.4-in. wheelbase, was powered by a 3.2-liter V-8 that made 220 bhp—barely adequate in the sport sedan segment. A year later, the power was addressed by adding an optional 3.6-liter V-6 making a more respectable 255 bhp.

The Sigma platform would also spawn the SRX, an SUV powered by a choice of the 3.6-liter V-6 or a 4.6-liter Northstar V-8. Completing the trio of Sigma-based product was the STS, a new flagship sedan that replaced the venerable Seville in 2005. The STS, which rides on a wheelbase three inches longer than that of the CTS, offered two engine choices: the 255-bhp 3.6-liter V-6 or a 320-bhp Northstar 4.6-liter V-8.

While Cadillac was busy rebuilding itself, Lincoln's European-influenced styling of the LS was far less distinctive and the car never quite caught on. Even though it shared its basic DEW98 platform with the Jaguar S-Type, upgrades to the British car reduced the commonality of the architecture and sacrificed economies of scale. Rather than spawning other variants like the Sigma platform, the DEW98 was deemed too expensive and inflexible to be of any use. Other than providing the underpinnings for the unsuccessful retro Thunderbird, the LS became an orphan in the Ford system and was dropped after the 2006 model year. The Wixom, Michigan plant that built the car was slated for closure.

290-291 Cadillac introduced its V-Series of high-performance models by wedging a 400-bhp 5.7-liter LS1 V-8. The CTS-V is distinguished by its mesh grille and more aggressive front fascia.

291 top It's all business in the cockpit of the CTS-V with minimal wood trim on the steering wheel and shift knob. Note that the only transmission available is a six-speed manual.

291 bottom The CTS-V rides about an inch lower than the stock model, has stiffer springs and shocks and underwent extensive testing on the famed North Loop (Nordschliefe) of the Nürburgring.

292 top Like its Mercedes-Benz sister division with its AMG line, Chrysler launched its SRT-8 family of Hemi-powered performance vehicles with a version of the 300C. In addition to more power under the hood, the SRT-8 is lower, sports a new front air dam and has larger wheels and tires.

292-293 Dodge entered the four-door executive express segment with its SRT-8 version of the Charger sedan. A large hood scoop announces the presence of a 425-bhp 6.1-liter Hemi V-8 beneath the hood.

Meanwhile, Chrysler, which had staked its fortunes on the advanced front-drive LH architecture, decided it too needed a modern full-size rear-wheel drive car to remain competitive.

Drawing on the synergies of its Daimler-Chrysler parent, the U.S. unit borrowed chassis technology from the Mercedes-Benz E-Class to develop the Chrysler 300, Dodge Magnum and Dodge Charger. This new rear-drive platform, known as LX, like Sigma, would be offered with an all-wheel drive option and for the first time in nearly two decades, a V-8 engine would power a Chrysler car.

The Chrysler 300 sedan and Dodge Magnum station wagon were the first to bow as 2005 models. Riding on a 120-in. wheelbase, both cars came with a standard 2.7-liter V-6 engine producing 190 bhp, while a 3.5-liter V-6 making 250 bhp was optional. But the star of the show was the 340-bhp 5.7-liter Hemi V-8 offered in the 300C and Magnum R/T.

In addition to offering tremendous power, the V-8 was equipped with an electronic engine-management system that would shut down four cylinders under light loads, especially during cruising, to boost fuel economy. The so-called Multi-Displacement System was good for a boost of about 10 percent in highway mileage.

Both cars were striking in appearance. The 300 had a small pillbox-like greenhouse, slab sides and an enormous grille that at first glance looked like a bargain basement Bentley. The Magnum sported a large cross-hair grille inspired by the Ram pickup and a tapered roofline that gave the wagon a sporty flair. Originally, Dodge was to offer only hatchbacks in its lineups, while the Chrysler brand would sell sedans.

That plan quickly unraveled as Dodge dealers demanded a sedan of their own and the company adapted the Magnum wagon body style for European sale, badged as a Chrysler.

In just over 18 months, Dodge developed the Charger sedan, resurrecting the name from a legendary late 1960s muscle car. The purists were aghast that Dodge would put such a revered name on a four-door sedan, although the same enthusiasts barely uttered a peep about the four doors on the 2000 Charger show car.

The Charger had a taller greenhouse than the 300, which improved interior headroom by an inch, and sported a shark nose that gave the front end a much more aggressive appearance than the Magnum.

The side featured an upswept rear fender, a cue from the mid-1950s Chevy Bel Air. The base engine on the Charger was the 250-bhp 3.5-liter V-6, while the 340-bhp 5.7-liter Hemi V-8 was standard on the R/T model.

Executive Express

These new rear-drive sedans opened the door for Cadillac and Chrysler to build high performance versions similar to the legendary BMW M-series and Mercedes-Benz AMG model.

At Chrysler, the Street and Racing Technology (SRT) group developed a potent 6.1-liter Hemi V-8 producing 425 bhp. It used this engine across the board in a series of SRT8 variants of the Chrysler 300C, Dodge Magnum and Dodge Charger. In addition to the beefed-up drive train, the SRT package included larger 20-in. wheels and tires, stiffer spring and shocks and enhanced brakes.

While the 300C and Magnum have understated looks, with small wings and rocker sill extensions, the Charger SRT8, introduced for the 2006 model year, had a much larger wing and a hood scoop.

Cadillac, through GM's Performance Division, developed the V-Series, which began with the 2004 CTS-V. This model was equipped with a 400-bhp LS6 5.7-liter V-8, an engine originally developed for the Corvette Z06. The CTS-V came with a 6-speed manual and featured a larger front fascia, mesh grille and high performance 18-in. wheels and tires.

Two years later, the STS received the V treatment. Although the STS-V had the same aggressive

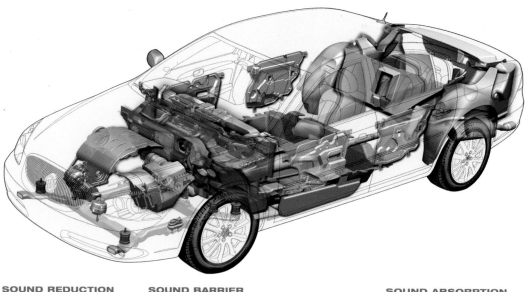

QUIETtuning
TOTAL PACKAGE
BUICK LUCERNE

SOUND REDUCTION COMPONENTS

- Quieter HVAC Module & Ducting
- QuietTuned Induction System
- Noise Reducing Mirrors
- Noise Reducing Tires
- QuietTuned Exhaust System
- Quiet Accessory Drive System

SOUND BARRIER COMPONENTS

- Laminated Vibration Dampening Steel
- Cast Foam Dash Mat, Heavy Weight Barrier Layer
- Exhaust Tunnel Full Length Acoustic Shield
- Enlarged Floor Damping
- Engine Cover
- Hydraulic Engine Mounts
- Isolated Cradle Mounts to Body
- Trunk Barrier
- Water Deflectors
- Laminated Side Glass
- Full Rear Wheelhouse Liners
- Rear Wheelhouse Insulators

SOUND ABSORPTION COMPONENTS

- Acoustic Absorption Pads in the Doors
- Thick Cast Foam Interior Carpet
- Engine Side Dash Mat
- Decklid Liner
- Trunk Liner Pad
- Trunk Trim Cotton Liner
- Trunk Floor Absorption Pad

294 The Buick Lucerne replaced two cars in the division's lineup, the Park Avenue and the LeSabre and, hoping to reassert itself in the luxury market, Buick is banking on extensive use of noise-quieting materials.

295 A clean modern design and bucket seats in the Lucerne does much to shake off Buick's stodgy image. The venerable fender-mounted portholes return in an updated fashion. True to tradition, four portholes signify a V-8, while three are used to designate a six-cylinder engine.

good looks as the CTS, with the same mesh grille treatment and aerodynamic bits, this flagship sedan was much more refined thanks to a 6-speed automatic transmission and a supercharged 4.2-liter V-8 pumping out 467 bhp. Built as more of an autobahn cruiser, the STS-V also had a high level of interior refinement that included a leather-covered dash and high-quality wood trim. Elsewhere at GM, the emphasis on performance also led to an expansion in V-8 power among its front-drive lineup. Before being dropped in 2006, the Pontiac Bonneville was offered in a GXP variant that used Cadillac's 280-bhp 4.6-liter Northstar V-8.

That car was later supplanted by the Grand Prix GXP equipped with a transversely mounted 5.3-liter V-8 producing 303 bhp. That engine was also fitted in the front-drive Impala SS and in 2007, the Buick LaCrosse Super. Even as it was transforming its Cadillac Division with the rear-drive Sigma platform, GM decided to retain its front-drive De Ville, although it renamed the vehicle DTS when it changed the car's sheetmetal over to the edgier Art & Science look of the other cars. In addition, it created a sister car for the Buick Division, called Lucerne that used the same 4.6-liter V-8 Northstar as the Cadillac, as well as adding a 3.8-liter V-6 as a base engine.

The Lucerne would replace two cars, the LeSabre and Park Avenue in Buick's lineup.

Ford Falls Back

While GM and Chrysler transformed themselves by creating a new generation of rear-drive models, Ford lost its bearings. By 2004, it was no longer the second largest auto manufacturer in the world. Toyota has passed the Dearborn automaker for the first time. In order to rebuild, Ford embarked on two critical product initiatives—a complete remake of the highly profitable F-150 full-size pickup (in anticipation of Nissan and Toyota entries in this previously untouched domestic domain), and a program to revitalize its car lineup.

Unfortunately, that plan wouldn't include an all-new rear drive platform as envisioned by the stunning 427 concept, a V-10 rear-drive sedan shown at the North American International Auto Show in 2003. Smaller and edgier than the aging Crown Victoria, the 427 was designed to compete head-on with the Chrysler 300C and Cadillac CTS.

But instead of going after its rivals with this car, Ford decided to tap into its global resources to find the underpinnings for its new North American products.

Ford's first stop on this global trek was Sweden, where Volvo mechanicals used on the S80 sedan and XC-90 SUV were utilized for the Ford Five Hundred and Mercury Montego. Powered by a transversely mounted 203-bhp 3.0-liter V-6, the Five Hundred and Montego were offered with a choice of front- or all-wheel drive. Two automatics were also offered, a conventional 6-speed transmission and a Continuously Variable Transmission (CVT). If Ford was expecting another breakthrough hit like the Taurus, it was sorely disappointed. The

generic styling and average performance of the Five Hundred limited its appeal. Sales hovered around 100,000 annually, far fewer than the nearly 200,000 aging Taurus models Ford managed to sell in 2004.

And management turmoil was having an effect on the product plan. The Five Hundred, Freestyle and Montego were developed under Chris Theodore, Ford's vice president of North American Product Development, whom Jacques Nasser recruited from Chrysler. Nasser's replacement as CEO, Nick Scheele, forced out Theodore and installed Phil Martens as the new product chief.

Martens moved over to North America working at Mazda in Japan and at Ford's European operations. From Mazda, Martens brought the Mazda 6 chassis, which was used to develop the Ford Fusion, Mercury Milan and Lincoln Zephyr (which, after just a year on the market, was renamed the MKZ). A base 2.4-liter four-cylinder engine and an optional 203-bhp 3.0-liter V-6 powered these front-drive sedans, which were later offered with an all-wheel-drive option. Later the 263-bhp 3.5-liter Cyclone V-6 was introduced in the MKZ.

Rather than using a "top hat" strategy in which a platform is topped off with distinctive sheetmetal depending on brand, Ford's approach was more classic badge engineering in which the differences between models is limited to grille inserts and interior detailing.

Lincoln, which had two unique products in the rear-drive LS and the V-8 powered front-drive Continental, would see those products replaced respectively by the Zephyr and the MKS, a four-door sedan based on the Five Hundred. This strategy was designed to broaden product offerings with minimal investment at a time when both GM and Chrysler were investing more heavily in product differentiation.

The American Exotic

Despite the struggles in the mass market, Detroit's automakers entered the 21st century displaying a talent for creating some remarkable performance cars that didn't cost a tremendous amount of money. The Dodge Viper and the Corvette Z06 both offered more than 400 bhp, terrific handling and great looks for well under $100,000.

Ford decided it needed to get into the act and its 100th anniversary in 2003 provided the right opportunity to create a halo car. At the 2002 North American International Auto Show, the company unveiled the Ford GT40 concept, a modern take on the legendary racers that dominated the 24 Hours of Le Mans in the mid-1960s. Powered by a 500 bhp mid-mounted supercharged 5.4-liter V-8, the GT40 was a sensation at the show. Bill Ford, Jr. quickly gave his blessing and within 16 months, three production versions were shown in the summer of 2003 at Ford's Centennial Celebration held at the company's world headquarters in Dearborn, Michigan.

Those three cars would be the only 2003 models offered as series production of what would become the Ford GT. Ironically, Ford didn't own the GT40 trademark; it had passed onto an aftermarket specialist which provided parts to the original race-cars now in private hands. Ford balked at paying royalties to the firm and decided to call the car the GT, noting that the new version stood 44.3 inches tall, while the original racer was only 40 inches high, a dimension that inspired the car's name.

The 2004 models that rolled off the assembly line rode on a 106.7-in. wheelbase and measured 182.8 inches in overall length. Power from the blown 5.4-liter V-8 had climbed to 550 bhp, although torque remained the same at 500 lb. ft. Though larger, the GT's look is faithful to the original GT40. Still, the differences are easy to spot.

The racer originally had its fuel tanks in the side rocker panels. The modern GT, for safety reasons, moved the fuel load inboard, putting it beneath a center console that the racer lacked. The GT also

featured such retro touches as toggle switches and the huge roof cutouts atop the doors. The GT production run lasted through the 2006 model year and approximately 3,000 cars were built. Best of all, this mid-engine exotic retailed for about $150,00, much less than the $200,000 commanded by the likes of the Ferrari F430 and Lamborghini Gallardo.

Dodge, which started the horsepower wars with the Viper in 1992, wasn't resting on its laurels. In 2003, it introduced the second generation Viper with a more curvaceous body and with an engine that cracked the 500 bhp level. Powered by an 8.3-liter V-10, the new roadster was built under the rubric 500/500/500: 500 cu. in. (actually 505 cu. in.),

500 bhp, 500 lb. ft. of torque. Equipped with 18-in. front and 19-in. rear wheels, the Viper stuck to the tarmac as well as it leapt off the starting line. The new roadster also featured a semi-hard manual top and a return to side exhausts.

Three years later, Dodge added a coupe version with design cues that echoed the 1996 GTS with a "double bubble" treatment providing additional headroom needed when wearing a helmet at track events. The rear end featured a hatch and ducktail spoiler. Power in the new coupe was upgraded to boost torque to 525 lb. ft.

Dodge skipped the '07 model year with the Viper because of a change in emission regulations, but came

back later in that calendar year with a 2008 Viper that had a significantly revised engine package. The V-10 now displaced 8.4 liters and featured a higher compression ratio and variable valve timing, which boosted output to 580 bhp and torque to 560 lb. ft. While the body style remained virtually unchanged, the '08 models are distinguished by larger hood louvers positioned farther forward on the hood.

298-299 To celebrate Ford's 100th anniversary, the company built a modern interpretation of the legendary GT40 racers that dominated Le Mans in the mid-1960s. The new-age GT featured a 550 bhp mid-mounted supercharged 5.4-liter V-8. Just over 3,000 units were produced.

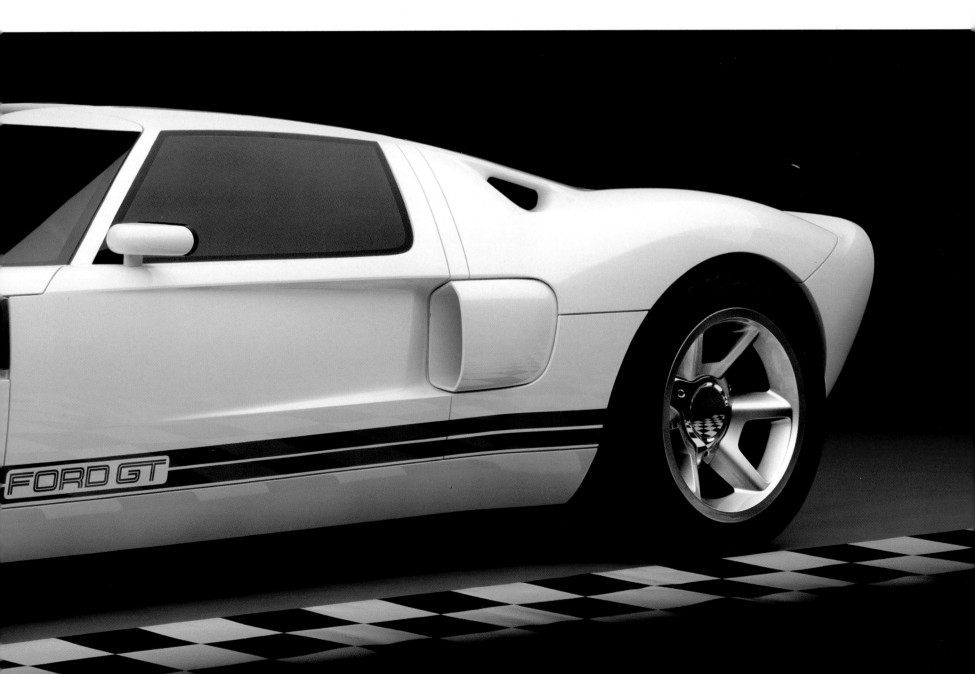

302 Two projector beam lamps and a turn signal are nestled in a body-colored bezel covered by a clear lens on the 2005 Corvette.

303 top The sides of the 2005 Corvette are very clean. The previous car had a single side strake which has been eliminated in the new design.

303 bottom The new Corvette has a single power bulge in the hood, a change from the previous double-bubble design. The Corvette badge also has been changed and no longer is encircled.

301 top The 2005 Corvette is shorter in overall length and shares the same wheelbase as the Cadillac XLR. Both two-seat sport cars are built at GM's Bowling Green, Kentucky, assembly plant.

301 center left In addition to capturing styling elements of previous generation Corvettes, designer Tom Peters was also inspired by the intakes of the F-22 Raptor fighter to create the car's side scoops.

301 center right Beneath the Corvette's composite body panels is the 6.0-lite LS6 V-8 engine mounted in a hydroformed steel chassis with aluminum suspension components.

301 bottom The designers wanted to give the 2005 Corvette a wide, aggressive stance, a single grille opening that recalls the first generation car, as well as the signature dual taillight treatment.

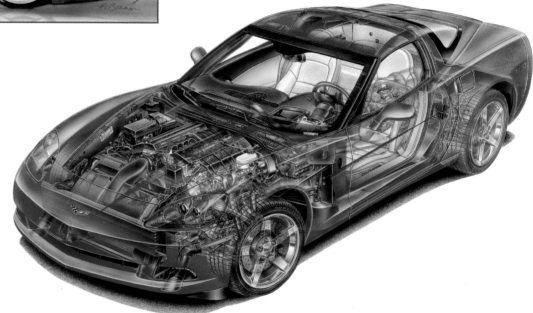

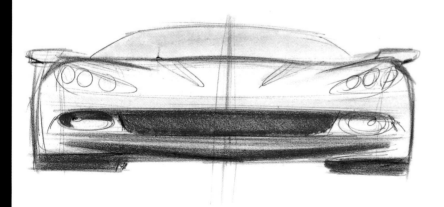

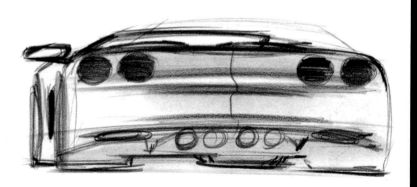

GM was also moving forward with a two-pronged effort aimed at the sports and luxury two-seater market. A sixth-generation Corvette was in the works, but before it launched, the company used this new architecture to develop for Cadillac the XLR, which was a two-seat roadster with a retractable hardtop.

This entry had its origins with the 1999 Evoq show car, a two-seat retractable hardtop designed by Simon Cox.

The concept, powered by a supercharged 405-bhp 4.2-liter Northstar V-8, was intended to showcase Cadillac's new Art & Science design philosophy. It proved so popular, GM decided to build it. Rather than create a costly new platform for aluminum-bodied Evoq, Cadillac would base the production car on the new Corvette C6 architecture already under development. Dave Hill, Corvette's chief engineer, had previously worked at Cadillac on that division's only other two-seater, the Allanté, in the early 1990s.

The XLR debuted in 2004 with a composite body and a 320-bhp 4.6-liter Northstar beneath the hood. The look remained faithful to the show-car, right down to the retractable hardtop. Positioned to compete with the Mercedes-Benz SL, the XLR was priced at $76,200.

A hotter version of the car, the XLR-V, debuted in 2006 with a supercharged 4.4-liter Northstar V-8 producing 443 bhp. Like other vehicles in the V-Series, the XLR sports a mesh grille, more aggressive front fascia and rocker moldings. Priced at $100,000, it was the most expensive production Cadillac ever.

Meanwhile, the long-awaited sixth generation Corvette debuted in 2005, a sleek, more compact design that featured exposed headlamps for the first time since 1962.

Designer Tom Peters' vision for the car was a contemporary shape that incorporated cues from previous generation cars. The egg-crate grille texture was taken from the 1955 model, a center

304 top Based on the same architecture as the Chevrolet Corvette, the Cadillac XLR serves a more luxury-oriented market with its retractable hardtop. The edgy shape of the XLR epitomizes Cadillac's "Art & Science" approach to design.

304 bottom The Northstar badge on the rear deck is another indication where the XLR differs from the Corvette, which uses a pushrod V-8 to provide motivation. The Cadillac has dual overhead cam V-8 displacing 4.6-liter and producing 320 bhp.

305 top The XLR was upgraded in 2006 to include a V-Series model with a supercharged 4.4-liter V-6 producing 443 bhp. Like other V models, the XLR-V sports a mesh grille and tauter handling.

305 bottom The interior of the XLR is more luxurious than the Corvette. Extensive use of aluminum accents and lightly toned wood contribute to this upscale aura. The XLR comes equipped with an automatic transmission—there is no manual-shift model.

spline running fore to aft and the fastback hatch recalled the '63 Sting Ray, while the Coke-bottle shape of the body paid homage to the '68 model.

The Corvette featured a new 6.0-liter V-8 producing 400 bhp mated to a choice of a 6-speed manual or 4-speed automatic.

A year later, a 6-speed automatic with paddle-shift sequential gear selection would supplant the 4-speed gearbox. Corvette returned with two body styles, a convertible and a hatchback coupe with a lift-out roof panel.

The hardtop Z06 was dropped until the 2006 model. That car returned as a hatchback with a fixed roof, a wider body, larger wheels and tires and beneath the hood, a 7.0-liter V-8 producing 505 bhp. The Z06 was distinguished by an additional hood inlet and rear side scoops for brake cooling, design cues lifted directly from the Corvette C6.R racer that won its class at the 24 Hours of Le Mans.

In addition, the Z06 was lightened with the use of aluminum instead of steel frame rails and magnesium structural pieces in the firewall and fixed roof. With a base price of just $65,690, the Z06 offered supercar performance at a breathtakingly low price.

Two for the Road

At the other end of the spectrum, GM was looking to put the full-court press on the entry-level two-seater market.

Behind this move was former Chrysler president Bob Lutz, who left that automaker in the wake of the Daimler-Benz merger. One of the first all-new products proposed by Lutz, who joined GM as vice chairman and was charged with global product development, was the Solstice, an entry level two-seater for Pontiac designed to go head-to-head with the Mazda Miata.

In 2002 concept form, the Solstice was initially shown as a roadster and coupe, but in production would be offered solely with a manual soft top. Built off the new rear-drive Kappa architecture, the Solstice was powered by a 2.4-liter four-cylinder engine producing 177 bhp.

It would be joined by a stablemate, the Saturn Sky, which used the same underbody structure but had unique exterior composite body panels and a more upscale appearance. The Solstice was priced at $20,000, while the better-equipped Saturn clocked in at about $22,000 when they were introduced in 2006.

Higher performance versions of both bowed a year later—the Solstice GXP and Sky Red Line. Both featured a turbocharged 2.0-liter four-cylinder engine making 260 bhp.

306 Looking to breath life into Saturn, GM developed a sister car to the Pontiac Solstice called the Sky. The Saturn version is mechanically identical to the Solstice, but sports a more upscale appearance thanks to the use of chrome body accents.

307 top The Pontiac Solstice serves two markets—an entry level segment priced at $20,000 and the enthusiast set with its high-performance GXP model that boasts a turbocharged 2.0-liter four making 260 bhp.

307 bottom Like Pontiac, Saturn offers the Sky in a higher level of tune. Called the Sky Red Line, this model features a larger front intake, dual rear exhaust and the same turbocharged 2.0-liter four as the Solstice GXP.

Ride that Pony!

Ford's perseverance with the Mustang at a time when GM was abandoning the pony car segment paid off. In 2003, the Chevrolet Camaro and Pontiac Firebird were dropped after years of shrinking sales, leaving the field to Ford.

Rather than embarking on yet another modification of the 25-year-old Fox platform or using the expensive DEW98 with its independent rear suspension, Ford started with a clean sheet of paper. The new car would employ an independent front suspension similar to the DEW98, but the rear would be a weight- and cost-saving solid axle. The 4.6-liter V-8 would be carried over from the previous model, but the sheetmetal would be all new.

J Mays, Ford's vice president of design, decided that the new Mustang should look the like original. Just as the GT was a faithful recreation of the GT40, this new-generation pony car would take many of its cues from the original fastback, circa

1968. It would have a more aggressive shark nose and although it looked like a hatchback, the Mustang would be a coupe with a conventional trunk. The retro styling was a huge hit when the car was introduced as a 2005 model.

Riding on a 107.1-in. wheelbase, the new Mustang measured 183.2 inches, up 4.4 inches from the previous model. The base models were equipped with a 4.0-liter V-6 making 221 bhp, while the more powerful GT extracted 300 bhp from its 4.6-liter ohc V-8. Within a year of the coupe's launch, a convertible was offered.

More than just reissuing an icon, the Mustang rekindled an interest in the sporty two-door market and opened up a wide range of special edition models inspired by the car's rich history. Shortly after the car's launch, Ford developed the GT-R concept, a racing version of the Mustang that recalled the car's triumphs in the TransAm racing series of

the late '60s and early '70s. This tangerine-orange show car sported a huge fixed rear wing, side exhausts and a 440-bhp 5.0-liter V-8. It was a sign of things to come.

308 Just reviving the Pony Car concept with the Mustang wasn't enough for Ford, which decided it should have a little fun along the way. The result was the GT-R concept which showed how the Mustang could be raced.

309 top Developed for the New York Auto Show, the GT-R features a paint job reminiscent of the 1970s factory-sponsored Trans-Am race car. The larger grille opening and revamped headlamps are two design elements that would be used on later models.

309 bottom left Inside, the GT-R is all business with a stripped-out interior, digital readouts, toggle switches and a slap-stick sequential shifter.

309 bottom right Like a true race car, the GT-R employs an unmuffled exhaust system with side exits. But because it's a show car, this element is chromed to highlight the feature.

Partnering with legendary racer Carroll Shelby, who built Ford-powered Cobras and specially modified Mustangs in the 1960s, Ford developed the Shelby GT500. By adapting the supercharged 5.4-liter V-8 engine used in the GT, the GT500 offered up 500 bhp for just $41,000.

The Shelby name would appear on two other Mustangs. The Shelby GT-H, a special black and gold edition producing 325 bhp, was available only for rent at Hertz agencies, a throwback to a similar car that Hertz rented in the 1960s.

The public would later be able to buy similarly equipped Shelby GTs in either black or white with silver stripes.

The popularity of the Mustang wasn't lost on Ford's ri-

vals. Pontiac, for its part, brought back the GTO for 2004, a version of the 2-door Monaro coupe built by Holden in Australia. It was powered by a 350 bhp LS1 V-8 and offered a choice of 6-speed manual or 5-speed automatic.

While some liked the spaciousness of the four-place cabin and understated looks, critics felt the modern GTO lacked the visual punch of the original. The following year, Pontiac facelifted the car with a more distinctive front end that included twin hood scoops and replaced the 5.7-liter LS1 with the 6.0-liter LS2, which took output up to an even 400 bhp. Despite the infusion of power and a more distinctive look, the GTO was dropped at the end of the 2006 model year.

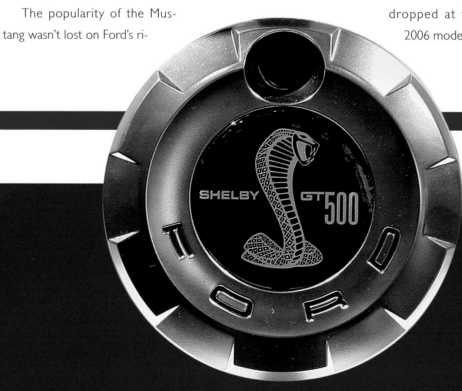

310 top Developed by Ford's Special Vehicle Team (SVT), the Shelby GT500 not only recalls previous Shelby efforts of the 1960s, but also marks the return of Carroll Shelby to the Ford fold.

310 bottom The Cobra is a recurring theme used on the gas cap and the grille to signify Carroll Shelby's involvement in the project.

310-311 The larger grille opening is similar to that used on the GT-R concept. It provides better breathing for the supercharged engine. Power comes from a supercharged 5.4-liter V-8, which makes 500 bhp. The raised hood with heat extractors is also required to accommodate the powerplant's taller deck height.

But the idea of the pony car didn't die with the GTO reissue. At the 2006 Detroit show, Chevrolet took the wraps off the Camaro concept and later that year promised to build it as a 2009 model. Taking its cue from the '69 Camaro, the concept is much more contemporary, not just a faithful reproduction of its ancestor.

Tom Peters, who developed the sixth-generation Corvette, oversaw Camaro development and took the same approach of using contemporary body forms and shapes and applying subtle cues from the original, such as the grille detailing and rake of the C-pillar.

Power for the concept came from the 400-bhp 6.0-liter LS2 V-8 found in both the Pontiac GTO and the base Corvette. In production, the Camaro would offer a choice of V-6 or V-8 powerplants. Chrysler's Dodge division decided it too needed to get into the act and at the same Detroit show took the wraps off the Challenger.

Like the Mustang, it is a more faithful recreation of the original 1970 model. Riding on an LX chassis shortened 4inches to a 116-in. wheelbase, the Challenger concept was equipped with a 6.1-liter Hemi V-8 rated at 425 bhp. Dodge estimated its 0-60 mph acceleration at 4.5 seconds. Like Chevrolet, Dodge promised the Challenger as a 2009 model.

312 top and 312-313 Tom Peters, who developed the sixth-generation Corvette, led the design team on the new Camaro. As a result, the exterior surface is clean and modern while retaining traditional Camaro design cues.

313 top Based on a new rear-drive platform known as Zeta and developed by GM's Holden unit in Australia, the Camaro was slated for a 2009 introduction with a choice of V-6 or V-8 power.

314 top The Challenger employs the same 425-bhp 6.1-liter V-8 used in the Charger and Magnum SRT-8 models. In production, buyers would be able to choose between a standard 5.7-liter Hemi and the larger engine.

314-315 The Challenger is a much more faithful remake of the 1970 classic. The long hood and short rear deck look is achieved by using a shortened wheelbase version of the LX platform that underpins the Dodge Magnum and Charger.

315 top The flavor of the '70s Challenger is captured in the interior, which features a pistol-grip shifter on the six-speed manual, the three-spoke design of the steering wheel and the round gauges in the instrument panel.

Crossovers: A New Way of Life

While trucks comprise nearly half the new vehicle market in America, a run-up in gasoline prices to over $3 per gallon in 2006 had people looking for alternatives to large truck-based sport-utility vehicles. These four-door all-wheel drive trucks had become to modern family transportation what the station wagon had been two generations earlier.

Auto manufacturers responded by creating a new category of vehicles that, while retaining rugged truck-like styling, were lighter and more fuel-efficient because of their use of car-based components. Rather than being body-on-frame behemoths, these so-called crossovers used unit-body construction and typically used transversely mounted engines driving the front wheels in two-wheel-drive mode.

Some of the first crossovers weren't too successful, like the homely Pontiac Aztek, which was based on GM's front-drive minivan platform. Others, like the Buick Rendezvous, which used the same architecture, but featured three-row seating and more conventional styling, were better accepted.

Chrysler blended the versatility of its minivan with SUV and station wagon styling cues in its 2003 Pacifica, an all-wheel drive vehicle powered by a transversely mounted 3.5-liter V-6. Ford had a similar vehicle called the Freestyle and used the same platform as the Ford Five Hundred.

By the end of the first decade of the new millennium, the crossover segment will be populated with variants in all size classes. Chrysler attacked the entry level with the Dodge Caliber, Jeep Compass and Jeep Patriot, a trio of compact people movers that feature hatchback styling, front- or all-wheel drive and fuel-efficient power from 2.0- and 2.4-liter four-cylinder engines.

Further up the scale, Ford introduced the Edge and Lincoln Aviator, a pair of five-passenger crossovers based on the Ford Fusion/Lincoln MKZ car platform. These mid-market entries are powered by a 265-bhp 3.5-liter V-6 and offer buyers a choice of front- or all-wheel-drive.

The most ambitious crossover program was GM's Lambda platform. This architecture spawned vehicles for GMC, Saturn and Buick. Designed as crossovers from the ground up, the GMC Acadia, Saturn Outlook and Buick Enclave feature three-row seating, rugged SUV-inspired looks and a high level of performance from a 275-bhp 3.6-liter V-6.

Crossovers are evidence that the only constant in the American automobile is change. While it's been said that Americans have a love affair with the automobile, the truth is that they are more in love with the convenience an automobile or truck affords them. From the self-starter to automatic transmissions, from air conditioning to DVD entertainment systems, and ultimately from the gasoline engine to fuel cell power, the history of the American car is a story of innovation to make cars easy to operate and widespread in ownership. It is automobility for everyman and, in a way, the embodiment of the American dream.

316 The Buick Enclave's flowing lines combines the styling of a luxury car with the muscular stance and all-wheel-drive capability of a sport-utility vehicle. This new crossover redefines the traditional roles of cars and trucks.

316-317 The Enclave offers three-row seating and a hose of amenities like on-board

entertainment systems. This environment offers all the functionality of a minivan in a much more stylish package.

317 bottom The instrumentation reflects Buick's drive to be perceived as a true luxury vehicle. Soft backlighting and chrome bezels give the gauges the look of a finely crafted watch.

BIBLIOGRAPHY

Automotive News, GM 75th Anniversary Issue, September 16, 1983

Automotive News, The Centennial Celebration of the Car, October 30, 1985

Automotive News, American Automotive Centennial, The 100 Year Alamanac, April 24, 1996

Automotive News, American Automotibile Centennial, 100 Events That Made The Industry, June 26, 1996

Automotive News, Ford-100, June 16, 2003

The American Automobile - A Centenary 1893-1993, Nick Georgano, Smithmark Publishers, 1992

American Cars, Leon Mandel, Stewart, Tabori & Chang, Inc. 1982

Billy Durant - Creator of General Motors, Lawrence Gustin, Craneshaw Publishers, 1984

Chevrolet Chronicle, Auto Editors of Consumer Guide, Publications International, 2002

Detroit Cars - 50 Years of the Motor City, Martin Derrick, PRC Publishing, 1999

Encyclopedia of American Cars, Auto Editors of Consumer Guide, Publications International, 2002

General Motors - The First 75 Years of Transportation Products, Editors of Automobile Quarterly, Automobile Quarterly Publishing, 1983

Motor City Muscle, Mike Mueller, Motorbooks International, 1997

The New Illustrated Encyclopedia of the Automobile, David Burgess Wise, Quarto Publishing, 1979

Setting the Pace - Oldsmobile's First 100 Years, Helen Jones Early and James R. Walkinshaw, Oldsmobile PR Dept., 1996

The Star and the Laurel - The Centennial History of Daimler, Mercedes and Benz, Beverly Rae Kimes, Mercedes-Benz North America, 1986

INDEX

PHOTOGRAPHIC CREDITS

Alamy Images: pages 66-67, 68-69, 147, 176-177, 184 bottom left, 254-255

Roger Viollet/Alinari: pages 38-39

AP Photo: page 35 top and bottom left

Archivio FIAT: pages 58, 59

Automedia: pages 14-15, 39 top, 200-201, 256-257, 257, 261 bottom, 269 bottom

Bettman/Corbis/Contrasto: pages 20, 20-21, 22, 23 top right and left, 27, 35 bottom right, 37, 39 bottom, 43 left and right, 44-45, 45 top and bottom, 46-47, 52, 53 top, 67, 70, 72-73, 76, 78 top, 119, 140, 142, 161 top left, 182, 202-203, 207, 228 top and bottom, 232 top, 234

The Peter Roberts Collection/Neil Bruce: pages 60-61, 61 bottom left and right, 74, 75 top right, bottom left and right, 77, 100-101, 104 top, 117 top, 121 top, 184 top right, 247 left

Neil Bruce: pages 24-25, 25 top, 34 top and bottom, 53 bottom left, 110-111, 114-115, 115 top 248-249, 249 top

Car Culture/Corbis: pages 312-313, 313

Giles Chapman Library: pages 189 top, 264

Corbis/Contrasto: pages 71, 129, 144 top

ICP/Double's: pages 36-37, 53 bottom left, 128, 138-139, 185 left

Andreas Conradt/Automedia: pages 64-65, 65 top left, 65 bottom, 158 top right, 158-159, 159 top right and left, 170

Daimler Chrysler Historical Collection: pages 232 bottom, 250-251

Daimler Chrysler Media Archive: pages 258-259, 260-261, 260 top, 261 top, 262 top, 263, 286 bottom, 286-287, 287

Richard Cummins: page 191 bottom

Richard Cummins/Corbis/Contrasto: pages 11, 178, 211, 300

Daimler Chrysler: pages 314, 315

Detroit Auto Dealers Association: page 312

Detroit Public Library/N.A.H.C.: pages 94-95, 188, 189 bottom

Mary Evans Pictures Library: pages 85 bottom, 120, 121 bottom

Ford Motors Company: pages 146 bottom left and right, 206-207, 214 top, 214-215, 215, 235 bottom center, 241, 270 top left and top right, 270 center right, 271 left and right, 272-273, 273, 276-277 bottom, 296, 297, 308-309, 309 top and bottom

Henry Ford Museum: pages 9, 23 bottom, 26-27, 28-29, 56 top left and right, 56-57, 102, 115 bottom, 116, 117 bottom, 123 top, 130, 134 bottom, 138 top, 139 top.

Ford Photomedia: page 240

Owen Franken/Corbis/Contrasto: pages 235 left

Michael Furman Photography: pages 2-3, 6-7, 8, 58-59, 96-97, 98-99, 102-103, 108-109, 124-125, 130-131, 132 top, 154-155, 160-161, 166-167, 173, 174-175, 196-197, 210-211, 218-219, 219 top, 224-225, 226-227

General Motors Corporation: pages 282, 283, 291 top, 294 top and bottom, 295 top and bottom, 304 top and bottom, 305 top and bottom, 306, 307 top and bottom, 316, 316-317, 317

General Motors Media Archive: pages 32, 32-33, 33, 51 bottom, 54-55, 61 top, 62, 73 top left and right, 78 bottom, 78-79, 118 top and bottom left, 118 bottom right, 120-121, 122 top and bottom, 129 top, 144 bottom, 144-145, 164, 165, 166, 167, 176, 177, 181, 183 top, 183 bottom left, 191 top, 192 top, 193 top and bottom, 204, 209 top and bottom, 212 top, 212-213, 216, 216-217, 217, 220, 221 top, 233 top, 236, 238, 238-239, 239, 246-247, 266 top and bottom left, 266-267, 268, 276-277, 277, 282, 283, 300, 301 top, center and bottom, 302, 303 top and bottom

Farrell Grehan/Corbis/Contrasto: page 208

Dave G. Houser/Corbis/Contrasto: pages 18-19

Hulton Archive/Laura Ronchi: pages 40-41, 41 top and bottom, 42, 183 bottom, 233 bottom.

Ron Kimball Photography: pages 10-11, 16-17, 42-43, 48-49, 136-137, 150-151, 156-157, 164-165, 170-171, 172-173, 185 right, 198-199, 214 bottom, 219 bottom, 220-221, 264-265, 269 top, 274-275, 276-277, 277, 288-289, 290-291, 291 bottom, 292, 292-293, 298-299, 310 top, 310-311, 314-315

David Kimber/The Car Photo Library: page 100

Kolvenbach/Alamy Images: page 254 top

Owaki Kulla/Corbis/Contrasto: page 1

John Lamm: page 30 top left

Cindy Lewis Photography: pages 103, 262-263

Reinhard Lintelmann/Automedia: pages 30 bottom, 30-31, 106, 227

Massimo Listri/Corbis/Contrasto: pages 180-181

Ludvigsen Library: pages 54, 55, 62-63, 94 top, 134

top, 163 bottom, 235 bottom, 235 right top center, 235 center, 235 right top, 237, 242 top center and bottom, 243 bottom, 247

Gjon Mili/Time Life Picture/Getty Images/Laura Ronchi: page 146 top

Francis Miller/Time Life Picture/Getty Images/Laura Ronchi: page 218 left

Minnesota Historical Society/Corbis/Contrasto: pages 82-83

Photos12: page 65 top right

Carl & Ann Purcell/Corbis/Contrasto: pages 152-153

Reuters/Contrasto: page 310 bottom

Rykoff Collection/Corbis/Contrasto: page 132 bottom

Schenectadi Museum; Hall of Electrical History Foundation/Corbis/Contrasto: pages 50-51

Bradley Smith/Corbis/Contrasto: page 212 center

Dennis Stock/Magnum Photos/Contrasto: page 161 top right

Studebaker National Museum, South Bend, Indiana: pages 139 bottom, 206

Harvey Swarts: pages 140-141

Harvey Swarts/Automedia: pages 270-271

TRH Pictures: pages 25 bottom, 30 top right, 101, 111, 249 bottom

Underwood Photo Archive: pages 229 top left and right, 229 bottom right and left

Peter Vann: pages 143 bottom, 243 top

Peter Vann/Automedia: pages 142-143, 158 top left, 160 top, 179 bottom

Zoomstock: pages 12-13, 168-169, 169, 179 top, 194, 226, 284-285, 285

Fotostudio Zumbrunn: pages 4-5, 5, 70-71, 80-81, 84-85, 85 top, 86, 86-87, 87 top left and right, 88-89, 89, 90, 90-91, 92-93, 93 top and bottom, 104 bottom, 105, 106-107, 107, 112 top and bottom, 113, 122-123, 126-127, 132-133, 135 top and bottom, 148-149, 162 top and bottom, 163 top, 186-187, 187, 190-191, 192-193, 195, 196, 197, 205 top and bottom, 222 top, 222-223, 230-231, 240-241, 244-245, 252-253, 253

Drawings by Angelo Colombo/Archivio White Star: pages 94 bottom, 143 top, 171, 192 bottom, 221 bottom, 222 center, 258, 266 bottom right, 271 bottom, 276, 286 top

AKNOWLEDGEMENTS

It is rare opportunity to chronicle the history of a country's automotive history and I appreciate all the efforts of many individuals who have made this work possible. Chief among them is photographer Jim Fets, a colleague and neighbor who made the necessary introductions to White Star Publishing. I also owe a debt of gratitude to my employer, Road & Track Editor-in-Chief Thos Bryant, whose patience and latitude allow me to indulge in such projects. But most of all, I want to thank my family for their support, especially my wife, Jane, who edits my work with consummate skill, and our children, Amy and Stephen.

Matt DeLorenzo

The publisher would like to thank:

Benson Ford Research Center, Henry Ford Museum - Michigan USA
GM Media Archive, General Motors Corp. - Michigan USA
Daimler Chrysler Corporate Historical Collection - Michigan USA
Daimler Chrysler Media Archive - Michigan USA
Detroit Auto Dealers Association - Michigan USA
The National Automotive History Collection, Detroit Public Library - Michigan USA
Studebaker National Museum - Indiana USA
Walter Reuther Library, Wayne State University - Michigan USA

324　This forward thrusting hood ornament from the 1947 Cadillac says much about the spirit of the American car—it's is always about looking ahead, looking for the next big idea.